THE TOS HANDBOOK OF TEXAS BIRDS

Number Thirty-six:
Louise Lindsey Merrick Natural Environment Series

D0965026

The TOS Handbook of Texas Birds

MARK W. LOCKWOOD & BRUSH FREEMAN

Texas A&M University Press ☀ College Station

The paper used in this book meets the minimum requirements
of the American National Standard for Permanence of Paper
for Printed Library Materials, z39.48-1984.
Binding materials have been chosen for durability.

LIBRARY OF CONGRESS CATALOGING-IN-PUBLICATION DATA

Lockwood, Mark.
    The TOS handbook of Texas birds / Mark W. Lockwood
and Brush Freeman. – 1st ed.
        p.cm. – (Louise Lindsey Merrick natural environment
series ; no. 36)
    Includes bibliographical references (p.   ).
    ISBN 1-58544-283-6 (cloth : alk. paper)
    ISBN 1-58544-284-4 (pbk. : alk. paper)
    1. Birds–Texas. I. Freeman, Brush. 1951– II. Title. III. Series.
QL684. T4 L633   2003
598'.09764–dc21   2003012952

TO GREG LASLEY —

Without his hard work and dedication

on behalf of the Texas Bird Records Committee

of the Texas Ornithological Society,

this book would not have been possible.

CONTENTS

PHOTOGRAPHS

ACKNOWLEDGMENTS

THIS BOOK reflects the efforts of ornithologists and birders alike who have reported their observations over the years. We thank everyone who has taken the time to submit their sightings to the Texas Bird Records Committee and to the journal now known as *North American Birds,* which has played a prominent role over the past 40 years in collecting and disseminating that information. Birders who formally contribute their sightings to the journal and to the Committee not only play an important role in documenting the ornithological history of Texas, but also generate the information so critical to the study of the status and distribution of birds on a larger scale.

The manuscript was reviewed by many past and present members of the TBRC, as well as by regional experts on the avifauna of Texas. We thank Keith Arnold, John Arvin, Kelly Bryan, Mel Cooksey, Bert Frenz, Tony Gallucci, John Gee, Petra Hockey, Greg Lasley, Guy Luneau, Terry Maxwell, Brad McKinney, Martin Reid, David Sarkozi, Willie Sekula, Ken Seyffert, Cliff Shackelford, Matt White, and Barry Zimmer for all their thoughtful comments, which greatly enhanced the quality of the book. We also want to thank David Riskind who kindly reviewed the introductory materials.

We were very fortunate to have many photographers graciously allow us the use of their photographs to illustrate this book. Their contribution to the final product is certainly greatly appreciated. These fine people include Tony Amos, John Arvin, Paul Bozzo, Kelly Bryan, Eric Carpenter, Bill Clark, Mel Cooksey, Jim Culbertson, Don Cunningham, Jack Eitniear, Ted Eubanks, Jim Flynn, Peter Gottschling, Michael Gray, Mary Gustafson, Kevin Karlson, Mike Krzywonski, Jimmy McHaney, Allan Mueller, Brent Ortego, Martin Reid, Heidi Schulz, Willie Sekula, Cliff Shackelford, Brian Small, Cliff Stogner, Vera and Bob Thornton, Tom Urban, Matt White, Alan Wormington, and Barry Zimmer. We would particularly like to thank Steve Bentsen, Tim Cooper, and Greg Lasley for the generous contribution of so many of their wonderful photographs.

Since the first TOS checklist was published in 1974, great changes in our knowledge of Texas birds have occurred. Everything we have learned over the last three decades is a direct reflection of observer participation in providing detailed data for the record. For example, our understanding of pelagic bird life was greatly enhanced during the 1990s, as was our understanding of the avifauna of the higher elevations of the mountain ranges of the Trans-Pecos.

Much is still to be learned about the avifauna in Texas and many counties remain to be explored in greater depth. It is our hope, and the hope of all those interested in preserving and building upon the record presented here, that observers will continue to gather and share their information about this state's diverse bird life.

INTRODUCTION

LTHOUGH THE TITLE has changed, this is the fourth edition of the *Check-list of the Birds of Texas* of the Texas Ornithological Society. As with previous editions, it is based on the observations of past and present ornithologists and naturalists, and is a continuation of an effort to accurately reflect the bird life of Texas.

Although John K. Strecker is best known as a herpetologist, he was also one of the most important late-nineteenth- and early-twentieth-century Texas ornithologists. During his tenure as curator at the Baylor University Museum, between 1903 and 1933, he compiled the first significant annotated checklist of the birds of Texas. His 69-page work, aptly titled *The Birds of Texas,* was published by the Baylor University Press in 1912. In those days the understanding of the distribution and abundance of a significant portion of the state's bird life was in its infancy, especially in the western half of the state. Much of what was known about a species' presence in many regions was based on the availability of specimens and the observations of a small, but skilled, group of keen observers and collectors.

L. R. Wolfe was the next ornithologist to catalog the avifauna of Texas. Upon the suggestion of Dr. Emerson Stringham, author of *Kerrville Texas and Its Birds* (1948), Wolfe compiled the known checklists and published materials on Texas Birds into his 1956 *Check-list of the Birds of Texas.* This checklist replaced Strecker's earlier effort and listed 521 species. By the mid-fifties, much more was known about the bird life of the state with Wolfe contributing to that knowledge with numerous articles on Texas birds and, in particular, Hill Country birds, including his *Check List of the Birds of Kerr County, Texas* (1965).

A contemporary of Strecker's was Harry C. Oberholser. Oberholser was charged with compiling data collected on birds during the Biological Survey of Texas. He began this effort in Big Bend in 1901 along with mammalogist Vernon Bailey, the leader of the survey. Oberholser's work was originally to be included in Bailey's 1905 report, but the manuscript was already too large for inclusion and therefore was to be published separately at a later date. Oberholser continued to collect information and add to his manuscript through the 1950s. Unfortunately, Oberholser never saw the publication of his life's work, for he died on Christmas Day 1963 at the age of 93. It was through the dedicated efforts of the late Edward B. Kincaid, with the assistance of many people, including Suzanne Winkler, John L. Rowlett, and several devoted sponsors, that *The Bird Life of Texas* was completed in 1974. This two-volume work remains a veritable classic, not only for Texas, but also for United States ornithological history. Although Oberholser's work is now somewhat dated, it continues to be a reference tool that is mandatory for anyone working on Texas' avifauna.

In 1953, a group of birding enthusiasts and conservationists from across Texas chartered the Texas Ornithological Society (TOS). The mandate of the newly-formed organization was, and still is, to promote the study, discovery, conservation, and dissemination of knowledge about the birds of Texas; to encourage the observation of birds; and to stimulate cooperation among professional and amateur ornithologists. As part of that mandate, Keith Arnold and Edward Kutac (1974) compiled the first *Check-list of the Birds of Texas* for TOS. When the Texas Bird Records Committee (TBRC) was formed by Arnold in 1972, it was charged with maintaining a state checklist and updating it every five years to reflect new information gained between intervals. This proved to be impractical and as a result a span of ten years passed before the second edition appeared (Arnold 1984). In 1995, the third edition of the checklist was published with TOS authorship. Those who were interested in the changes, in terms of additions or deletions to the TOS state list, during the intervening periods between checklists followed them through the annual reports of the TBRC published in the Bulletin of the Texas Ornithological Society (Arnold 1984, 1985; Haynie 1992a, 1992b, 1993, 1994, 1996, 1998; Lasley 1988, 1989, 1990; Lockwood 1998, 1999, 2000, 2001b, 2002).

This edition reflects the recent additions and deletions to the state list of birds due both to taxonomic revisions and to the actual changes in the distribution and abundance of Texas birds, where known. This edition has been substantially enlarged to incorporate additional introductory material, more detailed species accounts, and distributional maps.

The Texas List and Its Nomenclature

This fourth edition of the TOS "checklist" includes 623 species of birds accepted for the state by the TBRC. It represents an increase of 28 species since the third edition, 66 species since the second edition, and 89 species since the first edition in 1974. Most of these gains are the result of new discoveries or documented occurrences; however, a number also reflect recent taxonomic decisions by the American Ornithologists' Union (AOU) Committee on Classification and Nomenclature.

The taxonomic treatment and species sequence in this checklist follows the *Check-list of North American Birds, Seventh Edition* (AOU 1998), as currently supplemented. The last time the AOU treated subspecific taxonomy was in 1957. Previous editions of the TOS checklist followed that taxonomy. In the past 46 years many publications have influenced the treatment of subspecies for North American birds. We concluded that we did not have the needed information or the technical background to evaluate the merits of those publications as they relate to Texas avifauna. For this reason, mention of subspecies in this edition is restricted to a small number of species, predicated in many cases, on ongoing taxonomic work, some of which the AOU is currently considering.

Documentation

For a species to be considered for inclusion on the official Texas state list of birds of the Texas Ornithological Society, there must exist a known specimen, a recognizable and confirmed photograph or video, or a recognizable and confirmed audio recording. Any potential new state record must meet these criteria and be reviewed and accepted by the TBRC. The TBRC requests and reviews documentation on any report of a species that appears on its Review List or that has never been recorded in the state. Review Species occur, on average, fewer than four times per year for a ten-year period. Those on the current list are indicated in the species accounts, and a complete listing is found in Appendix D. Reports of Review List species are reviewed by the TBRC and if voted in favor of, are considered to be an "accepted" record. The review of such reports is a continuing process, and information about the number of accepted records of any particular review species is likely to have changed as of this book's publication date. The Review Species accounts are current as of 1 October 2003. For more information about TOS and the TBRC please visit http://www.texasbirds.org/.

Species Accounts

The purpose of this book is to define and update the known status and distribution of the birds of Texas, as defined by the TBRC. It is not intended as an identification guide, and the authors make no effort toward describing physiological features, vocalizations, other identifying traits, or a species' natural history. A broad range of excellent books in print already serve those purposes. Abundance and distribution are described for each season and for ecological regions if they differ; this information is augmented by a map for each species. Exceptional out-of-range records of non-review species are not presented on the associated maps but are instead covered within the text (see "Maps" below). For each species, where appropriate, we provide the typical migration periods, but do not try to present extreme arrival and departure dates. The issue of extreme migration dates is complex in Texas, where a lingering bird's presence is often overlapped by the arrival and departure dates of spring and fall migrants. In Texas, the lapse between late spring and early fall migration for some species can be as short as three weeks.

Each TBRC Review Species is noted as such in the species account header. For Review Species with five or fewer accepted records, each record is listed below the species account with date(s) of occurrence, location, the TBRC record number, and, if applicable, the Texas Photo Record File (TPRF) number. The photo file is housed at Texas A&M University in College Station. In a few cases, a specimen catalog number or the catalog number of an audio recording, archived at the Texas Bird Sounds Library (TBSL) located at Sam Houston State University in Huntsville, is also listed.

Maps

Each species account includes a map that is intended to reflect the typical expected range for that species, giving an overall picture of the species' distribution in Texas. We have attempted to make the maps as accurate as possible, but the very nature of bird distribution introduces some arbitrariness to the definition of the ranges. Many species are rare to very rare in areas outside the mapped range, and we did not attempt to map all the locations of the thousands of extralimital records that have occurred within the state. However, we do mention some of the more significant out-of-range records within the species account.

Status and Abundance Definitions

This book adheres roughly to the status and abundance codes as defined in the third edition of the TOS Checklist with a few variations.

permanent resident: Occurs regularly within the defined range throughout the year and implies a stable breeding population

summer resident: Implies a breeding population, although in some cases this population may be small

summer visitor: Implies a nonbreeding population or lingering migrants or winter residents

winter resident: Occurs regularly within the described range generally between December and February

winter visitor: Does not occur with enough regularity or in large enough numbers to be considered a winter resident

migrant: Occurs as a transient passing through the state in spring and/or fall (certain species may be migrants in some regions and residents in others)

local: May be found only in specific habitats or geographical area within any region, possibly in small numbers (e.g., Red-cockaded Woodpecker, Brown Jay, Colima Warbler, etc.)

abundant: Always present and in such numbers and with such general distribution in proper habitat that many may be found in a given day

common: Normally present and in such numbers that one may expect to find several in a day

uncommon: Normally present in proper habitat, but one cannot be sure of finding one in a day

rare: On the average, it occurs only a few times a year in a given area or not at all

very rare: Not expected, occurs regularly, although not on an annual basis

casual: Between 6 and 15 records accepted for the state by the TBRC; only one or a few records for any given area, but reasonably expected to occur again

accidental: Average of one or two records every 10 years
irregular: Present during most years, sometimes numerous, but absent during some years

Appendixes

Appendix A: Presumptive Species List

Sight records for these species have been accepted by the TBRC, but no specimen, photograph, video, or audio recording has been submitted so the species has not yet met the requirements for full acceptance on the Texas list.

Appendix B: Non-accepted Species

A number of species have not been accepted by the TBRC for inclusion on the Texas list or Presumptive Species List. These are species about which a legitimate debate may exist and/or a species for which published reports can be found in the literature, but are open to question.

Appendix C: Exotics, and Birds of Uncertain Origin

This list includes species that are known exotics or birds of uncertain origin. Some of these species may become established in small localized areas or are obvious escaped caged birds for which geographic range and species argue against a natural occurrence in Texas. The status of a very few of these may be subject to change in the future dependant upon decisions of the AOU or as a result of large expansions of introduced breeding populations. Examples of species formerly on this list that are now accepted by the TBRC include Red-crowned Parrot, Green Parakeet, Monk Parakeet, and Eurasian Collared-Dove.

Appendix D: List of Review Species

The TBRC requests documentation of all species that appear on the Review Species List. In general, this list includes birds that have occurred four or fewer times per year anywhere in Texas over a ten-year period. Guidelines for preparing rare bird documentation can be found in Dittmann and Lasley (1992).

NATURAL AREAS OF TEXAS

TEXAS CAN BE DIVIDED into natural or ecological regions that are defined by geology and vegetation. For the purposes of this book, we have chosen to follow the natural area boundaries developed by the Lyndon B. Johnson School of Public Affairs of the University of Texas at Austin (1978). The Lyndon B. Johnson School divided the state into 11 regions with some additional subregions. Although we are generally using these boundaries, some of the regions have been combined so that only eight natural areas are used in this book (see map p. xxvi). Some important subregions are specifically mentioned in the species accounts, however, and those are defined here as well.

Texas becomes more arid as one moves from east to west, and this, of course, has a definite impact on the vegetation present. Between the mesic Pineywoods in the east, which receives up to 50 inches of precipitation annually, and the deserts of far West Texas, where as little as eight inches of precipitation occurs each year, lies a complex assemblage of habitats that supports the diverse avifauna of the state. Riparian corridors along major river systems provide important habitats that are often very different from the surrounding vegetation.

The **Pineywoods** area is the easternmost ecological region in Texas. It covers 15.8 million acres or about 9.4 percent of the state. In general, the Pineywoods region is nearly level with some gently rolling to hilly country and elevations ranging from 200 to 500 feet above mean sea level. As the name implies, mixed pine-hardwood forests dominate the vegetational communities within the Pineywoods. Native pines common to the region are loblolly *(Pinus taeda)*, shortleaf *(P. echinata)*, and longleaf *(P. palustris)*. Slash pine *(P. elliottii)*, from the southeastern United States, has been widely introduced. Throughout the uplands, hardwoods are found in mixed stands with pines. Common hardwoods in the region include sweetgum *(Liquidambar styraciflua)*, various oaks *(Quercus* spp.), elms *(Ulmus* spp.), cottonwoods *(Populus* sp.), and hickories *(Carya* spp.), as well as

Average
Precipitation
in Inches

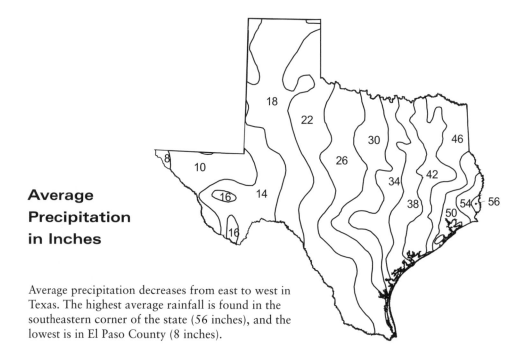

Average precipitation decreases from east to west in
Texas. The highest average rainfall is found in the
southeastern corner of the state (56 inches), and the
lowest is in El Paso County (8 inches).

Major Rivers
of Texas

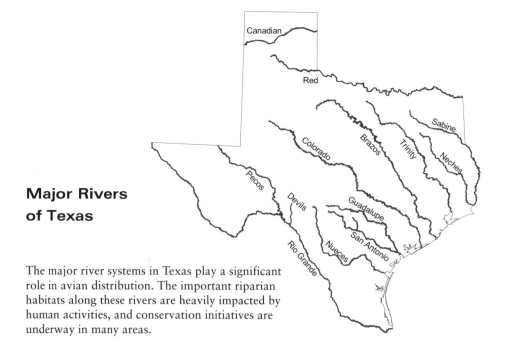

The major river systems in Texas play a significant
role in avian distribution. The important riparian
habitats along these rivers are heavily impacted by
human activities, and conservation initiatives are
underway in many areas.

water tupelo *(Nyssa aquatica)*, blackgum *(N. sylvatica)*, and bald cypress *(Taxodium distichum)*.

The **Coastal Prairies** is the smallest natural region in Texas covering 10.3 million acres or about 6.1 percent of the state. This region includes prairies, marshes, estuaries, and dunes on a nearly level plain that extends along the Gulf Coast from Mexico to Louisiana and includes the barrier islands. The Coastal Prairie reaches up to 80 miles inland from the Gulf with elevations ranging from sea level to 150 feet. The transition from Coastal Prairies to the Pineywoods and Post Oak Savannah is abruptly delineated except along drainages where riparian corridors extend into the prairies. The region grades more evenly into the South Texas Brush Country, narrowing to include the barrier islands and a thin corridor along the Laguna Madre south of Baffin Bay. The natural vegetation of the Coastal Prairies is tallgrass prairie and oak savannah. However, many of these grasslands have been invaded by trees and shrubs such as the exotic Chinese tallow *(Sapium sebiferum)*, native honey mesquite *(Prosopis glandulosa)*, and various acacias, in particular. Gulf cordgrass *(Spartina spartinae)*, big bluestem *(Andropogon gerardii)*, little bluestem *(Schizachyrium scoparium)*, indiangrass *(Sorghastrum nutans)*, and gulf muhly *(Muhlenbergia capillaris)* are common native grasses in these prairies.

An important natural region is the **Coastal Sand Plain.** This region is generally included as a subregion of the South Texas Brush Country. However, for ease in discussing bird distribution, this subregion is lumped into the Coastal Prairies (e.g. along the Coastal Prairies north to the central coast). The Coastal Sand Plain is an area of deep sands found south of Baffin Bay that borders the narrow extension of the Coastal Prairies inland to eastern Jim Hogg County. The sand plain is stabilized by vegetation, for the most part, and is largely dominated by live oak mottes.

West of the Pineywoods a large area with belts of forest, savannah, and grassland makes up the **Post Oak Savannah** and **Blackland Prairies** regions. These combined regions cover about 32.2 million acres or roughly 19.2 percent of the state. The Post Oak Savannah is found just to the west of the Pineywoods and grades into the Blackland Prairies to the south and west. This area is a gently rolling wooded plain with a distinctive pattern of post oak *(Quercus stellata)* and blackjack oak *(Q. marilandica)* in association with tall grasses. This basic vegetation type also characterizes the Cross Timbers subregion, which we also include in this region. The southwestern boundary with the South Texas Brush Country is indistinct. The Blackland Prairies intermingle with the Post Oak Savannah in the southeast and has divisions known as the Grand, San Antonio, and Fayette Prairies. This region was once an expansive tallgrass prairie dominated by little bluestem, big bluestem, indiangrass, tall dropseed *(Sporobolus asper)*, and Silveus dropseed *(S. silveanus)*. About 98 percent of the Blackland Prairies has been under cultivation for the past century. Many areas have been invaded by woody plants.

The **South Texas Brush Country** is an area of brushlands primarily found south of the Balcones Escarpment. The region covers 20.6 million acres or 12.2 percent of the state and is a moderately dissected, nearly level to rolling plain. Formerly, areas of dense brush were found only on ridges. Grazing and suppression of fires have altered the vegetation so that the region is now dominated by brushy species that include mesquite, live oak, several acacias, lotebush *(Zizyphus obtusifolia)*, spiny hackberry *(Celtis pallida)*, whitebrush *(Aloysia gratissima)*, and Texas persimmon *(Diospyros texana)*. The **Lower Rio Grande Valley** is found at the southern tip of this region. This distinctive subregion lies in the subtropical zone and is located within the delta of the Rio Grande and its alluvial terraces. Many species of plants reach their northern distribution in the Lower Valley. Historically, the floodplain of the Rio Grande supported a more diverse hardwood woodland which included sugarberry *(Celtis laevigata)*, cedar elm *(Ulmus crassifolia)*, ebony *(Pithecellobium ebano)*, and anacua *(Ehretia anacua)*. The Texas Sabal *(Sabal texana)* was a locally common component of that woodland. With the construction of numerous dams along the Rio Grande, the seasonal flooding that maintained the natural vegetation along the floodplain has ceased, and brush species from the north are invading this area.

The **Edwards Plateau** covers approximately 11.3 million acres or 10.6 percent of the state. This region also includes the Llano Uplift or Central Mineral Region. The Balcones Escarpment bounds the Edwards Plateau on the east and south. This region is deeply dissected with numerous streams and rivers. The Balcones Canyonlands form the true Hill Country along the escarpment and are dominated primarily by woodlands and forests with grasslands restricted to broad divides between drainages. Protected canyons and slopes support Ashe Juniper *(Juniperus ashei)*–oak forests. The dominant oak species differ depending on the location but include Lacey oaks *(Quercus laceyi)*, Texas red oak *(Q. buckleyi)*, and plateau live oak *(Q. fusiformis)*. Much of the northern and western plateau is characterized by semi-open grasslands and shrublands on the uplands with riparian corridors along the drainages.

The **Rolling Plains** cover 24 million acres or 14.3 percent of the state. The region is situated between the High Plains and the Cross Timbers and Prairies in the north-central part of the state. These plains are nearly level to rolling and were originally covered by prairie. The Rolling Plains are divided from the High Plains by the steep Caprock Escarpment. The vegetation of this region is tall and midgrass prairie with a wide variety of grasses present, including little bluestem, big bluestem, sand bluestem *(Andropogon gerardii* var. *paucipilus)*, sideoats grama *(Bouteloua curtipendula)*, Indiangrass, and Buffalograss *(Buchloe dactyloides)*. Many rivers and streams have eroded away the Caprock escarpment to form canyons. The largest and best known is **Palo Duro Canyon.** The canyons or breaks of the Canadian River are also included in this region. The Rolling Plains and the Edwards Plateau are ecologically similar, but a distinct geological change defines the boundary. The **Concho Valley** lies along this boundary. Overgrazing and reduction of fires have transformed much of the Rolling Plains from a mid-and tallgrass prairie to an open shrubland dominated by mesquite and juniper.

The **High Plains** region covers 19.4 million acres or about 11.5 percent of the state. The High Plains are bounded by the Caprock Escarpment and dissected by the Canadian River. These plains are nearly level with many shallow playa lakes. The original vegetation of the High Plains consisted generally of mixed and shortgrass prairie and was free from brush. The species of grasses present varied based on soil types. In areas with clay soils, blue grama *(Bouteloua gracilis)* and buffalograss were common, while on sandy soils grasses such as little bluestem, sideoats grama, and sand dropseed *(Sporobolus cryptandrus)* dominated. Today, about 60 percent of the High Plains is in agricultural production, much of that is used to produce row crops. The southern extension of the High Plains, south of the Canadian River, is known as the **Llano Estacado.** The area around Lubbock, including the surrounding counties, is known as the **South Plains.**

The **Trans-Pecos** of far west Texas includes the northern extension of the Chihuahuan Desert, and it coincides with the Basin and Range Physiographic Province. The region covers approximately 18 million acres or 10.7 percent of the state. Guadalupe Peak, at an elevation of 8,751 feet, is the highest point in Texas. There are many small mountain ranges within the region with the Davis, Chisos, and Guadalupe Mountains being the best known. Desert grasslands and desert scrub are found at lower elevations, although very little desert grassland persists today. The vegetation found at the mid-elevations in the mountain ranges is dominated by pinyon pines *(Pinus cembroides, P. edulis, and P. remota)* and junipers, while the upper elevations support pines *(P. ponderosa and P. arizonica).* Creosotebush

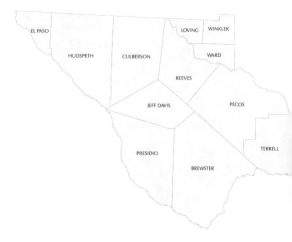

(Larrea tridentata), tarbush *(flourensia cernua),* and various acacias are found in the lowland basins. The **Stockton Plateau** is the subregion found west of the Pecos River and includes most of Terrell and southern Pecos Counties. This region is a transitional area between the Edwards Plateau and the Chihuahuan Desert. The dominant vegetation type is mesquite and Red-berry Juniper *(Juniperus pinchotii)* savannah. The Stockton Plateau is sometimes included as a subregion of the Edwards Plateau.

Texas Counties

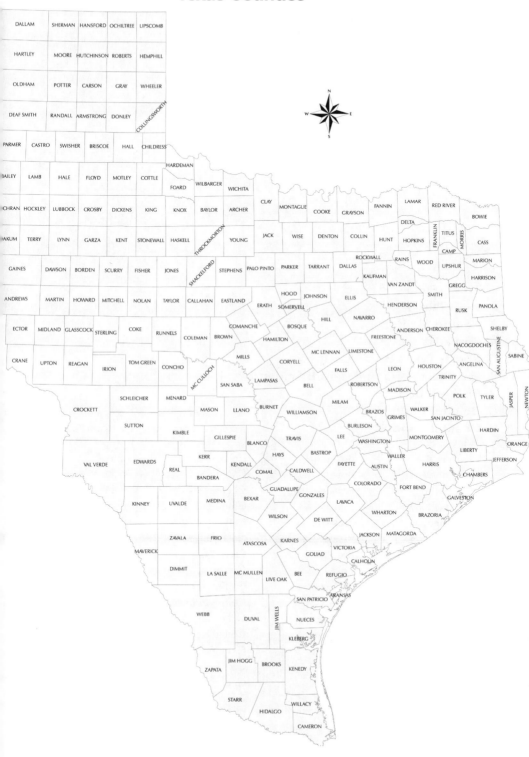

Counties Keyed to the Natural Areas of Texas

The Natural Areas of Texas as defined by the Lyndon B. Johnson School of Public Affairs of the University of Texas at Austin (1978).

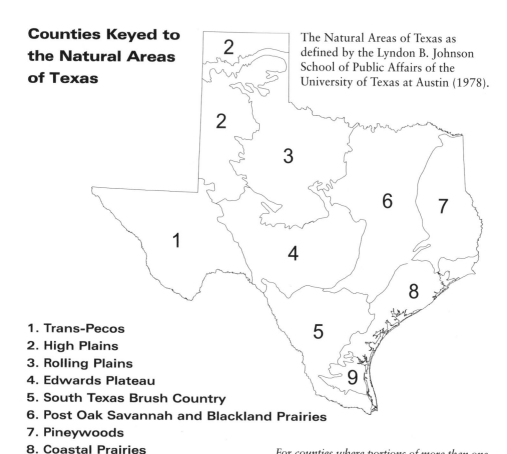

1. **Trans-Pecos**
2. **High Plains**
3. **Rolling Plains**
4. **Edwards Plateau**
5. **South Texas Brush Country**
6. **Post Oak Savannah and Blackland Prairies**
7. **Pineywoods**
8. **Coastal Prairies**
9. **Coastal Sand Plain**

For counties where portions of more than one Natural Area occur, all regions are listed.

Anderson 6, 7	Bosque 6	Castro 2	Crane 1
Andrews 1, 2	Bowie 6, 7	Chambers 8	Crockett 1, 4
Angelina 7	Brazoria 8	Cherokee 7	Crosby 2, 3
Aransas 8	Brazos 6	Childress 3	Culberson 1
Archer 3	Brewster 1	Clay 3	Dallam 2
Armstrong 2, 3	Briscoe 2, 3	Cochran 2	Dallas 6
Atascosa 5	Brooks 9	Coke 3, 4	Dawson 2, 3
Austin 6, 8	Brown 3, 4	Coleman 3	Deaf Smith 2, 3
Bailey 2	Burleson 6	Collin 6	Delta 6
Bandera 4	Burnet 4	Collingsworth 3	Denton 6
Bastrop 6	Caldwell 6	Colorado 6, 8	DeWitt 5, 6
Baylor 3	Calhoun 8	Comal 4	Dickens 3
Bee 5	Callahan 3, 4	Comanche 4, 6	Dimmit 5
Bell 4, 6	Cameron 5	Concho 3, 4	Donley 2, 3
Bexar 4, 5, 6	Camp 7	Cooke 6	Duval 5, 9
Blanco 4	Carson 2, 3	Coryell 4, 6	Eastland 3, 4, 6
Borden 3	Cass 7	Cottle 3	Ector 1, 2

Edwards 4
Ellis 6
El Paso 1
Erath 6
Falls 6
Fannin 6
Fayette 6
fisher 3
floyd 2, 3
Foard 3
Fort Bend 8
Franklin 6
Freestone 6
Frio 5
Gaines 2
Galveston 8
Garza 3
Gillespie 4
Glasscock 2, 4
Goliad 5, 8
Gonzales 5, 6
Gray 2, 3
Grayson 6
Gregg 7
Grimes 6
Guadalupe 6
Hale 2, 3
Hall 3
Hamilton 4, 6
Hansford 2
Hardeman 3
Hardin 7
Harris 8
Harrison 7
Hartley 2, 3
Haskell 3
Hays 4
Hemphill 2, 3
Henderson 6, 7
Hidalgo 5
Hill 6
Hockley 2
Hood 6
Hopkins 6
Houston 6, 7
Howard 3
Hudspeth 1

Hunt 6
Hutchinson 2, 3
Irion 3, 4
Jack 3, 6
Jackson 8
Jasper 7
Jeff Davis 1
Jefferson 8
Jim Hogg 5, 9
Jim Wells 5, 8
Johnson 6
Jones 3
Karnes 5
Kaufman 6
Kendall 4
Kenedy 9
Kent 3
Kerr 4
Kimble 4
King 3
Kinney 4, 5
Kleberg 8, 9
Knox 3
Lamar 6
Lamb 2
Lampasas 4
La Salle 5
Lavaca 6, 8
Lee 6
Leon 6
Liberty 7, 8
Limestone 6
Lipscomb 2
Live Oak 5
Llano 4
Loving 1
Lubbock 2, 3
Lynn 2, 3
Madison 6
Marion 7
Martin 2
Mason 4
Matagorda 8
Maverick 5
McCulloch 3, 4
McLennan 6
McMullen 5

Medina 4, 5
Menard 4
Midland 2, 4
Milam 6
Mills 3, 4
Mitchell 3
Montague 3, 6
Montgomery 7
Moore 2, 3
Morris 7
Motley 3
Nacogdoches 7
Navarro 6
Newton 7
Nolan 3
Nueces 8
Ochiltree 2
Oldham 2, 3
Orange 7, 8
Palo Pinto 3, 6
Panola 7
Parker 6
Parmer 2
Pecos 1
Polk 7
Potter 2, 3
Presidio 1
Rains 6
Randall 2, 3
Reagan 4
Real 4
Red River 6, 7
Reeves 1
Refugio 8
Roberts 2, 3
Robertson 6
Rockwall 6
Runnels 3
Rusk 7
Sabine 7
San Augustine 7
San Jacinto 7
San Patricio 8
San Saba 3, 4
Schleicher 4
Scurry 3
Shackelford 3

Shelby 7
Sherman 2
Smith 7
Somervell 6
Starr 5
Stephens 3
Sterling 3, 4
Stonewall 3
Sutton 4
Swisher 2
Tarrant 6
Taylor 3
Terrell 1
Terry 2, 3
Throckmorton 3
Titus 6, 7
Tom Green 3, 4
Travis 4, 6
Trinity 7
Tyler 7
Upshur 7
Upton 4
Uvalde 4, 5
Val Verde 1, 4
Van Zandt 6
Victoria 8
Walker 6, 7
Waller 6, 8
Ward 1
Washington 6
Webb 5
Wharton 8
Wheeler 2, 3
Wichita 3
Wilbarger 3
Willacy 5, 9
Williamson 4, 6
Wilson 5, 6
Winkler 1
Wise 6
Wood 6, 7
Yoakum 2
Young 3
Zapata 5
Zavala 5

Abbreviations

ANSP	Academy of Natural Sciences in Philadelphia
AMNH	American Museum of Natural History
NP	National Park
NWR	National Wildlife Refuge
SFASU	Stephen F. Austin State University
SP	State Park
TBRC	Texas Bird Records Committee
TBSL	Texas Bird Sounds Library, housed at Sam Houston State University
TCWC	Texas Cooperative Wildlife Collection, housed at Texas A&M University
TPRF	Texas Photo Record file, housed at Texas A&M University

Map Key

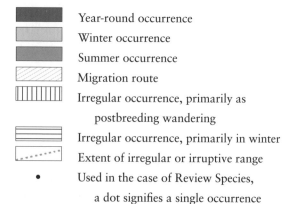

Year-round occurrence

Winter occurrence

Summer occurrence

Migration route

Irregular occurrence, primarily as
   postbreeding wandering

Irregular occurrence, primarily in winter

Extent of irregular or irruptive range

Used in the case of Review Species,
   a dot signifies a single occurrence

AN ANNOTATED LIST OF SPECIES

Sick or injured migratory waterfowl may summer virtually anywhere in Texas. Only those species that have shown a pattern of summer occurrence as healthy birds are included in the following accounts.

ORDER ANSERIFORMES

Family Anatidae: Swans, Geese, and Ducks

BLACK-BELLIED WHISTLING-DUCK
Dendrocygna autumnalis (Linnaeus)

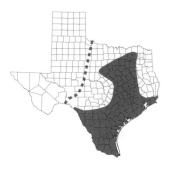

Uncommon to locally common resident, becoming less common in winter, throughout the South Texas Brush Country, north to the southern Edwards Plateau and northeast along the Coastal Prairies. Black-bellied Whistling-Ducks continue to expand their range northward and eastward and are now found north to Brazos and McLennan Counties and locally to Tarrant and Dallas Counties. Isolated breeding populations are also established on the southern Rolling Plains around Brownwood, Brown County. This species is an irregular to casual visitor to the remainder of the state, primarily between March and November. There are isolated breeding records outside of the mapped range.

FULVOUS WHISTLING-DUCK
Dendrocygna bicolor (Vieillot)

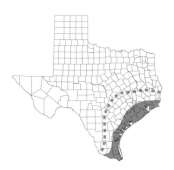

Common summer resident along the Coastal Prairie. Fulvous Whistling-Ducks are irregular summer residents in the eastern half of the Lower Rio Grande Valley, tending to occur only during wet years. This species is a rare to locally uncommon winter resident within its breeding range. The breeding population of Fulvous Whistling-Ducks arrives in early to mid-March and is present through October. They are also very rare and irregular spring visitors to the Blackland Prairies and Post Oak Savannah of east-central Texas north to Tarrant and Rains Counties. Fulvous Whistling-Ducks are accidental visitors to the Trans-Pecos (El Paso, Jeff Davis, and Reeves Counties), Panhandle (Randall County), and South Plains (Hale County).

GREATER WHITE-FRONTED GOOSE
Anser albifrons (Scopoli)

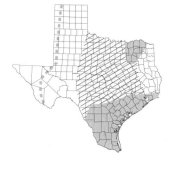

Common migrant through the central portion of the state, becoming uncommon in the Pineywoods and rare to uncommon in the western third of the state. White-fronted Geese are uncommon to locally abundant winter residents on the Coastal Prairies. They can also be found in agricultural areas from Medina and Uvalde Counties southward through the South Texas Brush Country and in northeast Texas. This species is a rare to locally uncommon winter visitor to the remainder of the state. Fall migrants normally appear in late September before other species of geese, and a few wintering birds often linger as late as early April.

SNOW GOOSE *Chen caerulescens* (Linnaeus)

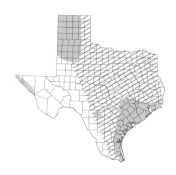

Common to abundant migrant in the eastern half of the state west to the Panhandle. Snow Goose is an abundant winter resident along the coast and is common to locally abundant on the High Plains from Lubbock County north. This species is also an uncommon and local winter resident in the western Trans-Pecos and in agricultural areas in Medina and Uvalde Counties. As with Greater White-fronted Geese, this species can occur as a winter visitor almost anywhere. Returning birds in fall normally appear in early October, often remaining until mid-March with a few lingering as late as early April. The blue morph, which is much less common than the white, was formerly considered a separate species called the Blue Goose.

ROSS'S GOOSE *Chen rossii* (Cassin)

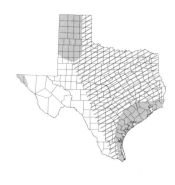

Uncommon, but increasing, winter resident in the Coastal Prairies and High Plains from Lubbock County northward. This species is also increasing as a winter resident in the central and western Trans-Pecos. The current wintering population in Texas is estimated at about 10,000 individuals. This species is an uncommon migrant in the central third of the state, primarily east of the Edwards Plateau, and is rare elsewhere. The seasonal occurrence of Ross's Goose is probably the same as that of Snow Goose. There is some evidence that Ross's arrive later and depart earlier, but additional observations are needed. The dark, or blue, morph of the Ross's Goose is very rare and makes up less than one percent of the population.

CANADA GOOSE *Branta canadensis* (Linnaeus)

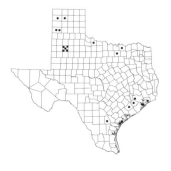

Uncommon to common migrant throughout the state. Canada Geese winter throughout the state, sometimes in large numbers, but are generally abundant only on the High Plains and common only along the upper and central coasts. This species can be rare along the lower coast some winters but locally uncommon during others. Fall migrants begin to appear in late September, with the majority of the wintering population arriving in late October. Most have departed by March. This species has become a summer resident, in small numbers, in the Panhandle. Some recent breeding records involve pairs where one individual was known to be injured. There are considerable differences in the size of the various subspecies of Canada Goose, causing some researchers to suggest that more than one species may be involved. Aldrich (1946) suggested that the smaller, more northern subspecies were specifically different from the larger forms, and a more recent genetics study supports that contention (Quinn, Shields, and Wilson 1991).

Review Species

BRANT *Branta bernicla* (Linnaeus)

Very rare to casual migrant and winter visitor to the state. There are 21 documented records. with most from the Panhandle, South Plains, and Coastal Prairies. Documented records occur between 20 November and 20 April. In many cases, Brants have been found with wintering Canada Geese. Both North American subspecies have been documented, with a few more records of "Atlantic" Brant *(B. b. bernicla)* than of "Black" Brant *(B. b. nigricans)*. There are 19 reports of Brant from prior to the development of the Review List in 1987 for which there is no documentation on file at Texas A&M University.

Review Species

TRUMPETER SWAN *Cygnus buccinator* Richardson

The Trumpeter Swan was a regular winter resident in the eastern two-thirds of Texas until the early 1900s. Nehrling (1882) reported large numbers in Galveston Bay and elsewhere along the upper coast in winter. Since then, there have been only four documented records for the state. In addition to these four records, there have been a number of sightings of birds from reintroduction projects located in the midwestern United States. These swans were not

considered for state records because such populations had not become established and self-sustaining. As of 2001, however, several of the states participating in this project have discontinued intensive management activities and consider the species established. For this reason, marked Trumpeter Swans from established populations documented in Texas after 2001 will be considered for state records.

28 DEC. 1989–14 JAN. 1990, FALCON DAM, STARR CO.
   (TBRC 1990-9; TPRF 936)
8 APR. 1993, NEAR VEGA, OLDHAM CO.
   (TBRC 1996-15; TPRF 1521)
7–26 DEC. 2000, HEMPHILL CO. (TBRC 2000-141; TPRF 1946)
2 JAN.–18 MAR. 2002, BRAZORIA NWR, BRAZORIA CO.
   (TBRC 2002-7; TPRF 1978)

TUNDRA SWAN *Cygnus columbianus* (Ord)

Rare to very rare and irregular winter visitor to all regions of the state. Tundra Swans occur annually only in the Panhandle. Most of the records of this species occur between late October and mid-March, but individuals have lingered as late as early April. Out-of-season reports include an adult in Moore County on 13 July 1985 and another in Potter County on 21 September 1995 (Seyffert 2001). Oberholser (1974) reports that this swan was a common to uncommon winter resident throughout the state prior to 1900.

MUSCOVY DUCK *Cairina moschata* (Linnaeus)

Rare and local resident along the Rio Grande, mainly in Starr and Zapata Counties. This Mexican species is generally more difficult to find during the summer. Muscovy Ducks were first discovered in Texas in December 1984. A small population, centered below Falcon Dam, became established and has persisted. The first reported nesting was near Bentsen–Rio Grande Valley State Park, Hidalgo County, during July 1994 (Brush and Eitniear 2002). An adult that was believed to be wild was along the Rio Grande in northern Maverick County on 5 June 2000, providing the northernmost report. This species is a commonly kept domestic duck and can be seen in parks and other areas throughout the state. These captive individuals very rarely exhibit wild-type plumage and normally have large areas of white on the body and extensive red warty protuberances on the face.

WOOD DUCK *Aix sponsa* (Linnaeus)

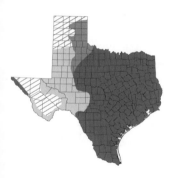

Locally uncommon to common resident in the eastern three-quarters of the state. Wood Ducks are summer residents as far west as the eastern Panhandle and western Edwards Plateau. This species is also an uncommon resident along the Rio Grande in the western Trans-Pecos and in Starr and Webb Counties in southern Texas, with the largest of these populations found in El Paso County. During the winter months, Wood Ducks largely withdraw from the Panhandle but are found more regularly westward on the South Plains and throughout the Trans-Pecos. This species becomes more common in winter in the eastern half of the state as migrants from more northerly populations arrive. Wood Duck populations have rebounded from a low point in the early 1900s. Strecker (1912) considered the species to be very rare and Simmons (1925) thought them to be almost extinct in the Austin area during that time.

GADWALL *Anas strepera* Linnaeus

Common to abundant migrant and winter resident throughout the state. Fall migrants arrive during October, and spring migrants are present as late as mid-May. This species is also a rare and somewhat local summer resident in the Panhandle, but reports of nesting are few. A four-year waterfowl survey made between 1974 and 1977 in the southwestern Panhandle reported only five broods, all from one year (Seyffert 2001). In addition to a few other scattered nesting records from that area, two more are from Dallas County in 1961, which have been questioned by Pulich (1988), and one from San Antonio in 1987. Gadwalls are known to summer irregularly in small numbers throughout the state.

Review Species

EURASIAN WIGEON *Anas penelope* Linnaeus

Casual visitor with 35 documented records for Texas. This species has occurred with greater frequency in the western half of the state and has become an almost annual occurrence in the El Paso area. As would be expected, all of the documented records are of the more conspicuous adult male. There are also a few documented occurrences of Eurasian Wigeon × American Wigeon hybrids. Careful examination of the feather pattern and coloration of the head, breast, and flanks is needed to identify hybrids. There are

24 reports of Eurasian Wigeons from prior to the development of the Review List in 1987 for which there is no documentation on file at Texas A&M University.

AMERICAN WIGEON *Anas americana* Gmelin

Common to abundant migrant and winter resident throughout the state. Fall migrants arrive in mid-September, and spring migrants depart during March with a few lingering into late May. American Wigeons also occur as local summer visitors to the Panhandle and are occasionally encountered elsewhere in the state during that season. There is no evidence of nesting in the state. The playa lakes of the High Plains are one of the primary wintering areas for this species.

Review Species

AMERICAN BLACK DUCK *Anas rubripes* Brewster

Accidental. Since 1950 there have been only four well-documented records for the state and a total of eight accepted records. American Black Duck appears to have been a more regular visitor prior to 1950, although detailed information about specific sightings is lacking. A factor that complicates documentation of American Black Duck is the identification challenge of separating them from the subspecies of Mottled Duck *(A. fulvigula maculosa)* that occurs in Texas. Male Mottled Ducks of this subspecies can be as dark as American Black Ducks, show a purple speculum (depending upon light angle), and have gleaming white wing linings. Documentation requires very careful study of the pattern, including the internal markings, of the feathers of the breast, scapulars, flanks, and back. Eliminating potential American Black Duck×Mallard hybrids only adds to the problem.

30 DEC. 1972, SHELDON LAKE, HARRIS CO.
  (TCWC 13716 AND 13717)
10 DEC. 1974, NEAR WELLS, CHEROKEE CO. (SFASU 2251)
DEC. 1991, SMITH POINT, CHAMBERS CO.
  (TBRC 1994-15; TPRF 1197)
9 DEC. 1998–2 JAN. 1999, FORT WORTH, TARRANT CO.
  (TBRC 1999-3; TPRF 1778)

MALLARD *Anas platyrhynchos* Linnaeus

Common to locally abundant winter resident in the northern half of the state, becoming increasingly less common farther south. Fall migrants arrive in mid-September, and spring migrants are present into late April. Mallards are an

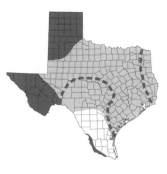

uncommon summer resident in the Panhandle and are rare and local breeders in many other parts of the state. Excluded are the numerous domesticated Mallards that are present throughout the state. A distinctive population of Mallard, known as "Mexican" Duck, is a rare to locally common resident throughout the Trans-Pecos and south along the Rio Grande to Hidalgo County. "Mexican" Ducks were formerly considered a separate species, but studies have shown that most if not all individuals in the United States are intergrades between green-headed Mallards and the true "Mexican" Duck *(A. p. diazi)* of central Mexico (AOU 1983).

MOTTLED DUCK *Anas fulvigula* Ridgway

Locally common resident along the Coastal Prairies. Wandering individuals, not limited to postbreeding dispersal, are regularly encountered as far inland as Travis County. Mottled Ducks have unexpectedly become an uncommon summer resident in eastern north-central and northeast Texas, north into Oklahoma and Kansas. Interestingly, the Texas Parks and Wildlife Department attempted to introduce this species into north-central Texas in the mid-1970s (Stutzenbaker 1988). However, monitoring of the introduced birds showed both poor survivorship and reproduction, making it unlikely that this project was the origin of the current population.

BLUE-WINGED TEAL *Anas discors* Linnaeus

Common to abundant migrant throughout the state. Spring migration includes all of March and April, and fall migration is from late July through October. This species is an uncommon summer resident throughout the Panhandle and South Plains and along the Upper Texas Coast. Blue-winged Teal are rare and local breeders throughout most of the remainder of the state. Blue-wingeds are uncommon to common winter residents along the Coastal Prairies and in the South Texas Brush Country. They become increasingly less common northward to Travis, Burleson, and Montgomery Counties and are generally absent farther north and west.

CINNAMON TEAL *Anas cyanoptera* Vieillot

Common migrant in the western half of the state, becoming uncommon to rare eastward. Cinnamon Teal are uncommon

and somewhat local winter residents along the coast. They are rare to very uncommon inland during the winter in much of the western half of the state from the South Plains southward with scattered records from farther east. This species is a local summer resident in the Panhandle and South Plains. There are also isolated breeding records from Bexar, Colorado, and El Paso Counties.

NORTHERN SHOVELER *Anas clypeata* Linnaeus

Common to abundant migrant and winter resident throughout the state. Northern Shovelers are present in large numbers between early September and mid-May. This species is an uncommon summer visitor to the Panhandle, with a few nesting records. Away from the Panhandle, Northern Shovelers are rare and local summer visitors over much of the rest of the state, with isolated breeding records from the Trans-Pecos and as far south and east as Bastrop and Bexar Counties.

Review Species

WHITE-CHEEKED PINTAIL *Anas bahamensis* Linnaeus

Accidental. There is only one accepted record for Texas. This single individual represents the westernmost record for the United States. The origin of White-cheeked Pintails found in the United States, including those from Florida, has been debated (AOU 1998). Seasonal movements are known for this species throughout its range, and this is true for populations from the West Indies.

20 NOV. 1978–15 APR. 1979, LAGUNA ATASCOSA NWR, CAMERON CO. (TPRF 141)

NORTHERN PINTAIL *Anas acuta* Linnaeus

Locally uncommon to abundant winter resident throughout the state. Northern Pintail is a rare to locally uncommon summer resident in the Panhandle and South Plains. There are also isolated breeding records from various other parts of the state, including Baylor, Calhoun, El Paso, Medina, and Wilbarger Counties, but most of these records date from the 1930s. Migrating Northern Pintails normally begin to arrive in Texas as early as late July and early August, with most of the wintering population in place by late September. Spring migrants and lingering individuals can often be found well into May.

Review Species

GARGANEY *Anas querquedula* Linnaeus

Accidental spring migrant. There are four documented records for the state, all pertaining to adult males. These sightings have occurred within a well-established pattern of spring Garganey records from the central United States. These individuals are believed to have wintered much farther south and were likely overlooked during fall migration when in basic plumage.

11 APR.–17 MAY 1985, NEAR RIVIERA, KLEBERG CO. (TPRF 354)
29 APR.–6 MAY 1994, PRESIDIO, PRESIDIO CO.
  (TBRC 1994-77; TPRF 1296)
17 APR. 1998, BOLIVAR PENINSULA, GALVESTON CO.
  (TBRC 1998-93)
4–7 APR. 2001, KING RANCH, KLEBERG CO.
  (TBRC 2001-88; TPRF 1968)

GREEN-WINGED TEAL *Anas crecca* Linnaeus

Common to abundant migrant, and uncommon to locally common winter resident throughout the state. Green-winged Teal is particularly abundant on the upper coast. Wintering birds are present from September through April. Fall migrants begin to appear in late August and spring migrants have lingered as late as early June. This species is a rare to occasional summer visitor to the Panhandle and Trans-Pecos. There are only two reports of breeding in Texas; a pair with young was found in Hutchinson County in 1975, and an unsuccessful nesting attempt was reported from Crosby County in 1982. Oberholser (1974) discounted a report of several nesting pairs in Dallam County from 1936, but Seyffert (2001) gave this report more weight based on the regular occurrence of this species in the area. The subspecies of Green-winged Teal present in Texas is *A. c. carolinensis,* but there is a single documented record of Eurasian Teal *(A. c. crecca)* from the Village Creek Drying Beds, Tarrant County, from 30 January to 1 February 1994 (TBRC 1994-135; TPRF 1279). The Association of European Rarity Committees recognizes Eurasian Teal as a separate species.

CANVASBACK *Aythya valisineria* (Wilson)

Uncommon to locally common migrant and winter resident throughout the state. Canvasbacks are present in Texas from mid-October to late March with a few lingering as late as early May. This species occasionally remains through the summer, but there are only a few nesting records. Four broods were discovered in the southwestern Panhandle in 1975 (Seyffert 2001), and a female with young was observed in Jeff Davis County on 13 May 1986.

REDHEAD *Aythya americana* (Eyton)

Uncommon to common migrant throughout the state. The Laguna Madre is the winter home to the largest concentration of Redheads in the world, and the species is considered a common to abundant winter resident along the central and lower coasts. They are also rare to locally common winter residents throughout the remainder of the state. This species is normally present between mid-October and early April. Redheads are uncommon to locally common summer residents in the Panhandle, but despite their relative abundance, they appear to be a fairly rare breeder (Seyffert 2001). Redheads also breed in small numbers in El Paso and Hudspeth Counties in the western Trans-Pecos.

RING-NECKED DUCK *Aythya collaris* (Donovan)

Uncommon to locally common migrant and winter resident throughout the state, Ring-necked Ducks are present from mid-October to mid-April. This species is a rare summer visitor to the Panhandle, South Plains, and Trans-Pecos. Despite the regular occurrence of this species in summer, there is no evidence of nesting in the state.

GREATER SCAUP *Aythya marila* (Linnaeus)

Rare to uncommon migrant in all parts of the state. Greater Scaup are rare to locally uncommon winter residents along the upper and central coasts and on reservoirs in the eastern half of the state. They are rare to very rare along the lower coast and in the western half of the state. Greater Scaup are present between early November and early March, but apparently healthy individuals have lingered to early June.

LESSER SCAUP *Aythya affinis* (Eyton)

Common to abundant migrant and winter resident east of the Pecos River. In the Trans-Pecos, they are common migrants and uncommon to locally rare winter residents. Lesser Scaup begin arriving in late September but are not common until late October. Most of the wintering population departs by late March, but some birds linger into mid-

May. This species is a rare summer visitor to virtually any part of the state. There are only two reports of breeding for the state: Muleshoe National Wildlife Refuge, Bailey County, in 1942 (Hawkins 1945) and a female with ducklings in southern Swisher County in early July 1977 (Seyffert 2001). Lesser Scaup populations are currently in sharp decline.

Review Species

KING EIDER *Somateria spectabilis* (Linnaeus)

Accidental. Texas has one documented record of this duck, a male in very worn plumage that was captured and transported to Ohio where it was rehabilitated. This record and two others from Louisiana all date from the late spring and early summer. Typically, King Eiders are not found farther south than New England during the winter. There is also a sight record of a male at Rockport on 23 October 1968, for which there is no documentation on file at Texas A&M University.

30 APR.–7 MAY 1998, QUINTANA, BRAZORIA CO.
  (TBRC 1998-59; TPRF 1729)

Review Species

HARLEQUIN DUCK *Histrionicus histrionicus* (Linnaeus)

Accidental. Texas has two documented records of Harlequin Duck: the first a male, the second a pair. Harlequin Ducks found in Texas may originate from either of the disjunct North American populations. The breeding range of the western population only reaches northwestern Wyoming, and these birds migrate to the Pacific for the winter. Winter records from the intermountain west are rare, and there is only one recent record for Colorado. Eastern birds breed east of Hudson Bay and on Greenland and winter along the Atlantic Coast as far south as Virginia. There are three sight records from Aransas County, two in January 1945 and one in November 1964; however, there is no documentation of these sightings on file at Texas A&M University.

30 JAN.–4 FEB. 1990, SOUTH PADRE ISLAND, CAMERON CO.
  (TBRC 1990-21; TPRF 858)
5 JAN. 1995, LAKE TAWAKONI, VAN ZANDT CO. (TBRC 1995-12)

SURF SCOTER *Melanitta perspicillata* (Linnaeus)

Rare migrant and winter visitor over most of the state and uncommon and local winter resident along the upper and central coasts. Surf Scoter is the most frequently encountered scoter species in Texas and has been found along the coast from late October to May, although most birds are seen between early December and early April. Migrants are most frequently encountered from late October to early December and mid-March to late April. The wintering population along the coast is mostly confined to saltwater habitats, such as bays and near-shore Gulf waters. The majority of Surf Scoters found in Texas are in first-winter plumage, although adults are present.

WHITE-WINGED SCOTER *Melanitta fusca* (Linnaeus)

Rare to very rare migrant and winter resident throughout the state, except the Trans-Pecos, where there is only one record. White-winged Scoters are more commonly encountered in saltwater habitats along the upper and central coasts than elsewhere. Most records occur between early November and mid-March. As is the case with the Surf Scoter, most reports involve individuals in first-winter plumage.

BLACK SCOTER *Melanitta nigra* (Linnaeus)

Very rare winter resident along the coast, primarily along the upper and central portions. As with other scoters, Black Scoters are found primarily in saltwater habitats and are casual inland. The period of occurrence for Black Scoter mirrors that of the White-winged Scoter with most records falling between early November and mid-March. Black Scoter is the least frequently encountered scoter in Texas.

LONG-TAILED DUCK *Clangula hyemalis* (Linnaeus)

Very rare migrant and winter visitor in nearly all parts of the state, although most frequently encountered along the coast. Most Long-tailed Duck records occur between mid-November and early April. As with the scoters, most individuals are in first-winter plumage and adult males are rarely observed. This species was formerly known as Oldsquaw.

BUFFLEHEAD *Bucephala albeola* (Linnaeus)

Common migrant and winter resident throughout the state. Buffleheads begin arriving in Texas in late October, and most have departed by early May. In most years, wintering populations along the coast and in the southern third of the state have migrated north by early April. Buffleheads very rarely linger later in the spring, but a few records exist from early June.

COMMON GOLDENEYE *Bucephala clangula* (Linnaeus)

Uncommon to rare winter resident in most of the state and uncommon to locally common along the upper and central coasts, becoming rare to very rare on the lower coast. Inland, Common Goldeneyes are most frequently encountered on larger reservoirs; however, they are sometimes found on small lakes and even on rivers. This species is present primarily between early November and early March. A few regularly linger into late April, particularly along the coast.

Review Species

BARROW'S GOLDENEYE *Bucephala islandica* (Gmelin)

Accidental. There are eight documented records of this species in the state. All but one, not surprisingly, have involved the more easily identified adult male. Barrow's Golden-eyes are regular winter visitors to northern New Mexico and Arizona and could be expected to occur in Texas more frequently than currently reported. The first record for the state was a male taken by a hunter near Greenville, Hunt County, on 6 November 1958 (TBRC 1989-202; TPRF 787). Reportedly, this bird was with two others of its kind. One other Texas record included more than a single bird: a pair was at Loy Lake, Grayson County, from 5 January to 22 February 2002 (TBRC 2002-12; TPRF 1981). All of the Texas records occur between 6 November and 22 February. There are six reports of Barrow's Goldeneyes from prior to the development of the Review List in 1987 for which there is no documentation on file at Texas A&M University.

HOODED MERGANSER
Lophodytes cucullatus (Linnaeus)

Uncommon to common migrant and winter resident throughout most of the state. Hooded Merganser is uncommon to rare and somewhat local on the Edwards Plateau and rare throughout the Trans-Pecos. They are rare summer visitors to the Pineywoods, and only a few breeding records are known. During the 1990s, the number of reported nesting attempts increased, many involving nests discovered in Wood Duck boxes. In some cases, female mergansers had laid eggs in active Wood Duck nests, and all young from the joint clutches were reared by the Wood Ducks. There are recent breeding records from Collin, Dallas, Fort Bend, Harrison, Lee, Liberty, Rusk, and Upshur Counties.

COMMON MERGANSER *Mergus merganser* Linnaeus

Uncommon to occasionally abundant winter resident on the High Plains, from the Panhandle south to the San Angelo area, and west through the Trans-Pecos, where they are locally common. This species is rare eastward to north-central Texas and absent throughout the remainder of the state. Common Merganser is very rarely found in saltwater habitats, although there are a small number of coastal records. This species is a rare summer visitor to the Panhandle.

RED-BREASTED MERGANSER
Mergus serrator Linnaeus

Common winter resident along the coast and uncommon to rare on inland reservoirs in the eastern two-thirds of the state, including Amistad Reservoir, Val Verde County. Red-breasted Merganser is a rare winter resident in the western third of Texas, where most birds are in female-like plumage. This species is present along the coast throughout the year, although rare during the summer. There is one breeding record from the state: two females with young were discovered at Laguna Atascosa National Wildlife Refuge, Cameron County, during May and June 1995 (Rupert and Brush 1996). One fledgling was found dead and preserved as a specimen in the collection at the University of Texas–Pan American.

Review Species

MASKED DUCK *Nomonyx dominicus* (Linnaeus)

Rare and irregular visitor along the coast and in the Lower Rio Grande Valley. Masked Ducks are absent during most years but can be locally uncommon during invasion periods (Lockwood 1997). Large concentrations have been noted during these invasions, including a total of 37 individuals on a lake in San Patricio County in February 1993 (Blankenship and Anderson 1993). Of the 62 documented records for the state, only two are away from the coastal plains: one in El Paso County on 11 July 1976 (TBRC 1999-42) and another in Hays County from 20 September to early October 1980 (TPRF 211). Only one well-documented nesting record exists for the state, a female with young at Anahuac National Wildlife Refuge, Chambers County, in 1967. Reports of nestings have come from Brooks, Brazoria, Cameron, Colorado, Jefferson, Hidalgo, and San Patricio Counties. This species has been widely reported as a rare permanent resident in Texas; however, there is very little evidence to support this contention. There are 76 reports of Masked Ducks from prior to the development of the Review List in 1987 for which there is no documentation on file at Texas A&M University.

RUDDY DUCK *Oxyura jamaicensis* (Gmelin)

Common migrant and winter resident throughout most of the state, but rare in winter in the Panhandle. Ruddy Ducks arrive in Texas in early September and depart by mid-May. Although uncommon, this small duck is regularly encountered in Texas during the summer months. Their elaborate courtship ritual can be seen during the late spring throughout the state, but breeding records are few. This species is a locally common summer resident in El Paso County and can be found nesting at resacas along the Rio Grande in Presidio County when conditions are favorable, as was the case in 1991 when there were many successful nestings.

ORDER GALLIFORMES

Family Cracidae: Curassows and Guans

PLAIN CHACHALACA *Ortalis vetula* (Wagler)

Uncommon to common resident in the Lower Rio Grande Valley north to Willacy and Zapata Counties. Plain Chachalacas formerly occurred north to Webb County. A small population has been discovered in Kenedy County, but these are probably remnants of a 1987 release on a private ranch. Similar releases occurred during the mid- to late 1980s in Brooks, Dimmitt, Jim Wells, Kleberg, LaSalle, Nueces, and San Patricio Counties, which likely account for the occasional reports from those counties.

Family Phasianidae: Pheasants, Grouse, and Allies

RING-NECKED PHEASANT
Phasianus colchicus Linnaeus

Common resident in the northern and western parts of the Panhandle, becoming increasingly less common southward

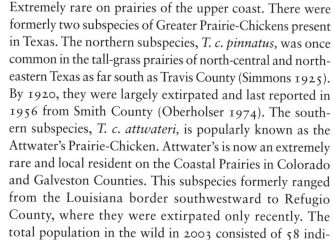

onto the northern South Plains and farther east. A small population of this introduced species is still present in eastern Chambers County near Anahuac. Ring-necked Pheasants were formerly more widespread but have declined in many areas, including most of the South Plains. Small populations were once established near El Paso and Balmorhea, Reeves County, but their status there is uncertain. The Ring-necked Pheasant was introduced into Texas for hunting beginning in the 1930s, and both Texas Parks and Wildlife Department and private releases have occasionally supplemented these populations, producing temporary, nonviable populations elsewhere in the state.

GREATER PRAIRIE-CHICKEN
Tympanuchus cupido (Linnaeus)

Extremely rare on prairies of the upper coast. There were formerly two subspecies of Greater Prairie-Chickens present in Texas. The northern subspecies, *T. c. pinnatus,* was once common in the tall-grass prairies of north-central and northeastern Texas as far south as Travis County (Simmons 1925). By 1920, they were largely extirpated and last reported in 1956 from Smith County (Oberholser 1974). The southern subspecies, *T. c. attwateri,* is popularly known as the Attwater's Prairie-Chicken. Attwater's is now an extremely rare and local resident on the Coastal Prairies in Colorado and Galveston Counties. This subspecies formerly ranged from the Louisiana border southwestward to Refugio County, where they were extirpated only recently. The total population in the wild in 2003 consisted of 58 individuals, many of which originated from a captive breeding program.

LESSER PRAIRIE-CHICKEN
Tympanuchus pallidicinctus (Ridgway)

Rare to uncommon and local resident in the Panhandle and South Plains. There are currently two disjunct populations in Texas. The population on the western South Plains extends from Bailey County southward to Gaines and possibly Andrews Counties. There have been recent sightings as far north as Parmer and Deaf Smith Counties. Whether these sightings pertain to a resident population or birds wandering northward from established populations is not known. The population in the eastern Panhandle is found from Lipscomb County south to Collingsworth County. Lesser Prairie-Chickens formerly ranged south to Menard and Jeff Davis Counties (Strecker 1912). They have been reported to have formerly ranged as far east as Cooke and Tarrant Counties. Pulich (1988) questioned the validity of the easternmost reports and postulated that the eastern boundary was probably several counties farther west. Pulich also noted that G. H. Ragsdale is credited with collecting both Greater and Lesser Prairie-Chickens from Cooke County in January 1878, which he considered unlikely. Lesser Prairie-Chickens formerly wandered southward during the winter months. The last incursion into the western Edwards Plateau was during the winter of 1885–86 (Lacey 1911). This species was last documented in the San Angelo area in 1912 and was present in Howard County until at least 1945 (T. Maxwell, pers. comm.).

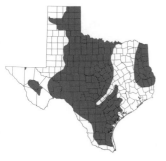

WILD TURKEY *Meleagris gallopavo* Linnaeus

Common to uncommon resident from the eastern Panhandle southward through the Rolling Plains to the Edwards Plateau. This species is also common to uncommon in the South Texas Brush Country north of the Lower Rio Grande Valley, on the Coastal Prairies to Jackson County, and in the mountains of the central Trans-Pecos. Wild Turkey was formerly a common resident in the eastern half of the state. In many of these areas today, turkeys are very rare. The Texas Parks and Wildlife Department has reintroduced Wild Turkey to many areas of the state with mixed results, and these activities continue. Within Texas, there have been considerable efforts to bolster or restore local populations.

Family Odontophoridae: New World Quail

SCALED QUAIL *Callipepla squamata* (Vigors)

Uncommon to locally common resident in the Trans-Pecos and from the Panhandle south through the Rolling Plains (east to Wichita and Coleman Counties), to the western South Texas Brush Country. Scaled Quail populations from the South Plains to the western Edwards Plateau have experienced sharp declines in recent years. The reasons behind this decline are presently unclear but are probably related to habitat loss. Scaled Quail formerly ranged eastward to the eastern Rolling Plains and Edwards Plateau (Strecker 1912; Simmons 1925).

GAMBEL'S QUAIL *Callipepla gambelii* (Gambel)

Common resident in El Paso and western Hudspeth Counties southward along the Rio Grande to Presidio County. Gambel's Quail are colonizing areas away from the floodplain of the Rio Grande (Peterson and Zimmer 1998). They appear to be rare and very localized residents throughout Hudspeth County and possibly in extreme western Culberson County south of the Guadalupe Mountains. Gambel's Quail have also been found irregularly on the upland plateaus of Big Bend Ranch State Park in southern Presidio County. As a result, the actual range of this species away from El Paso County and the Rio Grande floodplain are uncertain.

NORTHERN BOBWHITE *Colinus virginianus* (Linnaeus)

Locally uncommon to rare throughout the state east of the Pecos River. Northern Bobwhite is a rare and local resident in southern Reeves County and has been reported from Jeff Davis and Pecos Counties. The origin of these populations has been debated. Northern Bobwhite populations have declined significantly, particularly in the eastern half of the state where they have become rare in many areas. They are still locally common in the eastern half of the state but are more evenly distributed in the Panhandle, South Plains, and western Rolling Plains. The innumerable releases of pen-raised birds have confused distributional ranges of the subspecies and obscured the actual status of the species as a whole.

MONTEZUMA QUAIL *Cyrtonyx montezumae* (Vigors)

Uncommon and local resident in the Davis and Del Norte Mountains of the Trans-Pecos. This quail is rare to locally uncommon in the Chinati and Glass Mountains, as well as the Sierra Diablo and Sierra Vieja. A relict population still exists on the western Edwards Plateau and is centered in Edwards County. Due to the skulking habits of this quail, they are easily overlooked and may occur in other mountain ranges in the Trans-Pecos. There have been attempts at reintroduction into the Guadalupe and Chisos Mountains but with minimal success, and the occasional sightings in Dog Canyon on the north side of Guadalupe Mountains National Park are presumed to be remnants of these attempts. Montezuma Quail have been shown to be sensitive to changes in the quality of the grasslands and savannas they inhabit. Albers and Gehlbach (1990) showed that when 40 to 50 percent of tall-grass cover is removed, the quail are extirpated. Montezuma Quail formerly occurred over much of the Edwards Plateau and southward into Maverick County.

ORDER GAVIIFORMES

Family Gaviidae: Loons

RED-THROATED LOON *Gavia stellata* (Pontoppidan)

Very rare winter resident along the upper coast and on lakes and reservoirs in the northeastern sector of the state. Red-throated Loon is considered accidental to most other areas of Texas. There are 48 documented records of this species with the majority since the early 1990s. Whether this represents an increase in frequency or greater observer awareness is uncertain. Documented records of this species exist between 26 October and 3 May. This species was removed from the Review List in 2002; at the time there were 48 documented records. There are 52 additional reports of Red-throated Loons from prior to the development of the Review List in 1987 for which there is no documentation on file at Texas A&M University.

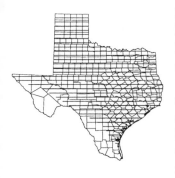

PACIFIC LOON *Gavia pacifica* (Lawrence)

Rare to very rare winter visitor along the coast and on larger lakes and reservoirs throughout most of the state. Pacific Loons occur with greater frequency, and are more evenly distributed statewide, than Red-throated Loons. Prior to 1980, there were only four documented records from the state. That number grew to over 60 by 1996 when the species was removed from the Review Species list. Wintering birds have lingered into spring with one individual from Galveston County remaining through June. Other summer records include single birds in Aransas County on 9 July 1994 and San Antonio, Bexar County, on 17 June 2001.

Most records pertain to single individuals although groups of up to nine have been recorded. This taxon was previously included under Arctic Loon, *Gavia arctica* (AOU 1957). Reports of Pacific Loon prior to 1985 may be listed as *G. arctica,* but in fact probably are *G. pacifica.* No accepted records of *G. arctica* exist for Texas.

COMMON LOON *Gavia immer* (Brünnich)

Uncommon to rare migrant throughout the state. This species is a common winter resident in bays and estuaries along the coast where loose groups exceeding 60 individuals are occasionally found in late winter. Common Loons are uncommon to locally common on inland lakes and reservoirs, especially where water depths are adequate for deep dives. They are decidedly less common and more local in the western third of the state, particularly on the High Plains. This species arrives as early as mid-September and departs by mid-April. Common Loons occur infrequently during the summer months, and then most often along the coast. These summering individuals are nonbreeders and typically retain basic plumage.

Review Species

YELLOW-BILLED LOON *Gavia adamsii* (Gray)

Accidental. Texas has five documented records of Yellow-billed Loon. A bird of the high Arctic, it has occurred with greater frequency in the interior United States over the past two decades (Patten 2000). Prior to 1970, this species was virtually unknown away from the Pacific Coast and was so unexpected in Texas that the first occurrence was thought to be an atypical Common Loon. Examination of the photographs six years later proved beyond doubt that the bird was in fact a Yellow-billed Loon. To date, all individuals discovered have been in first-winter plumage. The Cameron County individual appears to be the southernmost ever documented in the New World.

2 DEC. 1981–9 JAN. 1982, BUFFALO SPRINGS LAKE, LUBBOCK CO.
(TBRC 1988-276; TPRF 696)

12–14 JAN. 1992, LAKE O' THE PINES, MARION CO.
(TBRC 1992-23)

25 NOV.–10 DEC. 1993, BALMORHEA LAKE, REEVES CO.
(TBRC 1993-149; TPRF 1243)

21 DEC. 1996–3 JAN. 1997, BALMORHEA LAKE, REEVES CO.
(TBRC 1997-5; TPRF 1528)

23 DEC. 2000–26 MAY 2001, SOUTH PADRE ISLAND, CAMERON CO.
(TBRC 2001-39; TPRF 1967)

ORDER PODICIPEDIFORMES

Family Podicipedidae: Grebes

LEAST GREBE *Tachybaptus dominicus* (Linnaeus)

Uncommon to locally common resident of the Lower Rio Grande Valley north along the Coastal Prairies to the central coast. They are low density residents, or at least occasional breeders, eastward along the coast to Harris County and north to Bastrop and Bexar Counties. Least Grebes are rare and very local visitors at all seasons farther up the coast to Jefferson County and inland to at least Travis County. The greatest population densities are found from Brooks, Kenedy, and Kleberg Counties southward to Cameron and Hidalgo Counties. Least Grebes occur irregularly farther inland to Kerr and Val Verde Counties and have been documented as far west as Brewster County (TPRF 128). The number of individuals present fluctuates greatly from year to year depending on rainfall and therefore habitat availability. Populations may also decline temporarily in response to stress resulting from unusually cold weather (James 1963). Some individuals retreat southward during the winter, particularly those from the northernmost portions of their range. Breeding may occur during any month in the Lower Rio Grande Valley. Nesting sites usually are on small, shallow, secluded bodies of water protected by trees, brush, and other vegetation.

PIED-BILLED GREBE *Podilymbus podiceps* (Linnaeus)

Uncommon to common migrant and winter resident throughout the state. This species is a rare to uncommon, but irregular, breeder in most areas, although they may be locally common during a given year when conditions are favorable. Nonbreeding Pied-billed Grebes are also frequently found during the summer. Preferred nesting habitat in Texas appears to be much like that of Least Grebe; however, Pied-billeds do seem to tolerate slightly more open and less protected locations.

HORNED GREBE *Podiceps auritus* (Linnaeus)

Rare to locally common winter resident along the coast, particularly along the upper portion. Horned Grebes are

generally rare to uncommon inland, except in the northeastern quarter of the state, where they are locally common. They are most often found on large bodies of water. Horned Grebes are very rare to casual in the South Texas Brush Country and along the lower coast. This species generally occurs between late October and late March, although birds have lingered through May.

Review Species

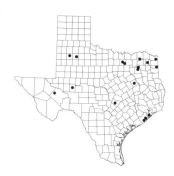

RED-NECKED GREBE *Podiceps grisegena* (Boddaert)

Very rare winter visitor for which there are 17 documented records. The first to be documented was found at Big Lake, Reagan County, from 23 to 30 November 1975 (TBRC 1992-129). Nearly half of those documented have been from north-central and northeast Texas. The greatest number of individuals present for a single accepted record was three at White River Lake, Crosby County, from 21 to 22 January 1978. Extreme dates of occurrence are 5 November and 30 March. There are 35 reports of Red-necked Grebe from prior to the development of the Review List in 1987 for which there is no documentation on file at Texas A&M University.

EARED GREBE *Podiceps nigricollis* Brehm

Common to uncommon migrant throughout the state. Eared Grebes are uncommon to common winter residents in most areas, except for the High Plains, where they are very rare. This grebe is common to locally abundant along the coast, where flocks of several hundred are occasionally encountered. This species is an uncommon to rare summer resident in the Panhandle and Trans-Pecos. Large concentrations of breeding birds have occasionally been reported from the Panhandle, including a total of 61 nests on a single playa in Randall County in 1999. Breeding records are rare in other areas of the state, but exist from as far south as Bee County. Nonbreeding Eared Grebes are frequently found summering throughout the state, including coastal bays.

WESTERN GREBE *Aechmophorus occidentalis* (Lawrence)

Common to uncommon migrant and winter resident in the Trans-Pecos. Western Grebes are rare migrants and winter visitors east of the Pecos River and are annual as far east as north-central Texas. The wintering population in the Trans-

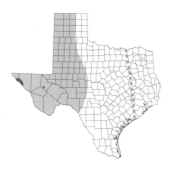

Pecos, and to a lesser extent farther east, has increased steadily during the 1990s. Concentrations of up to 70 individuals have been noted in Hudspeth County. Since 1991, small numbers of individuals have remained through the summer on reservoirs in the Trans-Pecos. The first nesting record of Aechmophorus grebes in Texas consisted of a mixed pair of Western/Clark's found at Balmorhea Lake, Reeves County, in 1991 (Lockwood 1992). Another mixed pair was discovered building a nest in Hudspeth County in 1994. The first breeding record involving only Western Grebes was discovered at McNary Reservoir, Hudspeth County, in December 2001, and several pairs nested there in 2002. Many reports of "Western" Grebe prior to the elevation of Clark's Grebe to species status in 1985 lack sufficient detail for identification to species.

CLARK'S GREBE *Aechmophorus clarkii* (Lawrence)

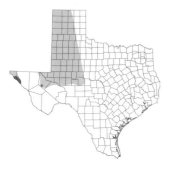

Uncommon to rare winter resident in the Trans-Pecos and very rare migrant and winter visitor to the High Plains and Concho Valley. Clark's Grebe is a winter vagrant farther east. As with the Western Grebe, the wintering population of Clark's Grebe in the Trans-Pecos has increased significantly during the 1990s. A small but increasing summer population is now also present, particularly at reservoirs in Hudspeth and El Paso Counties and at Balmorhea Lake, Reeves County. Breeding pairs of Clark's Grebes have been noted at McNary Reservoir, Hudspeth County, since 1997 and the number of pairs has increased each year. In 2001, eight pairs with chicks were noted, with similar numbers reported in 2002. There are a few instances of breeding resulting from Clark's/Western pair bondings (see Western Grebe account).

ORDER PROCELLARIIFORMES

Family Diomedeidae: Albatrosses

Review Species

YELLOW-NOSED ALBATROSS
Thalassarche chlororhynchos (Gmelin)

Accidental. There are four documented records of this species for the state. Three were found on beaches, two on the

lower coast and one on the central coast. Two were found dead or dying and were preserved as specimens. Yellow-nosed Albatross is found primarily south of the Tropic of Capricorn in the southern oceans.

14 MAY 1972, PORT ISABEL, CAMERON CO. (TBRC 1988-50)
28 OCT. 1976, SOUTH PADRE ISLAND, WILLACY CO. (TPRF 118)
11 JULY 1997, SAN JOSE ISLAND, ARANSAS CO.
  (TBRC 1997-129; TPRF 1651)
26 SEP. 2003, OFF SOUTH PADRE ISLAND, WILLACY CO.
  (TBRC 2003-74; TPRF 2119)

Family Procellariidae: Shearwaters and Petrels

Review Species

BLACK-CAPPED PETREL *Pterodroma hasitata* (Kuhl)

Accidental. There are two records of this species from the offshore waters of Texas. Both records involve single individuals discovered 60+ miles offshore from Port O'Connor, Calhoun County. Black-capped Petrel is a casual visitor to the Gulf of Mexico; most other sightings are off the western coast of Florida.

28 MAY 1994, OFF PORT O'CONNOR, CALHOUN CO.
  (TBRC 1996-129; TPRF 1631)
26 JULY 1997, OFF PORT O'CONNOR, CALHOUN CO.
  (TBRC 1997-118; TPRF 1633)

Review Species

STEJNEGER'S PETREL

Pterodroma longirostris (Stejneger)

Accidental. A single record of this species exists for Texas. A decomposing carcass was retrieved from a beach near Port Aransas, Nueces County. Specific identification was made by comparing the skeleton to that of other similar-sized *Pterodroma* species (S. Olson and D. Lee, pers. comm.). Stejneger's Petrel is primarily found in the southern Pacific, and its occurrence in the Gulf of Mexico was quite unexpected.

15 SEPT. 1995, PORT ARANSAS, NUECES CO.
  (TBRC 1997-59; TPRF 1746)

Review Species

WHITE-CHINNED PETREL

Procellaria aequinoctialis (Linnaeus)

Accidental. There is a single record of this species for Texas. The bird was discovered floundering in the surf and was taken to a wildlife rehabilitator where it later died. Unfortunately, the specimen was not saved. This individual repre-

sented the first documented occurrence for North America; however, the AOU (1998) questions its origin. A second sighting of a White-chinned Petrel, this one from the North Atlantic, was made off North Carolina in 1996. Although this petrel was perhaps correctly identified, the North Carolina Bird Records Committee decided that the report was not documented thoroughly enough to be accepted. The species is found primarily in the southern oceans.

27 APR. 1986, ROLLOVER PASS, GALVESTON CO.
(TBRC 1990-129; TPRF 957)

CORY'S SHEARWATER *Calonectris diomedea* (Scopoli)

Uncommon, but regular, offshore along the entire Texas coast during summer and fall. This species is rare to very rare through the winter and spring. They appear to be most common between July and September in the western Gulf of Mexico. The status of Cory's Shearwater was not well understood until waters along the Continental Shelf were visited more regularly. Unlike other tubenoses, Cory's Shearwaters were regularly encountered in waters near the Continental Shelf during the 1970s and 1980s.

Review Species

GREATER SHEARWATER *Puffinus gravis* (O'Reilly)

Casual visitor to offshore waters along the upper and central coasts of the Gulf. There are 11 documented records of this species with most falling between late June and mid-October, although single records exist for April, November, and December. Six of these records involve dead or dying birds discovered on beaches, five of which are preserved as specimens. The first record for Texas was found at Galveston on 4 November 1973 (TCWC 9316).

Review Species

SOOTY SHEARWATER *Puffinus griseus* (Gmelin)

Casual visitor to the offshore waters of the Gulf. There are 13 documented records of this species in Texas. Of these, 11 involved beached individuals, with seven preserved as specimens. Records are from almost every season of the year; however, none exist from February through April. Given the difficulty of distinguishing Sooty from Short-tailed Shearwater, the TBRC voted to label all records that include only written documentation (no photos or specimens) as Sooty until Short-tailed is documented anywhere in the Gulf of Mexico or the northern Atlantic Ocean.

Review Species

MANX SHEARWATER *Puffinus puffinus* (Brünnich)

Accidental. There are six documented records of this species for the state. All of these records involve individuals discovered on Mustang Island, Nueces County, or North Padre Island, Nueces or Kenedy Counties. When found they were either dead or barely alive and in poor condition; five were preserved as specimens. The first record for the state was discovered on North Padre Island on 15 February 1975. Four of the Texas records are from the fall, ranging from mid-August to mid-November. There are also single summer and winter records.

AUDUBON'S SHEARWATER

Puffinus lherminieri Lesson

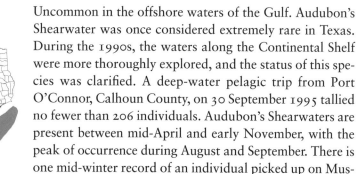

Uncommon in the offshore waters of the Gulf. Audubon's Shearwater was once considered extremely rare in Texas. During the 1990s, the waters along the Continental Shelf were more thoroughly explored, and the status of this species was clarified. A deep-water pelagic trip from Port O'Connor, Calhoun County, on 30 September 1995 tallied no fewer than 206 individuals. Audubon's Shearwaters are present between mid-April and early November, with the peak of occurrence during August and September. There is one mid-winter record of an individual picked up on Mustang Island, Nueces County, on 23 January 1989. Audubon's Shearwater was a Review Species until 1997.

Family Hydrobatidae: Storm-Petrels

Review Species

WILSON'S STORM-PETREL

Oceanites oceanicus (Kuhl)

Accidental. Texas has one documented record of the species. There are eight additional reports of this species without supporting documentation, some of which are of multiple birds and date as far back as 1912. Possible confusion with the more commonly occurring Band-rumped Storm-Petrel casts doubt on these reports. Surprisingly, Wilson's is the most frequently encountered storm-petrel in Louisiana's offshore waters, particularly east of the Mississippi Delta; hence, this species might be expected to occur in Texas waters between April and September.

8 AUG. 1979, OFF PORT ARANSAS, NUECES CO. (TPRF 567)

Review Species

LEACH'S STORM-PETREL
Oceanodroma leucorhoa (Vieillot)

Rare to very rare in the offshore waters of the Gulf. There are 22 documented records for the state, some involving multiple birds and all from May through September. As with other tubenoses, the exploration of waters along the Continental Shelf during the 1990s greatly enhanced our understanding of this species' occurrence in Texas. Before 1991, there were only three accepted records for the state. As these organized pelagic trips continue on a regular basis, it is plausible that enough data will be collected to remove it from the Review List. Extreme dates of accepted records are 28 May and 30 September.

BAND-RUMPED STORM-PETREL
Oceanodroma castro (Harcourt)

Uncommon to rare summer visitor offshore. Band-rumped Storm-Petrel was considered accidental in Texas prior to the mid-1990s, but since that time it has been found on virtually every deep-water pelagic trip made between May and September. The highest count to date was 70 individuals found on 14 July 2000 off South Padre Island, Cameron County. There are two documented inland records: three individuals were discovered near Edinburg, Hidalgo County, after Hurricane Alice on 25 June 1954 and a single bird near San Antonio, Bexar County, on 14 June 1984. Band-rumped Storm-Petrel was a Review Species in Texas until 1997.

ORDER PELECANIFORMES

Family Phaethontidae: Tropicbirds

Review Species

RED-BILLED TROPICBIRD
Phaethon aethereus Linnaeus

Accidental. The six documented records fall between 8 June and 13 November. Three of these refer to stranded and weak individuals that later died during rehabilitation and were preserved as specimens. One of these was a bird found in a Zapata County yard more than 140 miles from the Gulf. This species was not known in the state until 1985, when one was found stranded in Houston, Harris County, on 13 November (TCWC 11576). Prior to the discovery of the first Red-billed Tropicbird in the state, it was generally thought that White-tailed was more likely to occur.

Family Sulidae: Boobies and Gannets

MASKED BOOBY *Sula dactylatra* Lesson

Uncommon to rare migrant and nonbreeding summer resident offshore and rare to very rare along the immediate coast. They are considered very rare during the winter. Masked Boobies found on coastal beaches are frequently injured or sick. The plumage similarity of sub-adult and immature Masked Boobies and Northern Gannets often causes confusion and is an underappreciated identification challenge.

Review Species

BLUE-FOOTED BOOBY *Sula nebouxii* Milne-Edwards

Accidental. One documented record exists for this species in Texas. Remarkably, this bird occurred well inland. An immature bird appeared at Granite Shoals, Burnet County, in early June 1993 and remained for almost 16 months. It roosted on a diving board throughout its stay before eventually disappearing. It reappeared at Lake Bastrop, Bastrop County, about 80 miles downstream along the Colorado River drainage, where it again remained for almost four months. An immature sulid photographed on 5 October 1976 at South Padre Island, Cameron County, had previously been reported as a Blue-footed Booby; however, reexamination of the photographs showed it to be a Masked Booby.

2 JUNE 1993–6 OCT. 1994, LAKE LYNDON B. JOHNSON, GRANITE SHOALS, BURNET/LLANO CO. AND 10 DEC. 1994–12 APR. 1995, LAKE BASTROP, BASTROP CO. (TBRC 1993-110; TPRF 1168)

Review Species

BROWN BOOBY *Sula leucogaster* (Boddaert)

Very rare visitor to offshore waters and along the coast. There are 19 documented records, including two specimens. Although primarily found during the summer and fall, there are three records from December and January. A majority of the records for the state are of immature birds. The first documented record for the state is from August 1967. An unexpected concentration of six birds was recorded on 30 March 1990 offshore from Freeport, Brazoria County.

There are 13 reports of Brown Booby from prior to the development of the Review List in 1987 for which there is no documentation on file at Texas A&M University.

Review Species

RED-FOOTED BOOBY *Sula sula* (Linnaeus)

Accidental. There is one documented record of this species for the state. A single Red-footed Booby was photographed on a petroleum platform in 1983, offshore from Galveston. A bird reported to have been mounted by a Rockport taxidermist prior to 1910 has since been lost (Oberholser 1974). Another sighting reported by Oberholser from Cameron County in 1968 had insufficient details for acceptance by the TBRC.

27 MAR. 1983, OFF GALVESTON, GALVESTON CO.
  (TBRC 1988-258; TPRF 758)

NORTHERN GANNET *Morus bassanus* (Linnaeus)

Uncommon to common migrant and winter resident offshore and along the immediate coast. This species is often found in large numbers, with reports of as many as 1500 observed in a single day. Northern Gannets are primarily found between late September and early May. There are many reports from the summer, but these usually involve sick or injured birds. Despite their relative abundance in the Gulf and having been found in every coastal county, there are no records from inland locations in Texas. Immature Gannets are sometimes confused with other members of the family Sulidae, the Masked Booby in particular.

Family Pelecanidae: Pelicans

AMERICAN WHITE PELICAN
Pelecanus erythrorhynchos Gmelin

Uncommon to common migrant over the eastern half of the state, while decidedly less common in the western half. White Pelicans are common winter residents in the southern half of the state, particularly along the coast, and locally on inland reservoirs in the northern half and the Trans-Pecos. During migration, flocks of 4,000–11,000 birds have been reported. There are only two nesting colonies of White Pelicans in Texas; one on Pelican Island, Nueces County, and the other near South Bird Island, Kleberg County. Nonbreeding summer birds may be encountered, sometimes in fairly large numbers, at numerous locations statewide.

BROWN PELICAN *Pelecanus occidentalis* Linnaeus

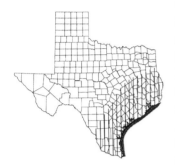

Common to uncommon resident along the coast. Brown Pelicans routinely wander inland along the Coastal Prairies, primarily in the late summer and fall. They are casual to accidental farther inland with records from as far west as El Paso and as far north as Lubbock and Fort Worth. Most of these vagrants are immature or hatch-year birds. Large nesting colonies are present on the upper and central coasts. Although none are known to breed along the lower coast, as the population continues to increase, colonies may become established there. It is estimated that 10–15 percent of the birds in Texas are the "red-pouched" form more typical of the Pacific coast. Brown Pelicans were once nearly decimated by the use of pesticides, and their recovery represents one of the greatest success stories for an Endangered Species. In the 1970s, the total population in Texas may have dropped to as low as 12 to 15 individuals. The reintroduction of additional breeding stock, conservation efforts, and tighter controls on pesticide use, especially DDT, have given the species the opportunity to flourish, and there are once again many thousands of these birds along the coast.

Family Phalacrocoracidae: Cormorants

NEOTROPIC CORMORANT
Phalacrocorax brasilianus (Gmelin)

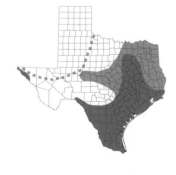

Uncommon to common summer resident along the upper and central coasts and inland through the Coastal Prairies, south to the Lower Rio Grande Valley. This cormorant is rare to locally uncommon at scattered inland locations away from the Coastal Prairies. Neotropic Cormorants are uncommon and somewhat more local during the winter, particularly inland. Inland populations are found on lakes and reservoirs in the eastern half of the state. This species is a summer visitor westward through the Edwards Plateau and Concho Valley, although breeding sites have not been discovered. There is a sizable colony established farther west at McNary Reservoir, Hudspeth County. Neotropic Cormorants are casual visitors to the South Plains but are undocumented from the Panhandle (Seyffert 2001). Like the Brown Pelican, this species has experienced a notable comeback since populations declined during the 1970s. This species was formerly called Olivaceous Cormorant.

DOUBLE-CRESTED CORMORANT
Phalacrocorax auritus (Lesson)

Uncommon to abundant migrant throughout the state. Double-crested Cormorant is a common to abundant winter resident along the coast, becoming uncommon to locally abundant inland through most of the state. In the Panhandle and northern Rolling Plains, this species is a rare winter resident and in recent years has become common in a few localities during summer. This species is a rare to uncommon summer resident along the upper and central coast. There are inland breeding records from the 1930s from Baylor, Matagorda, and Wilbarger Counties (Oberholser 1974). In recent decades, Double-crested Cormorants have established breeding colonies at reservoirs at scattered inland locations as far west as McNary Reservoir, Hudspeth County, in the Trans-Pecos and as far north as Palo Duro Lake, Hansford County, in the Panhandle.

Family Anhingidae: Darters

ANHINGA *Anhinga anhinga* (Linnaeus)

Uncommon summer resident along the Coastal Prairies and northward through the eastern half of the state. Anhingas are rare to locally uncommon winter residents throughout the South Texas Brush Country and along the Coastal Prairies. They are generally less common and more local inland through the eastern third of the state, with sightings during the winter north to Angelina, Freestone, Harrison, McLennan, and Wood Counties. This species is a very rare postbreeding stray to areas west of the breeding range. Anhingas have been found in the Panhandle on three occasions (Seyffert 2001) and in the Trans-Pecos once. Anhingas begin migrating northward in late February, and northern breeding populations depart by late October, with a few individuals lingering as late as December.

Family Fregatidae: Frigatebirds

MAGNIFICENT FRIGATEBIRD
Fregata magnificens Mathews

Uncommon summer and fall visitor along the coast. Magnificent Frigatebirds can be locally common in the Gulf and in larger bays, where high counts of over 100 individuals have been noted. This species can generally be found in Texas between early May and mid-September with a few individuals lingering through October and rarely into November. They are rare from late March through April. Frigatebirds are very rare inland in the eastern half of the state, with records north to Denton and Nacogdoches Counties. These inland occurrences are typically associated with severe weather, such as tropical storms, along the coast. There is one breeding record from Aransas County from 6 June 1931 (Oberholser 1974).

ORDER CICONIIFORMES

Family Ardeidae: Bitterns and Herons

AMERICAN BITTERN *Botaurus lentiginosus* (Rackett)

Rare to locally uncommon migrant in the eastern third of the state and generally rare west to the Trans-Pecos where very rare to casual. In winter, this species is a rare to uncommon resident on the Coastal Prairies and at scattered localities farther inland, as far north as the Panhandle. They are very rare summer visitors locally throughout the state. There are breeding records from Chambers, Galveston, and Wilbarger Counties and indications of possible breeding from Delta, Grayson, and El Paso Counties.

LEAST BITTERN *Ixobrychus exilis* (Gmelin)

Rare to locally common summer resident throughout much of the eastern half of the state, west to the Balcones Escarpment, and south to the Lower Rio Grande Valley. Least

Bittern is a very rare and local summer resident in the western half of Texas, probably due to a lack of habitat. There are isolated breeding records from El Paso, Hemphill, Midland, Presidio, Reeves, Tom Green, and Val Verde Counties. This bittern is a rare to uncommon migrant throughout the state. The species is a very rare winter resident in the Coastal Prairies.

GREAT BLUE HERON *Ardea herodias* Linnaeus

Uncommon to common summer resident throughout much of the state. Great Blue Heron is especially common along the Coastal Prairies and immediate coast. This species is less common as a winter resident away from the Coastal Prairies, as northern birds move south to more favorable conditions. Large rookeries containing hundreds of nests have been found at scattered locations across the state, especially on coastal islands. Most inland rookeries typically contain from five to 30 nesting pairs. There are four documented records of the white subspecies, *A. h. occidentalis,* from the upper and central coasts. This subspecies was formerly known as Great White Heron and was once considered a separate species (AOU 1957). There is some question whether the "Great White" Heron is actually a morph, rather than a subspecies.

GREAT EGRET *Ardea alba* (Linnaeus)

Common resident along the Coastal Prairies and locally common as a summer resident in the eastern and central portions of the state, north to the Oklahoma border. The species is an uncommon year-round visitor to the Trans-Pecos, with sporadic nesting at McNary Reservoir, Hudspeth County (Peterson and Zimmer 1998). Great Egret is a rare to common postbreeding visitor to most of the state and can often be found in very large flocks in late summer and early fall. These flocks may include upwards of 700 individuals at inland wetlands, and even larger groups have been noted along the coast. Away from the Coastal Prairies, this species is an uncommon to rare, and irregular, winter visitor northward to the South Plains.

SNOWY EGRET *Egretta thula* (Molina)

Uncommon to common summer resident throughout much of the state west to the Rolling Plains and south along the

Coastal Prairies to the Lower Rio Grande Valley. Snowy Egrets are rare to locally common summer residents in the Trans-Pecos and rare summer visitors to the High Plains, with two nesting records at Buffalo Lakes National Wildlife Refuge, Randall County. In winter, this species is an uncommon resident along the Coastal Prairies, becoming rare farther inland. In general, Snowy Egrets are rare to common migrants throughout the state. As with many other egrets and herons, this species suffered greatly in the nineteenth and early twentieth centuries from plume hunters. Conservation initiatives have been successful and populations of Snowy Egret have flourished.

LITTLE BLUE HERON *Egretta caerulea* (Linnaeus)

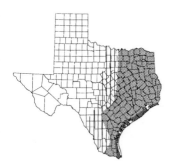

Common summer resident in the eastern third of the state, becoming locally abundant along the Coastal Prairies to the Lower Rio Grande Valley. Little Blue Heron is a rare to locally uncommon postbreeding wanderer to the western two-thirds of the state. In winter, small numbers of Little Blue Herons are present along the Coastal Prairies and are rare inland east and south of the Edwards Plateau to north-central and northeast Texas. This species has been noted in large numbers as migrants over the open waters of the Gulf.

TRICOLORED HERON *Egretta tricolor* (Müller)

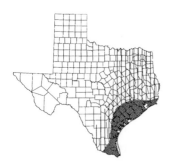

Common summer resident along the immediate coast and locally common on the Coastal Prairies. This species is an uncommon to rare visitor to the eastern third of the state in late summer and fall, becoming increasingly less common farther west. Spring records for this region are increasing, and this species is an irregular breeder as far north as north-central and northeast Texas. Tricolored Herons have been recorded twice in the Panhandle during September, in Donley and Gray Counties, and are casual visitors to the South Plains as postbreeding wanderers. In recent years, this heron has occurred almost annually in the Concho Valley and westward through the Trans-Pecos during all seasons except winter. This species is uncommon to locally common along the Coastal Prairies during the winter and rare and local farther inland to Bexar County. They are very rare farther inland during this season, although there are several winter records from northeast Texas.

REDDISH EGRET *Egretta rufescens* (Gmelin)

Uncommon to locally common resident along the coast, being most numerous from Matagorda Bay southward. Reddish Egret is a very rare postbreeding visitor inland through the eastern third of the state. An interesting phenomenon is the almost annual occurrence during all seasons of this species at reservoirs in the Trans-Pecos, particularly Balmorhea Lake, Reeves County. In contrast, one has been found on the High Plains, and there are only two records from the Edwards Plateau and two from the western Rolling Plains (Jones and Taylor Counties). This egret has been found on several occasions in the Concho Valley. Reddish Egret is listed as threatened by the Texas Parks and Wildlife Department. A high count of 399 individuals was recorded in Cameron County on 1 January 1996.

CATTLE EGRET *Bubulcus ibis* (Linnaeus)

Common to abundant summer resident throughout most of the state, but locally distributed on the High Plains, Rolling Plains, Edwards Plateau, and Trans-Pecos. During migration, Cattle Egrets are locally common to abundant in the eastern half of the state and along the coast. In winter, they are uncommon to rare along the Coastal Prairies, becoming rare to very rare inland and generally absent from the High Plains and northern Rolling Plains. This species was unknown in Texas until late November 1955 when one was found in Nueces County (Oberholser 1974). The first breeding record for the state was discovered three and one-half years later at Rockport, Aransas County, on 10 May 1959. Cattle Egrets are colonial nesters, and very large rookeries can be found at scattered locations through the eastern half of the state. In the western half, breeding is very localized and usually involves only a few pairs.

GREEN HERON *Butorides virescens* (Linnaeus)

Common summer resident throughout the eastern two-thirds of the state, becoming uncommon westward across the Edwards Plateau and High Plains. Green Herons are uncommon and local in the Trans-Pecos. As a migrant, they are uncommon to common statewide. Most Green Herons leave the state during the winter, becoming locally uncommon to rare along the coast and in the Lower Rio Grande Valley. This species is very rare to rare during the winter inland and is generally absent from the Panhandle, South Plains, and Trans-Pecos away from the Rio Grande.

BLACK-CROWNED NIGHT-HERON
Nycticorax nycticorax (Linnaeus)

Common resident along the coastal plain. Inland, this species is a locally common to uncommon summer resident west of the Pineywoods. The exception is from Lubbock County northward through the Panhandle, where they are fairly common to locally abundant. Black-crowned Night-Herons are rare to locally uncommon winter residents inland except in the Panhandle and Pineywoods, where they are casual visitors. Given its nocturnal nature, this species often goes undetected and is probably more common in any given region than is readily apparent.

YELLOW-CROWNED NIGHT-HERON
Nyctanassa violacea (Linnaeus)

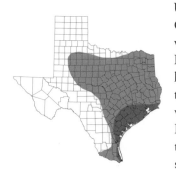

Uncommon to locally common summer resident along the Coastal Prairies and through the eastern third of the state, westward through the central Rolling Plains and eastern Edwards Plateau. This species is a casual visitor to the Panhandle and Trans-Pecos between late April and early September. Yellow-crowned Night-Herons are locally common winter residents along the coast, primarily from Matagorda Bay southward and are rare to casual elsewhere, including the Panhandle. Like the Black-crowned Night-Heron, this species is often present in larger numbers than is realized, especially during the summer months. With the exception of the forested eastern third of the state, Yellow-crowned Night-Herons are generally less common than Black-crowneds in Texas.

Family Threskiornithidae: Ibis and Spoonbills

WHITE IBIS *Eudocimus albus* (Linnaeus)

Common to abundant resident along the immediate coast and Coastal Prairies. White Ibis is particularly abundant along the upper coast during the summer. In the last few decades, numbers have skyrocketed, and immense rookeries are now found in a few locations. One rookery in

1. As recently as the 1960s, Black-bellied Whistling-Ducks *(Dendrocygna autumnalis)* were found only in the Lower Rio Grande Valley and up the Coastal Prairies almost to Corpus Christi. They are now found throughout much of the southern half of the state and locally as far north as the Dallas–Fort Worth area.   *Photograph by Tim Cooper.*

2. Trumpeter Swans *(Cygnus buccinator)* were once regular visitors to the eastern two-thirds of Texas until the late 1800s. In part because of reintroduction programs in the Midwest, Trumpeter Swans have begun to reappear in Texas. This individual was photographed at Brazoria National Wildlife Refuge on 23 February 2002 and represents the fourth recent record of this species. *Photograph by Paul W. Bozzo.*

3. Muscovy Ducks *(Cairina moschata)* are widespread throughout the Neotropics but did not reach Texas until 1984. A small population has since become established along the Rio Grande, mainly in Starr and Zapata Counties. *Photograph by Greg W. Lasley.*

4. The Eurasian Wigeon *(Anas penelope)* has occurred with greatest frequency in the western half of the state. The vast majority of individuals found in Texas have been alternate-plumaged males. This one was photographed in Amarillo, Potter County, on 24 November 1995.
Photograph by Peter Gottschling.

5. Mottled Ducks *(Anas fulvigula)* are common residents along the Coastal Prairies and locally inland to north-central and northeastern Texas. The darker-plumaged males are sometimes confused with the very rare American Black Duck.
Photograph by Tim Cooper.

6. The striking plumage of the male Cinnamon Teal *(Anas cyanoptera)* makes it a favorite among birders. This drake was photographed at Port Aransas, Aransas County. *Photograph by Mark W. Lockwood.*

7. There are four documented records of Garganey *(Anas querquedula)* from Texas. These records all involve alternate-plumaged males found during spring migration. This one was at Presidio, Presidio County, from 29 April to 6 May 1994 and was the second documented in the state. *Photograph by Mark W. Lockwood.*

8. This subadult male King Eider *(Somateria spectabilis)* is the only one thus far documented in the state. It had very worn plumage during its stay on the beach at Quintana, Brazoria County, from 30 April to 7 May 1998. It was eventually captured for rehabilitation.   *Photograph by Steve Bentsen.*

9. The occurrence of Masked Ducks *(Nomonyx dominicus)* in Texas appears to be highly cyclical. There have been "invasions" about every twenty to thirty years since the 1890s, with only scattered records in the intervening periods. The most recent invasion lasted from 1992 to 1996. This male was photographed at Brazos Bend State Park, Fort Bend County. *Photograph by Mark W. Lockwood.*

10. Plain Chachalaca *(Ortalis vetula)* is the only guan, Family Cracidae, found in the United States. They are only present in southernmost Texas, although this species has been released at various locations as far north as Dimmitt and San Patricio Counties. *Photograph by Mark W. Lockwood.*

11. As of 2003, the population of Greater (Attwater's) Prairie-Chicken *(Tympanuchus cupido attwateri)* on the Texas Coastal Prairies had fallen to fewer than 68 birds. Conservation initiatives are underway, and the population is being bolstered by releasing captive-raised birds into the wild. *Photograph by Clifford E. Shackelford.*

12. Lesser Prairie-Chicken *(Tympanuchus pallidicinctus)* populations are declining in Texas, and the species appears imperiled. A little known fact provided by Rylander (2002) is that this species also displays to a lesser extent in October and November due to a slightly elevated testosterone level that occurs in the fall.
Photograph by Mark W. Lockwood.

13. Populations of Scaled Quail *(Callipepla squamata)* have dramatically declined in many areas of their range. The reasons for this change are not known but are probably tied to changes in land-use practices and loss of preferred habitat. Unlike the Northern Bobwhite, coveys of Scaled Quail may contain as many as 125 to 150 individuals.
Photograph by Mark W. Lockwood.

14. The plumage of the male Montezuma Quail *(Cyrtonyx montezumae)* is certainly one of the most strikingly patterned of the native galliformes. Their legs and feet are strong and well adapted to scratch and dig in the hard, rocky soils that characterize their preferred habitats.
Photograph by Mark W. Lockwood.

15. There are five documented records of Yellow-billed Loon *(Gavia adamsii)* for Texas, two of which were found at Balmorhea Lake, Reeves County. This individual was photographed there on 27 November 1993.
Photograph by Greg W. Lasley.

16. Least Grebes *(Tachybaptus dominicus)* are widespread throughout the Neotropics and reach the northern extent of their range in Texas. They frequent small ponds with abundant emergent vegetation.
Photograph by Greg W. Lasley.

17. The populations of Clark's (*Aechmophorus clarkii*) and Western Grebes (*A. occidentalis*) have increased dramatically in Texas over the past decade. They were once uncommon and local winter residents. Today they are uncommon summer residents and common in winter on water impoundments in El Paso and Hudspeth Counties.
Photograph by Barry Zimmer.

18. Although common in the Gulf Stream off the southeastern United States, Black-capped Petrels (*Pterodroma hasitata*) are rare in the Gulf of Mexico. This individual was photographed on 26 July 1997 off Port O'Connor, Calhoun County, and was just the second documented in Texas waters.
Photograph by Michael Gray.

19. White-chinned Petrels (*Procellaria longirostris*) are denizens of the southern oceans. This individual was found on the beach near Rollover Pass, Galveston County, on 27 February 1986 and represents the only record for North America.
Photograph by Allan J. Mueller.

20. There is a single record of Blue-footed Booby *(Sula nebouxii)* for the state. This bird resided at Lake Lyndon B. Johnson, Burnet/Llano County, for more than a year. It had molted to adult plumage when this photograph was taken on 14 September 1994. *Photograph by Greg W. Lasley.*

21. The Brown Pelican *(Pelecanus occidentalis)* population in Texas dipped to a low of fewer than 20 individuals in the 1970s but has rebounded thanks to concerted conservation efforts and the ban of DDT. *Photograph by Mark W. Lockwood.*

22. In recent decades, the range of Neotropic Cormorant *(Phalacrocorax brasilianus)* has greatly expanded, and breeding colonies are found far from the coast, including up the Rio Grande to McNary Reservoir in Hudspeth County and at scattered locations across north Texas. *Photograph by Steve Bentsen.*

23. *(below left)* The only breeding population of Magnificent Frigatebird *(Fregata magnificens)* in the United States is in Florida, but they are uncommon postbreeding wanderers to Texas. A few nonbreeding birds can be found as early as April along the coast, but most arrive in late summer and early fall. *Photograph by Mark W. Lockwood.*

24. In the United States, Reddish Egrets *(Egretta rufescens)* are found along the Gulf Coast from Texas to Louisiana and in Florida. Although the dark morph is more common, white morphs are a regular sight along the Texas Coast. *Photograph by Mark W. Lockwood.*

25. Although once considered very rare in Texas, the Glossy Ibis *(Plegadis falcinellus)* has become resident in Texas and is now locally uncommon along the Coastal Prairies south to Corpus Christi. *Photograph by Greg W. Lasley.*

26. The Roseate Spoonbill *(Platalea ajaja)* is a common sight along the Gulf Coast and certainly a favorite among birders. They are also well known for wandering inland after the breeding season and have been documented from as far west as the Trans-Pecos and north to the Panhandle. *Photograph by Mark W. Lockwood.*

27. Jabiru *(Jabiru mycteria)* has been documented in Texas on seven occasions. All have been postbreeding wanderers that reached the state between late July and late October. This individual was one of two found near Encino, Brooks County, on 29 October 1979. *Photograph by Tom Urban.*

28. Wood Storks *(Mycteria americana)* occur in Texas primarily as postbreeding wanderers from breeding populations in Florida and Mexico. They are found in highest numbers between late June and early November. *Photograph by Brush Freeman.*

29. Greater Flamingos *(Phoenicopterus ruber)* are accidental visitors along the Texas coast, presumably from breeding colonies on the Yucatan Peninsula in Mexico. Careful scrutiny is needed for each sighting as other species of flamingos have escaped captivity, including Greater Flamingos of the Old World subspecies *(P. r. roseus)*. This individual was photographed in Aransas Bay, Aransas County, on 27 April 2000. *Photograph by Mel Cooksey.*

30. The northern edge of Hook-billed Kite's *(Chondrohierax uncinatus)* range just reaches Texas in the Lower Rio Grande Valley. These raptors feed primarily on land snails for which they use the extended hook on the tip of the upper mandible to extract the snail from its shell.
Photograph by Jim Culbertson.

31. Swallow-tailed Kites *(Elanoides forficatus)* were a common breeding species in eastern Texas until the early 1900s. By 1915, the breeding population had all but disappeared, but over the last two decades they have been found with increasing frequency during the summer in the southeastern quadrant of the state and as migrants elsewhere. *Photograph by Tim Cooper.*

32. There is only one record of Crane Hawk *(Geranospiza caerulescens)* for the United States. This adult spent almost four months at Santa Ana National Wildlife Refuge, Hidalgo County, during the winter of 1987–88. *Photograph by Kevin T. Karlson.*

33. The hunting style of Gray Hawks *(Asturina nitida)* is reminiscent of accipiters and falcons. Fast and agile, they dart through woodlands snatching prey items from branches and foliage of the understory. *Photograph by Bill Clark.*

34. White-tailed Hawks *(Buteo albicaudatus)* are widespread throughout the American tropics, but within the United States they are found only in Texas. This species is well known for preying on small animals fleeing grassland fires and will respond to smoke signaling the presence of fires from more than 10 miles away. *Photograph by Tim Cooper.*

35. Crested Caracaras *(Caracara cheriway)* are conspicuous birds of the southern portion of the state. With their long legs, they are the most agile of all North American raptors on the ground. They also have the most varied diet, often scavenging carcasses, which is surprising behavior from such an otherwise very specialized family.   *Photograph by Tim Cooper.*

36. Prior to about 1920, Aplomado Falcons *(Falco femoralis)* were summer residents across the Trans-Pecos and South Texas Brush Country. A reintroduction project that started in 1989 has returned this grassland falcon to some of its former haunts. This banded adult was one of the birds released at Laguna Atascosa National Wildlife Refuge, Cameron County, as part of the program. *Photograph by Tim Cooper.*

37. This Gyrfalcon *(Falco rusticolus)* faithfully roosted on a water tower in Lubbock from 21 January to 7 April 2002 and was the first to be documented in the state. This record appears to be the southernmost in North America.
Photograph by Jimmy McHaney.

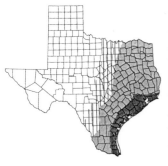

Galveston County was estimated to contain 20,000 breeding pairs in 2001 (W. Burkett, pers. comm.). This species has expanded its breeding range inland to include the entire eastern third of the state, most notably in the northeast and north-central portions. The majority of White Ibis retreat from the northern half of the state in the winter, with only a few lingering through the season. They are casual visitors to the eastern Edwards Plateau and accidental in the Trans-Pecos.

GLOSSY IBIS *Plegadis falcinellus* (Linnaeus)

The status of Glossy Ibis in Texas is poorly understood. This species was unknown in the state prior to November 1983, but by the early 1990s Glossy Ibis were being found with increasing regularity on the upper and central coasts. Currently, Glossy Ibis is a rare to locally uncommon resident on the Coastal Prairies from Jefferson County to Calhoun County, becoming rare to very rare on the lower coast. The first nesting was discovered in 1997 on Sundown Island in Matagorda Bay, Matagorda County. No additional nesting records were obtained until 2002 when a survey of colonial nesting birds revealed 23 pairs of Glossy Ibis in Matagorda Bay on Snake Island, Calhoun County. This species is increasing elsewhere in the eastern half of the state at all seasons. There are documented records of this species from as far west as El Paso, but there are none for the Panhandle or Edwards Plateau.

WHITE-FACED IBIS *Plegadis chihi* (Vieillot)

Common to uncommon resident along the coast. The population along the Coastal Prairies swells during the winter as migrants arrive. White-faced Ibis is a rare and localized breeder away from the coast as far north as the Panhandle. This species occasionally lingers through the winter inland, as far west as the Trans-Pecos. White-faced Ibis have not been recorded from the Panhandle and South Plains past November. They are uncommon to common migrants in most regions of the state.

ROSEATE SPOONBILL *Platalea ajaja* (Linnaeus)

Locally common summer resident along the coast, becoming uncommon in the winter. Roseate Spoonbills are well

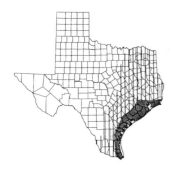

known as postbreeding wanderers to inland locations. They are rare to very rare visitors inland to the eastern third of the state during the summer and fall. Farther west, spoonbills are casual to accidental, with scattered records west to the Trans-Pecos and north to the Panhandle. These postbreeding wanderers are encountered with greater frequency in the southern half of the state.

Family Ciconiidae: Storks

Review Species

JABIRU *Jabiru mycteria* (Lichtenstein)

Casual. Jabirus found in Texas have been postbreeding wanderers. All those documented are from the Coastal Prairies, with the exception of one from the Lower Rio Grande Valley. The first individual discovered in Texas was present from 11 August to 8 September 1971 at Escondido Lake, Kleberg County (TPRF 22; Haucke and Keil 1973). All seven records occurred between late July and late October. The closest breeding populations of Jabirus are on the Yucatan Peninsula and in Tabasco, Mexico.

WOOD STORK *Mycteria americana* Linnaeus

Uncommon to locally common postbreeding visitor to the coast and inland to the eastern third of the state. They generally occur between early June and late October. Most Wood Storks are found east of a line from Dallas to San Antonio to Zapata. West of this line, they are very rare and generally absent. Wood Storks are very rarely found in Texas during the winter, though there are a few records from the coast and the South Texas Brush Country. During fall migration, as many as 5,000 birds have been reported passing over hawk watches in a single day along the central and upper coasts. Wood Storks formerly nested in Chambers, Jefferson, and Harris Counties (Oberholser 1974).

Family Cathartidae: New World Vultures

BLACK VULTURE *Coragyps atratus* (Bechstein)

Common to locally abundant resident in the eastern two-thirds of the state. Black Vultures are casual summer and fall visitors to the South Plains and most of the Rolling

Plains. This species is a locally uncommon resident along the Rio Grande from eastern Val Verde County to northern Presidio County in the Trans-Pecos. Some Black Vultures retreat from the northern portions of their range in Texas during the winter, although the species may continue to be locally common as migrants from more northern populations arrive to take their place.

TURKEY VULTURE *Cathartes aura* (Linnaeus)

Common to locally abundant summer resident throughout the state. Turkey Vultures withdraw from most of the western half of the state during the winter, although small numbers remain on the eastern Edwards Plateau. They are common during winter in the eastern half of the state and in the South Texas Brush Country. In late fall, vast numbers of migrating Turkey Vultures pass through southern Texas on their way to wintering areas farther south.

ORDER PHOENICOPTERIFORMES

Family Phoenicopteridae: Flamingo

Review Species

GREATER FLAMINGO *Phoenicopterus ruber* Linnaeus

Accidental. There are four accepted records of this species from Texas, although there have been numerous others reported. Unaccepted reports lack sufficient detail to eliminate other flamingo species or involve individuals of questionable origin. There have been well-documented occurrences of escaped Greater Flamingos of the Old World subspecies, *P. r. roseus,* including one that was present at Laguna Atascosa National Wildlife Refuge, Cameron County, from 1995 to 1997. The first accepted record for the state was a bird discovered in spring 1978 at Bird Island, Kleberg County; it remained through the summer, returning each spring from 1979 through 1982.

26 APR. 1978+, SOUTH BIRD IS., KLEBERG CO. (TPRF 219)
5 APR.–6 JULY 2000, ARANSAS BAY, ARANSAS CO.
  (TBRC 2000-49; TPRF 1900)
15–16 APR. 2000, ESPIRITU SANTO/SAN ANTONIO BAYS,
  CALHOUN CO. (TBRC 2000-50; TPRF 1901)
28 APR. 2001, MATAGORDA ISLAND, CALHOUN CO.
  (TBRC 2001-92; TPRF 2024)

ORDER FALCONIFORMES

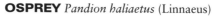

Family Accipitridae: Osprey, Eagles, Kites, and Hawks

OSPREY *Pandion haliaetus* (Linnaeus)

Uncommon to rare migrant throughout most of the state. In general, the migration periods for this species extend from mid-March to late May and from early September to mid-November. Osprey is a common to uncommon winter resident along the coast, becoming uncommon to rare in the eastern third of the state. They are very rare to casual winter visitors to the High Plains and Trans-Pecos. This species is a very rare and local breeder in the Pineywoods and along the upper coast, typically near larger reservoirs. Nonbreeding individuals are rare summer visitors along the coast and through the eastern third of the state. Like many other birds of prey, the population of this species has increased significantly since the early 1970s following the ban on DDT.

HOOK-BILLED KITE

Chondrohierax uncinatus (Temminck)

Rare to locally uncommon permanent resident in Hidalgo and Starr Counties of the Lower Rio Grande Valley. There is a single sight record from Cameron County. Hook-billed Kites were first found in Texas, and the United States, in 1964 when a pair nested at Santa Ana National Wildlife Refuge, Hidalgo County (Fleetwood and Hamilton 1967). This species was not reported in Texas again until 1976 when another nesting pair was discovered. Brush (1999b) reported that Hook-billed Kites might be somewhat nomadic, following changes in the populations of their favored food item, tree snails *(Rabdotes alternatus)*. This may explain the variability in the number of individuals reported from year to year.

SWALLOW-TAILED KITE

Elanoides forficatus (Linnaeus)

Rare to uncommon migrant through the Coastal Prairies and the eastern third of the state. Swallow-tailed Kite is a

casual migrant west to the eastern Edwards Plateau, where it appears to be more regular during fall migration. They are accidental to casual migrants west to the Trans-Pecos, and there are records from Floyd, Midland, Lubbock, and Oldham Counties on the High Plains. This species is a rare to locally uncommon summer resident in southeast Texas with recent breeding records from Chambers, Liberty, Orange, and Tyler Counties. Swallow-tailed Kite was formerly a common summer resident in the eastern half of the state and nested as far west as Bastrop and Medina Counties until about 1915 (Attwater 1892; Simmons 1925; Oberholser 1974). The migration periods are between mid-March and early May and from late August to mid-October.

WHITE-TAILED KITE *Elanus leucurus* (Vieillot)

Uncommon to common resident along the Coastal Prairies, the southern half of the Post Oak Savannahs, and in the eastern South Texas Brush Country. They occasionally form large winter roosts in the South Texas Brush Country and Lower Rio Grande Valley, sometimes including more than 100 individuals. White-tailed Kites are rare to locally uncommon summer residents in the northern half of the Post Oak Savannahs to the Oklahoma border. This species is a rare and local resident along the Rio Grande to Val Verde County and is a rare visitor, with records from all seasons, to the Edwards Plateau and the Trans-Pecos. White-tailed Kites are also very rare to casual visitors to the Rolling Plains with records as far north as Clay, Crosby, Dickens, and Young Counties. Formerly considered conspecific with the Old World Black-shouldered Kite *(E. caeruleus)*.

Review Species

SNAIL KITE *Rostrhamus sociabilis* (Vieillot)

Accidental. Texas has two documented records of this tropical species. The first was an immature bird found in Jim Wells County during the summer of 1977; this individual reportedly returned in 1978, but supporting documentation is lacking. The second was an adult female. The northern extent of the Snail Kite's range in Mexico is in central Veracruz.

22–26 JULY 1977, LAKE ALICE, JIM WELLS CO. (TPRF 127)
17–29 MAY 1998, NEAR BENTSEN–RIO GRANDE VALLEY SP,
  HIDALGO CO. (TBRC 1998-119; TPRF 1724)

MISSISSIPPI KITE *Ictinia mississippiensis* (Wilson)

Common to uncommon migrant throughout the state. Mississippi Kites are common summer residents on the High Plains and Rolling Plains. They are also uncommon, but increasing, summer residents in El Paso County and rare and very local summer residents in the Pineywoods. There is an isolated breeding population present on the central and upper coasts in Fort Bend, Matagorda, Wharton, Jackson, and Victoria Counties. In addition, there are scattered breeding records across the Blackland Prairies and Post Oak Savannah from Washington County northward to Grayson and Wilbarger Counties. Mississippi Kites sometimes migrate in large flocks, as was the case on 18 April 1998 when approximately 16,000 to 18,000 were observed in northern Kenedy County. Migration occurs between early April and mid-May and late August to mid-October.

BALD EAGLE *Haliaeetus leucocephalus* (Linnaeus)

Rare and local summer resident primarily in the eastern third of the state. Current population estimates indicate there are about 140 breeding pairs present, some inland as far west as Llano County and as far south along the coast as Nueces County. Where these birds go after the nesting season is unclear. An adult Bald Eagle banded as a nestling in Matagorda County was discovered nesting in Arizona. The last nesting record from the Panhandle was in 1916. During migration and winter, Bald Eagles are more widely distributed in Texas, and can be found throughout the northern two-thirds of the state beginning in mid-October. However, they are locally common only on large reservoirs in the eastern third. In the South Texas Brush Country, Bald Eagles are casual mid-winter visitors. Two subspecies occur in the state: *H. l. leucocephalus,* the breeding population, and *H. l. alascanus,* the wintering population. Interestingly, breeding and wintering activities overlap.

NORTHERN HARRIER *Circus cyaneus* (Linnaeus)

Common to uncommon migrant and winter resident in all parts of the state. Northern Harriers are particularly common on the Coastal Prairies in winter. This species is a rare summer visitor to most regions with breeding activity noted on very rare occasions. The majority of breeding records come from native grasslands on the Coastal Prairies and in the Panhandle. There is evidence that adult male Northern Harriers make up a larger percentage of the overall wintering population in the northern half of the state but are still outnumbered by female and immature birds in all regions. Migration occurs between early April and mid-May and late August to mid-October.

SHARP-SHINNED HAWK *Accipiter striatus* Vieillot

Uncommon to common migrant, and uncommon winter resident throughout the state. Sharp-shinned Hawk is a very rare and local summer resident in the Pineywoods (Shackelford, Saenz, and Schaefer 1996) and at higher elevations in the Guadalupe, Davis, and Chisos Mountains of the Trans-Pecos. There are isolated nesting records from Wise, Hays, and Hidalgo Counties. Migrant and wintering Sharp-shinned Hawks arrive in mid-September and most depart by early May.

COOPER'S HAWK *Accipiter cooperii* (Bonaparte)

Uncommon to rare migrant and winter resident throughout the state. In general, Cooper's Hawk is slightly less common as a migrant and wintering bird in Texas than Sharp-shinned Hawk. This species is a rare to locally uncommon summer resident in all areas except the High Plains and the Coastal Prairies south to Matagorda Bay. Migrants arrive in Texas beginning in mid-September, and the wintering population has generally departed by late April. In recent years, urban populations in the southern half of the state seem to be expanding and possibly coinciding with the expansion of White-winged Dove populations.

Review Species

NORTHERN GOSHAWK *Accipiter gentilis* (Linnaeus)

Casual winter visitor to the state. There are 16 documented records of Northern Goshawk in Texas. The majority of these records are from the Trans-Pecos and Panhandle, with others scattered across the northern two-thirds of the state. There are over 70 undocumented reports of Northern Goshawk, including several involving specimens supposedly collected between 1885 and 1934. Interestingly, despite the frequency with which this species has been reported, only three have been documented with photographs. Most documented records occur between 1 November and 18 March, but there is one from Big Bend National Park, Brewster County, on 9 September 1999. There are 64 reports of Northern Goshawks from prior to the development of the Review List in 1987 for which there is no documentation on file at Texas A&M University.

Review Species

CRANE HAWK *Geranospiza caerulescens* (Vieillot)

Accidental. Certainly one of the highlights of the Texas ornithological record is the Crane Hawk found on 20 December 1987, at Santa Ana National Wildlife Refuge, Hidalgo County. Not only did it represent a first for Texas but also a first for the United States. The Crane Hawk's range extends only to the central portions of Tamaulipas, Mexico (Howell and Webb 1995; J. Arvin, pers. comm.).

20 DEC. 1987–9 APR. 1988, SANTA ANA NWR, HIDALGO CO. (TBRC 1988-87; TPRF 595)

GRAY HAWK *Asturina nitida* (Latham)

Rare to locally uncommon resident along the Rio Grande corridor from Hidalgo County to Webb County. Gray Hawks are very rare to casual residents north along the Coastal Prairies to southern Kleberg County. They are rare and local summer residents in the Trans-Pecos at Big Bend National Park and very rare west along the Rio Grande in Presidio County and in the Davis Mountains. There are out-of-range records from El Paso, Refugio, and Val Verde Counties.

COMMON BLACK-HAWK
Buteogallus anthracinus (Deppe)

Rare and local summer resident in the Davis Mountains in the Trans-Pecos. There are also small populations of this species in Big Bend National Park, along the Devil's River in central Val Verde County, and in the Concho Valley. A pair of Common Black-Hawks nested unsuccessfully in Lubbock County in 1982 and 1983, while a single bird was found in Potter County on the northern High Plains in April 1999. Historically, this species was resident in the Lower Rio Grande Valley up river to Webb County. In recent years, Common Black-Hawks have been very rare visitors to this area with most records coming from the winter.

They formerly nested in western Presidio County, and vagrants have been reported in Bandera, Bexar, Culberson, Duval, El Paso, and San Saba Counties.

HARRIS'S HAWK *Parabuteo unicinctus* (Temminck)

Common to uncommon resident in the South Texas Brush Country north to the southern edge of the Edwards Plateau and east to the Goliad-Victoria County line. This hawk is found with decreasing frequency up the coast from Refugio and western Calhoun Counties to the upper coast, where it is very rare. Harris's Hawk is a locally uncommon to rare resident along the Rio Grande from Big Bend northwest to El Paso County. There is also a resident population in the southern High Plains from Cochran and Winkler Counties southeastward to Schleicher County on the northwestern Edwards Plateau. This species formerly occurred northward to Travis County east of the Balcones Escarpment. Harris's Hawks are vagrants elsewhere in the state. This hawk is known for its social behavior with groups of six or more often sighted.

Review Species

ROADSIDE HAWK *Buteo magnirostris* (Gmelin)

Accidental. The first documented record of this species for Texas, and the United States, is from Cameron County on 2 April 1901. Since that date, there have been only three other documented records, all from the Lower Rio Grande Valley. These birds were found between 7 October and 2 April. Roadside Hawks are reported almost every year, but definitive documentation has rarely accompanied these reports. This species is very common from southern Tamaulipas in northeastern Mexico southward through northern South America.

2 APR. 1901, CAMERON CO. (OHIO STATE MUSEUM 5676, TPRF 1943)

7 JAN. 1979, SANTA MARGARITA RANCH, STARR CO. (TBRC 1989-187)

7 OCT. 1982–MID-FEB. 1983, BENTSEN–RIO GRANDE VALLEY SP, HIDALGO CO. (TPRF 283)

11–15 DEC. 2000, BENTSEN–RIO GRANDE VALLEY SP, HIDALGO CO. (TBRC 2001-6; TPRF 1969)

RED-SHOULDERED HAWK *Buteo lineatus* (Gmelin)

Common to uncommon resident throughout the eastern two-thirds of the state, becoming rare to casual farther west

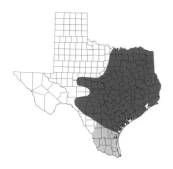

primarily along wooded drainages. The resident population of Red-shouldered Hawks ranges west to the Concho Valley and western Edwards Plateau and south to the Nueces River. South of the Nueces River, Red-shouldered Hawks are primarily a winter resident, although there are records from all seasons and this species may have formerly bred (McKinney 1998). One of the most interesting records of this hawk involved an unsuccessful nesting attempt with a Gray Hawk in Big Bend National Park in 1989.

BROAD-WINGED HAWK *Buteo platypterus* (Vieillot)

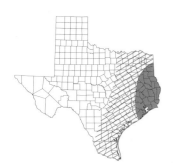

Common to abundant migrant throughout the eastern half of the state. On certain days, it is possible to see over a hundred thousand of these small buteos as they migrate along the coastal plain. A small percentage of migrating birds pass over the eastern portion of the Edwards Plateau where this species is uncommon to rare, but farther west they are casual to rare at best. Typical migration dates are between mid-March and mid-May and from early September to mid-October. Broad-winged Hawk is a rare and local breeder in the Pineywoods and locally west to north-central Texas and the eastern edge of the Edwards Plateau. There are a few scattered winter records from along the coast and the Lower Rio Grande Valley.

Review Species

SHORT-TAILED HAWK *Buteo brachyurus* Vieillot

Casual visitor to the Lower Rio Grande Valley and accidental northward to the Edwards Plateau. Texas has 17 documented records of this tropical hawk. The first was an adult found at the Santa Margarita Ranch, Starr County, on 22 July 1989 (TBRC 1989-179; TPRF 833). Since then, most records are from Hidalgo County, but the species has occurred four times on the Edwards Plateau. There are also single records from Brewster and Nueces Counties. Ten records fall between 15 February and 28 July with two others from October. All but two of the birds documented in Texas have been light morph individuals.

SWAINSON'S HAWK *Buteo swainsoni* Bonaparte

Common to locally abundant migrant in the western three-quarters of the state. Like the Broad-winged Hawk, this species can occasionally be seen in very large migrating

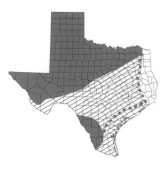

flocks, particularly along the Coastal Prairies. Spring migrants are present between late March and mid-May, although small numbers are occasionally seen as late as mid-June. During the fall, migrants are present from early August to early November. Swainson's Hawks are uncommon to common summer residents from the Panhandle, south through the Rolling Plains to the northern Edwards Plateau, and west through most of the Trans-Pecos. They are also rare summer residents across north-central Texas and in the western South Texas Brush Country south to northern Hidalgo and Starr Counties. This species is an irregular summer visitor east of the normal breeding range into the Blackland Prairies and Post Oak Savannahs of central Texas. There are isolated breeding records within this region from the Oklahoma border south to Travis and Williamson Counties. Swainson's Hawks have also been reported with increasing frequency along the Coastal Prairies, and breeding has been reported at a few scattered locations on the upper coast. This species is a rare to very rare winter resident along the Coastal Prairies from Calhoun County southward to the Lower Rio Grande Valley, and the vast majority of wintering birds are immature. The northernmost winter record was an immature bird photographed in Tom Green County on 2 February 1993 (TPRF 1958).

WHITE-TAILED HAWK *Buteo albicaudatus* Vieillot

Uncommon to locally common resident in the Coastal Prairies. The breeding population of White-tailed Hawks is found primarily south of Matagorda Bay, along the central and lower coasts. This species is a very rare visitor farther inland, primarily during the fall and winter, to Bexar and Travis Counties. Unexpected records have come from Brewster and Uvalde Counties to the west and Delta County in the northeast. White-tailed Hawks are found from Texas southward through the tropics. Despite habitat loss the species appears to have made a comeback from decades of DDT use and persecution.

ZONE-TAILED HAWK *Buteo albonotatus* Kaup

Uncommon and local summer resident in the mountains of the central Trans-Pecos, east through the southern Edwards Plateau. There is a single breeding record from Taylor County (Oberholser 1974). Zone-tailed Hawk is a rare

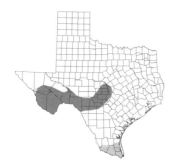

summer visitor to the Guadalupe Mountains, although it is unrecorded from the northwestern Trans-Pecos. This species is a rare migrant and winter resident in the Lower Rio Grande Valley and an irregular visitor there during the summer. Zone-taileds are rare and local winter visitors from Tom Green and Irion Counties southward to east-central Texas. Although there is no consistent wintering area east of the Balcones Escarpment, there are numerous records from Bell and Bastrop Counties south to Bexar, Colorado, and Victoria Counties. Vagrants have also been noted in the South Texas Brush County and as far north as Rains County in north-central Texas.

RED-TAILED HAWK *Buteo jamaicensis* (Gmelin)

Common resident virtually statewide. Red-tailed Hawks are common to uncommon summer residents throughout most of the state, except for the southern South Texas Brush Country where they are uncommon and the Lower Rio Grande Valley where they are absent as breeders. They are common migrants and winter residents in all areas. There are five subspecies present in Texas, including the very distinctive "Harlan's" *(B. j. harlani)* and "Krider's" *(B. j. krideri)* Hawks, both of which are migrants and winter residents arriving in mid-October and remaining until mid-March.

FERRUGINOUS HAWK *Buteo regalis* (Gray)

Common to locally uncommon winter resident in the High Plains and Trans-Pecos. Ferruginous Hawks are uncommon to rare winter residents through the remainder of the western two-thirds of the state, including the Coastal Prairies and associated barrier islands from Waller County southward. This hawk is a very rare to rare winter visitor east through the Post Oak Savannah region of Texas. They are typically present from mid-October to late March. Ferruginous Hawk is a rare summer resident in the central and western portions of the Panhandle. Strecker (1912) stated that the species "breeds abundantly" in the Panhandle, though this is certainly no longer the case. Due to steep population declines continent-wide, this species has been considered for inclusion on the list of Endangered Species.

ROUGH-LEGGED HAWK *Buteo lagopus* (Pontoppidan)

Uncommon to rare winter resident in the Panhandle and South Plains, becoming increasingly rare farther east and south. Rough-legged Hawks arrive late in the fall and depart early in the spring. They very rarely arrive before mid-October in the Panhandle (Seyffert 2001). Rough-legged Hawks reported in Texas from September are questionable, as are reports from May. The latest spring date from the Panhandle is 19 April 1970 (Seyffert 2001). This species is casual in the Trans-Pecos and rare south of the Rolling Plains to about Travis and Brazos Counties. They are very rare wanderers to the Coastal Prairies and are accidental in the South Texas Brush Country. Many, though certainly not all, reports of dark morph individuals along the coast and in southern Texas probably pertain to other similarly plumaged raptors, particularly "Harlan's" *(B. jamaicensis harlani)* and immature White-tailed Hawks *(B. albicaudatus).*

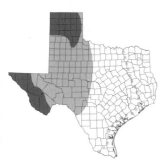

GOLDEN EAGLE *Aquila chrysaetos* (Linnaeus)

Rare to locally uncommon resident in the Panhandle and western and central Trans-Pecos. There have been isolated breeding records as far east as central Val Verde County during the 1990s. Golden Eagles are rare to uncommon winter residents on the remainder of the High Plains and Trans-Pecos as well as the Rolling Plains and western Edwards Plateau. This species is rare to very rare in winter from the Coastal Bend eastward to Colorado and Fort Bend Counties and very rare to casual throughout the remainder of the state. The breeding range of the Golden Eagle has been much reduced in the last century. Oberholser (1974) cites breeding records eastward through the Edwards Plateau. Like the Ferruginous Hawk, this species has often been observed frequenting prairie dog towns in west Texas.

Family Falconidae: Falcons

Review Species

COLLARED FOREST-FALCON
Micrastur semitorquatus (Vieillot)

Accidental. Texas has the only record of this tropical species for the United States. A light morph adult was discovered at

Bentsen–Rio Grande Valley State Park, Hidalgo County, during the winter of 1994. Collared Forest-Falcons occur within 150 miles of Brownsville in central Tamaulipas, Mexico.

22 JAN.–24 FEB. 1994, BENTSEN–RIO GRANDE VALLEY SP, HIDALGO CO. (TBRC 1994-40; TPRF 1227)

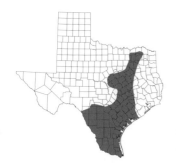

CRESTED CARACARA *Caracara cheriway* (Jacquin)

Uncommon to common resident in the South Texas Brush Country and Coastal Prairies, including associated barrier islands. This species occurs up the coast irregularly as far north as Chambers County. Crested Caracaras are locally common to uncommon residents in the Blackland Prairies and Post Oak Savannahs north to Kaufman County and occur irregularly to Delta and Hunt Counties. They are rare and very localized summer residents on the Edwards Plateau and casual to the Trans-Pecos at all seasons. Seasonal movements do occur, as birds retreat somewhat from the northernmost portions of the range during cooler winters. Crested Caracara is a species of open rangeland and brush country and is absent from forested regions such as the East Texas Pineywoods.

AMERICAN KESTREL *Falco sparverius* Linnaeus

Common to abundant migrant and winter resident throughout the state. American Kestrels are uncommon to common summer residents in the High Plains and Trans-Pecos. They are also rare to uncommon in the Pineywoods and locally east to Tarrant County and the western South Texas Brush Country, south to Starr County. There are isolated breeding records for other areas, but they are generally absent from the remainder of Texas during the summer. The two breeding populations in Texas represent different subspecies, with *F. s. sparverius* in the west and *F. s. paulus* in the Pineywoods.

MERLIN *Falco columbarius* Linnaeus

Rare to uncommon migrant and winter resident throughout the state. Merlins are low density winter residents throughout most of the state and are most common on the Coastal Prairies. They arrive in the state in mid-September and most depart by late April. The majority of those found in Texas belong to two subspecies, *F. c. columbarius* and *F. c. richardsoni*. There are two photographically documented records of the Pacific Northwest subspecies, *F. c. suckleyi*, one from Bee County (TPRF 1959) and the other from Galveston County (Wheeler and Clark 1995).

APLOMADO FALCON *Falco femoralis* Temminck

Rare to locally uncommon resident along the Coastal Prairies from Calhoun County southward, including associated barrier islands. Beginning in 1989, the Peregrine Fund, Inc. and the United States Fish and Wildlife Service began a reintroduction program, and to date there have been almost 700 captive-raised individuals released. In 1995, a pair successfully nested in Cameron County followed by other nestings from Cameron to Calhoun Counties. Aplomado Falcons from this project have wandered as far up the coast as Jefferson County. This species may be a very rare to casual visitor to mid-elevation grasslands in the Trans-Pecos with single records from Culberson and Presidio/Jeff Davis Counties during the 1990s. These sightings, along with several others from southern New Mexico, are believed to be of individuals originating from a natural population in northern Chihuahua, Mexico. Aplomados were released in Jeff Davis and Presidio Counties beginning in the summer of 2002, which may cloud the origin of any future sightings from the Trans-Pecos. Prior to 1919, this falcon was a summer resident from the central Trans-Pecos east to Midland and in the South Texas Brush Country. There were scattered records from Cameron County and the western Trans-Pecos until the early 1950s. The future looks much brighter for this Endangered species in Texas.

Review Species

GYRFALCON *Falco rusticolus* Linnaeus

Accidental. There is only one record of this arctic falcon for Texas. An immature gray morph bird remained in Lubbock, Lubbock County, for over two months during the late winter and early spring of 2002. This individual faithfully roosted on a water tower within the city limits during its stay. This is the southernmost record for this species in the New World.

21 JAN.–7 APR. 2002, LUBBOCK, LUBBOCK CO.
  (TBRC 2002-16; TPRF 1982)

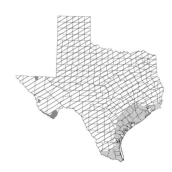

PEREGRINE FALCON *Falco peregrinus* Tunstall

Uncommon to rare migrant throughout the state. Peregrine Falcons are locally uncommon winter residents *(F. p. tundrius)* on the Coastal Prairies and can be common at times along the immediate coast, particularly near bays and estuaries. This species is a rare to very rare winter resident, primarily in urban areas, inland to north-central Texas. Peregrines are very local summer residents *(F. p. anatum)* in the Trans-Pecos with breeding populations confined to the Guadalupe and Chisos Mountains and the cliffs that line the Rio Grande in southern Brewster County north to Presidio County. Fall migrants are noted around the state as early as mid-July, and spring birds may linger as late as early May. This falcon, once listed as Endangered, has made a remarkable comeback and was delisted in 1999.

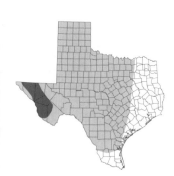

PRAIRIE FALCON *Falco mexicanus* Schlegel

Rare and local summer resident in the central mountains of the Trans-Pecos. Previous editions of this checklist implied breeding in the Panhandle, but there is only one recent nesting record from that region (Seyffert 2001). There have been a number of recent summer sightings from the Panhandle suggesting possible breeding. Prairie Falcons are rare to uncommon migrants and winter residents in the High Plains, western Rolling Plains, and Trans-Pecos. This species is a rare and local winter visitor across the eastern Rolling Plains and south to the South Texas Brush Country. Prairie Falcons are casual winter visitors farther east and south but have not been documented from the Pineywoods.

ORDER GRUIFORMES

Family Rallidae: Rails, Gallinules, and Coots

YELLOW RAIL *Coturnicops noveboracensis* (Gmelin)

Rare migrant through the eastern third of the state. This species is a rare to locally common winter resident on the upper and central coasts. They are generally present between early October and late April. Surveys in appropriate habitat, including rice fields, have uncovered large numbers of this species. Its status away from the Coastal Prairies is poorly known. Yellow Rails have been found during migration and winter as far west as the High Plains in Bailey, Lubbock, and Randall Counties. There is also a record from Big Bend National Park, Brewster County, from 31 January 1976. On 16 October 1960, Pulich (1961a) picked up 13 dead Yellow Rails at the base of a television tower in Dallas County. These unexpected records underscore how little is known about this species in Texas. Yellow Rails do not breed in Texas as far as is known.

BLACK RAIL *Laterallus jamaicensis* (Gmelin)

Rare migrant in the eastern third of the state, east of the Balcones Escarpment. Migrants have been reported as far west as the High Plains (Bailey, Crosby, Lubbock, and Randall Counties). There is only one documented record of this species from the Pineywoods. Black Rails are rare to locally uncommon residents on the upper and central coasts. Vocalizing birds have been found at several locations along the lower coast during the spring and summer, which may suggest some localized breeding. An exceptional record involved a calling individual in the Panhandle, Hutchinson County, on 1 July 1979 (TBSL 31-1). Many reports of Black Rails seen out of proper habitat or during the breeding season probably pertain to the similar-looking dark chicks of King and Clapper Rails.

CLAPPER RAIL *Rallus longirostris* Boddaert

Common resident in brackish and salt marshes along the coast. There is only one well-documented inland record of Clapper Rail: one was netted and photographed in Tom Green County on 20 August 1986 (Burt et al. 1987; TPRF 402). Clapper and King Rails are very similar in appearance, and some individuals can be very difficult to identify with certainty. This identification challenge clouds inland reports of Clappers. This species is not known to occupy freshwater habitats in Texas, although they do elsewhere in their range.

KING RAIL *Rallus elegans* Audubon

Common to locally abundant resident in freshwater marshes, irrigation ditches, and weedy lakes on the Coastal Prairies from the Louisiana border south to Kenedy County. King Rails are uncommon southward to the Lower Rio

Grande Valley. This species is very rare and local elsewhere in the eastern half of the state during the summer. There are documented breeding records from the Panhandle (Hutchinson County in 1950) and the Edwards Plateau (Crockett County in 1977). This species formerly bred across north-central Texas; the only recent records are from Delta County (White 2002). There are interesting summer records from the Trans-Pecos from El Paso County and Balmorhea Lake, Reeves County. The species is either a rare or seldom observed migrant throughout the state.

VIRGINIA RAIL *Rallus limicola* Vieillot

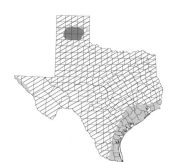

Uncommon migrant in all parts of the state. Virginia Rails are uncommon to locally common residents in the central Panhandle (Seyffert 2001). There are isolated nesting records from various locations across the state, mostly in the western third, suggesting a more widespread breeding range. This species is an uncommon to common migrant along the Coastal Prairies. Virginia Rails are uncommon to rare winter residents along the coast and are found inland at scattered locations throughout the state.

SORA *Porzana carolina* (Linnaeus)

Uncommon to locally common migrant throughout the state. Soras are common to locally abundant migrants and winter residents along the Coastal Prairies. There was an extraordinary count of up to 622 individuals from rice fields on the central coast on 14 October 1998. This species is rare to uncommon, or undetected, inland during the winter. Sora is also a rare summer resident throughout the state. Breeding records for this species are rare, and nesting activity appears to be irregular even at known locations along the Coastal Prairies and elsewhere.

Review Species

PAINT-BILLED CRAKE *Neocrex erythrops* (Sclater)

Accidental. There are only two documented records of this species from the United States. The Texas record was first and involved a single bird captured in a mammal trap (Arnold 1978b). Paint-billed Crakes are found discontinuously from Costa Rica south to northern Argentina.

17 FEB. 1972, NEAR COLLEGE STATION, BRAZOS CO. (TCWC 8930)

Review Species

SPOTTED RAIL *Pardirallus maculatus* (Boddaert)

Accidental. There is one documented record of this tropical rail for Texas. This individual also represents the second record for the United States (Parkes, Kibbe, and Roth 1978). Spotted Rails are known for dispersing long distances from population centers (AOU 1998). Spotted Rails occur from central Mexico and the Greater Antilles southward to northern Argentina.

9 AUG. 1977, NEAR BROWNWOOD, BROWN CO. (TCWC 10400)

PURPLE GALLINULE *Porphyrio martinica* (Linnaeus)

Rare to uncommon migrant in the eastern half of Texas and very rare to accidental in the western half. This species is a rare to locally common summer resident in the eastern third of the state, west to Gonzales and Hidalgo Counties. They are most common during the summer along the upper and central coasts. Purple Gallinules are very rare winter residents along the coast and in the Lower Rio Grande Valley. Migration occurs between mid-April and late May and from early August to late October.

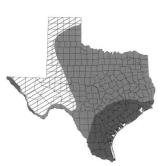

COMMON MOORHEN *Gallinula chloropus* (Linnaeus)

Uncommon to locally abundant resident from the Lower Rio Grande Valley and Coastal Prairies inland to Bastrop and Brazos Counties. Common Moorhens are rare to locally uncommon summer residents throughout the eastern two-thirds of the state, including the Panhandle. In the Trans-Pecos, Common Moorhens are uncommon residents in El Paso, Hudspeth, and Presidio Counties. During the winter, this species is most common from the central coast southward. This species was formerly known as the Common Gallinule.

AMERICAN COOT *Fulica americana* Gmelin

Uncommon to common summer resident in nearly all regions of the state. Despite the widespread occurrence of American Coots in Texas, breeding has only been reported from scattered locations statewide and has been very localized. This species is a common to abundant winter resident statewide. During the winter, some water impoundments support large populations of coots, sometimes numbering in the thousands.

Family Gruidae: Cranes

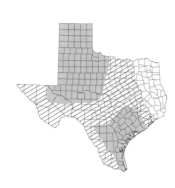

SANDHILL CRANE *Grus canadensis* (Linnaeus)

Uncommon to common migrant throughout much of the state. There are two population centers of wintering Sandhill Cranes in Texas: the High Plains and Rolling Plains to the north and the Coastal Prairies to the south. This species winters locally elsewhere in the western two-thirds of the state, although they are rare in the Trans-Pecos during mid-winter. Migrants can be found throughout the state, although this species is generally rare in the forested areas of east Texas. Sandhill Cranes are noisy diurnal migrants, arriving in mid-October with most departing by mid-March. This species was formerly a rare resident in the coastal marshes of southeast Texas (Strecker 1912). Sandhill Cranes are now only occasional summer visitors to the Coastal Prairies. It is assumed that physiological problems prevent these birds from migrating. A lone Sandhill Crane spent the summer of 2003 near Lubbock, providing one of the very few records for the High Plains for that season.

WHOOPING CRANE *Grus americana* (Linnaeus)

This critically Endangered species is an uncommon winter resident in Aransas and Calhoun Counties. They arrive in late October to early November with stragglers coming in as late as mid-December. Northward migration begins in late March; most birds depart by mid-April but some occasionally linger into May. On rare occasions, this species has oversummered on the Texas coast, but most of these records pertained to sick or injured birds. Whooping Cranes are rarely encountered as they migrate along a narrow corridor down the middle of the state. Migrants are occasionally found, often with Sandhill Cranes, just west and east of the traditional migration route between the Texas coast and Wood Buffalo National Park, Alberta. Out-of-range birds have also been reported west to Uvalde County and east to Jefferson and Smith Counties. As of this writing, the wintering population in Texas consists of approximately 185 birds. There were only 14 individuals in the wild in the late 1930s when concerted conservation efforts were initiated. An attempt to establish a second migrating population that summered in Idaho and wintered in New Mexico failed.

ORDER CHARADRIIFORMES

Family Burhinidae: Thick-knees

Review Species

DOUBLE-STRIPED THICK-KNEE
Burhinus bistriatus (Wagler)

Accidental. Texas has one record for this species. This unusual nocturnal shorebird that resembles a giant plover was an unexpected find and represents the only record for the United States. Double-striped Thick-knees have been found irregularly as far north as southern Tamaulipas in northeastern Mexico and could potentially occur again on the Coastal Prairies of southern Texas.

5 DEC. 1961, KING RANCH, KLEBERG CO. (USNM 478866)

Family Charadriidae: Plovers

BLACK-BELLIED PLOVER
Pluvialis squatarola (Linnaeus)

Uncommon to common migrant through the eastern half of the state, becoming increasingly less common westward. Black-bellied Plover is common to abundant on the coast in winter and rare to uncommon inland in the southeastern quarter of the state. They are also a rare to uncommon summer visitor along the coast, although this species does not breed. These nonbreeding individuals usually retain basic plumage. The Black-bellied Plover is the largest plover found in Texas.

AMERICAN GOLDEN-PLOVER
Pluvialis dominica (Müller)

Common spring migrant in the eastern half of the state, becoming very rare to casual west of the Balcones Escarpment. Large concentrations, sometimes including up to 20,000 individuals, have been noted on the central and upper coasts. American Golden-Plovers are rare to uncommon fall migrants in the eastern half of the state. In the western half of Texas, these plovers occur with greater regularity in the fall, although they are still rare to very rare. Spring migrants are present between early March and mid-May, with a few lingering into early June. Fall migrants arrive in mid-

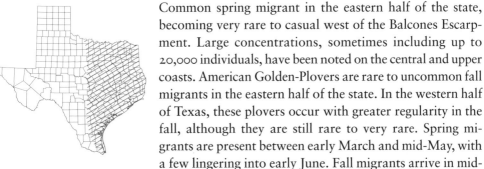

August and are present through late October. Wintering birds are very rarely found along the coast and are casual inland. This species is often confused with the smaller Mountain Plover. No doubt many reports of Mountain Plovers from along the coast and elsewhere pertain to this species, especially in the spring when most American Golden-Plovers are still in basic, or winter, plumage.

COLLARED PLOVER *Charadrius collaris* Vieillot

Review Species

Accidental. Collared Plover is yet another tropical species for which Texas holds the only record for the United States. An adult was discovered during the 1992 spring Texas Ornithological Society meeting in Uvalde, Uvalde County. Given that this species occurs as far north as southern Tamaulipas in northeastern Mexico, it is surprising that more Collared Plovers have not been discovered.

9–12 MAY 1992, UVALDE NATIONAL FISH HATCHERY, UVALDE CO. (TBRC 1992-70; TPRF 1099)

SNOWY PLOVER *Charadrius alexandrinus* Linnaeus

Uncommon summer resident along the coast from Galveston County southward. Snowy Plovers are rare to locally uncommon summer residents, primarily on saline lakes, at scattered locations in the western half of the state. This species is a casual summer resident along major waterways of the Panhandle (Canadian River and the Prairie Dog Fork of the Red River). They are very rare to casual migrants through the eastern quarter of the state. Migrants are found from late March through early May and late July through mid-September. Snowy Plovers are rare to locally uncommon winter residents along the coast and are rare to very rare inland to north-central Texas. They are possibly most common during the winter at salt lakes in Willacy and Hidalgo Counties, where concentrations of several hundred birds have been reported.

WILSON'S PLOVER *Charadrius wilsonia* Ord

Common summer resident along the immediate coast. Wilson's Plover is a casual visitor inland, primarily to the southeastern quarter of the state. They are very rare and local along the coast in the winter, although they occur with greater frequency on the central and lower coasts. This plover is a rare to locally uncommon breeder up to 60 miles inland, primarily at salt lakes, in Willacy, Hidalgo, and western Kenedy Counties. Summer residents begin returning to the coast in mid-February but are not common until early March. Most depart by late September.

SEMIPALMATED PLOVER
Charadrius semipalmatus Bonaparte

Common winter resident along the coast, rare to very rare inland. Semipalmated Plovers are uncommon to common migrants in the eastern two-thirds of the state, becoming uncommon farther west. Semipalmated Plovers may at times congregate in large flocks along the coast during spring migration, sometimes including up to 1,000 individuals. The migration periods for this species are between late March and mid-May and from mid-July to mid-October. This species is a rare summer visitor on the coast.

PIPING PLOVER *Charadrius melodus* Ord

Uncommon to locally common winter resident along the coast. Piping Plover is a rare visitor along the coast in the summer. Piping Plovers are not often observed during migration at inland locations, but most appear to pass east of the Balcones Escarpment. This species is a very rare to casual migrant in the western two-thirds of the state. Recent surveys indicate that the Piping Plover continues to decline in numbers in the state (Eubanks 1994). In 2000, the Canadian Wildlife Service estimated the world's population to be around 5,900 individuals. Piping Plover is listed as Endangered by the U.S. Fish and Wildlife Service.

KILLDEER *Charadrius vociferus* Linnaeus

The Killdeer is one of the most ubiquitous birds in Texas. They are common to abundant summer residents in all parts of the state and increase in numbers in the central and southern parts of the state during the winter. Killdeer populations fluctuate greatly during the winter in the Panhandle where they can be common some years and virtually absent in others.

MOUNTAIN PLOVER *Charadrius montanus* Townsend

Very rare summer resident in the mid- and upper elevation grasslands of the Trans-Pecos and in open grasslands of

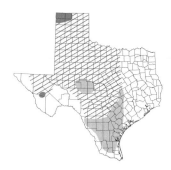

the northwestern Panhandle. Mountain Plovers are rare and local winter residents from the southern Blackland Prairies south to the central Coastal Prairies. In recent years, they appear to occur with more consistency on the Blackland Prairies. This species also winters very locally in the Trans-Pecos, South Texas Brush Country, Concho Valley, and northwestern Edwards Plateau. Wintering birds arrive in late September to early October and are present until early April. Migrants are very rarely encountered away from the Panhandle and South Plains. Occasionally, Mountain Plovers are reported from unlikely locations when American Golden-Plover are migrating through. These reports probably pertain to basic-plumaged American Golden-Plovers. The Mountain Plover is a candidate for the Threatened Species list, and population estimates indicate that there are fewer than 9,000 individuals remaining.

Family Haematopodidae: Oystercatchers

AMERICAN OYSTERCATCHER

Haematopus palliatus Temminck

Locally common resident along the central coast. This species is rare to locally uncommon along the upper and lower coasts. American Oystercatchers nest primarily on or near shell ridges and are seldom found far from areas that provide an ample supply of salt water mollusks on which they feed. Breeding activities are underway in late February, and young can be encountered after mid-April.

Family Recurvirostridae: Stilts and Avocets

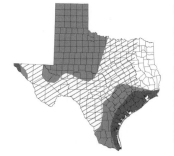

BLACK-NECKED STILT *Himantopus mexicanus* (Müller)

Common summer resident along the Coastal Prairies and locally common inland to the South Texas Brush Country and southern Blackland Prairies. Isolated breeding populations are also present in north and north-central Texas. Black-necked Stilts are uncommon to rare summer residents on the High Plains, western Rolling Plains, and northeastern Trans-Pecos. They are uncommon to common in El Paso and

Hudspeth Counties in summer. As migrants, Black-necked Stilts are rare to uncommon in all areas except the Pineywoods where they are very rare. They are rare to locally uncommon along the Coastal Prairies and in El Paso and Hudspeth Counties during winter and very rare at other inland locations.

AMERICAN AVOCET *Recurvirostra americana* Gmelin

Common to locally abundant winter resident on the coast. Wintering avocets arrive in mid-August, and most depart by mid-May. They are typically absent from the northern half of the state in winter, and individuals present after mid-November are very rare. This species is a common summer resident on the High Plains and in El Paso and Hudspeth Counties. American Avocets are also rare and local summer residents along the coast. This species is a common to uncommon migrant through the western half of the state, becoming generally uncommon farther east. In the Pineywoods, they are rare in spring and uncommon in fall. In general, avocets occur in greater numbers in the fall than in the spring. Migration periods are from early April to mid-May and between early August and late October. Large concentrations of these birds can sometimes be found during peak migration, and up to 14,000 birds have been noted at one location in Galveston County.

Family Jacanidae: Jacanas

Review Species

NORTHERN JACANA *Jacana spinosa* (Linnaeus)

Very rare visitor, primarily during the winter, to the Lower Rio Grande Valley. Northern Jacanas have been found along the Coastal Prairies and inland north to Travis County. There are single records from the Edwards Plateau (Kerr County) and the Trans-Pecos (Brewster County). Thirty documented records exist for Texas, covering every month of the year. The majority of these sightings have been between November and April. Northern Jacana appears to have been a rare resident in the Lower Rio Grande Valley prior to 1910. Interestingly, a resident population of over 40 jacanas became established at Maner Lake, Brazoria County, between the winter of 1967 and April 1978. There are 44 reports of Northern Jacanas from prior to the development of the Review List in 1987 for which there is no documentation on file at Texas A&M University.

Family Scolopacidae: Sandpipers, Phalaropes, and Allies

GREATER YELLOWLEGS *Tringa melanoleuca* (Gmelin)

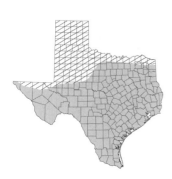

Uncommon to common migrant across the state. Spring migration occurs mainly between late March and early May while fall migration averages longer, from late July to mid-November. Greater Yellowlegs is a rare winter visitor to the Panhandle and South Plains and is uncommon elsewhere, including the Trans-Pecos. Along the Coastal Prairies, this species is uncommon to locally common during the winter. In general, Greater Yellowlegs are rare summer visitors, yet in winter they are more likely to be encountered than the Lesser Yellowlegs.

LESSER YELLOWLEGS *Tringa flavipes* (Gmelin)

Common migrant throughout the state between late March and early May and from early July to mid-October. Lesser Yellowlegs may be present in Texas every month of the year because in the Panhandle the earliest fall migrants arrive in mid-June. This species is an uncommon to locally common winter resident on the coast, becoming rare to uncommon inland in southern Texas. Lesser Yellowlegs is casual to very rare in most of the northern half of the state and Trans-Pecos in winter. During peak migration in the spring, concentrations of over 1,000 birds have been noted with some regularity along the coast.

Review Species

SPOTTED REDSHANK *Tringa erythropus* (Pallas)

Accidental. There is one record of this Old World species in Texas. Spotted Redshank is a rare, but regular, migrant through western Alaska and a casual migrant farther south along the Pacific Coast to California. There are a few scattered records from the interior of North America, including one from Kansas, and one from along the Atlantic Coast as far south as North Carolina.

28, 29, OR 30 SEPT. 2000, AUSTIN, TRAVIS CO.
  (TBRC 2001-129; TPRF 1983)

SOLITARY SANDPIPER *Tringa solitaria* Wilson

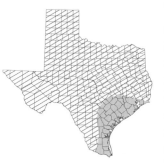

Uncommon to common migrant throughout the state. This species lives up to its name and is very seldom found in flocks of any size, though many may be found loosely scattered at any one location during peak migration. Spring migration extends from mid-March to mid-May with a peak in mid-April, and fall migration is from mid-July to late October, peaking from late August to mid-September. Solitary Sandpiper is a rare winter resident along the coast and casual to very rare inland east of the Balcones Escarpment. They are very rare to casual summer visitors statewide.

WILLET *Catoptrophorus semipalmatus* (Gmelin)

Common to abundant resident along the coast. Willets are rare to uncommon migrants throughout the state. This species is a rare to casual wanderer inland during the late summer and early fall. Migration dates are between late March and mid-May and from mid-July to mid-September. Willets are one of the few shorebirds to breed in the state, but nesting is restricted to the coast.

Review Species

WANDERING TATTLER *Heteroscelus incanus* (Gmelin)

Accidental. There is one documented record of this species for Texas. This species normally frequents rocky shorelines, and the seawall in Galveston, Galveston County, approximates that habitat type. Wandering Tattlers are typically found along the Pacific Coast, and this is one of only four documented records east of the Rocky Mountains.

23 APR.–9 MAY 1992, GALVESTON, GALVESTON CO. (TBRC 1992-64; TPRF 1090)

SPOTTED SANDPIPER *Actitis macularia* (Linnaeus)

Common migrant throughout the state. Migrants are generally present from late March to early May and between early July and mid-October. Spotted Sandpipers are common winter residents in the southern half of the state but are absent from the Panhandle and very rare on the remainder of the High Plains. They are uncommon elsewhere in the northern half of the state and in the Pineywoods and Trans-Pecos. The distribution of this species during winter fluctuates greatly depending on the severity of the season. Spotted Sandpipers are casual breeders in the Panhandle

(Seyffert 2001) and are believed to have nested on the Edwards Plateau (Lockwood 2001b). Oberholser (1974) also cites a breeding record reported by John J. Audubon from Harris County in 1837.

UPLAND SANDPIPER *Bartramia longicauda* (Bechstein)

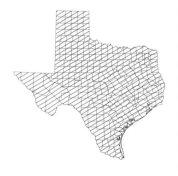

Common spring migrant and uncommon to common fall migrant east of the Pecos River. This species is a rare spring and uncommon fall migrant in the Trans-Pecos. The flight calls of migrating Upland Sandpipers are familiar sounds to those well acquainted with the species. Once greatly reduced in numbers due to market hunting, this species has since rebounded somewhat. Migrants can be found between mid-March and early May and from July to very early October. This species was reported to have bred in the northern Panhandle as late as 1945 and eastward across north-central Texas to Cooke County during the 1890s. Occasionally, summering birds are found in those areas today, suggesting breeding may still occur on an irregular basis.

Review Species

ESKIMO CURLEW *Numenius borealis* (Forster)

The last fully documented record of this small curlew in Texas was in April 1962. Eskimo Curlews were formerly regular spring migrants in the state, with records falling between 8 March and 23 April. This species once migrated along the east coast of North America during the fall, and, as expected, there are no records for this season in Texas. Available records suggest that the majority of Eskimos Curlews migrated east of the Edwards Plateau but west of the Pineywoods. There are 41 published reports of this small curlew from Texas between 1850 and 1905, including specimens collected as far west as Pecos County in the Trans-Pecos (Oberholser 1974). This information suggests that large numbers of Eskimo Curlews migrated through Texas until the very early 1900s. Strecker (1912) listed them as a common migrant in the eastern half of the state. There are 19 accepted records (those from 1959 and 1962 being the only ones from this century), and while Eskimo Curlews have been reported several times since the spring of 1962, incontrovertible evidence of their presence has not been obtained.

WHIMBREL *Numenius phaeopus* (Linnaeus)

Uncommon to rare migrant along the coast, becoming rare inland in the eastern half of the state excluding the Pineywoods, where they are very rare. Whimbrels are most commonly encountered on the Coastal Prairies. In the western half of the state, this species is a very rare to casual migrant. Therefore, it appears that the majority of Whimbrels pass along a narrow corridor down the center of the state. Migration periods are between late March and late May and from late July to late October. This species is a rare winter resident and summer lingerer on the coast.

LONG-BILLED CURLEW

Numenius americanus Bechstein

Common to locally abundant winter resident on the coast where flocks of several hundred are not unusual. Wintering Long-billed Curlews are uncommon to rare farther inland to the southern Blackland Prairies as far north as Bell County and locally common west to El Paso and Hudspeth Counties. They are casual winter visitors in most other areas of the state although very locally in the Panhandle. This species is a locally common summer resident in the northwestern Panhandle, and there are reports of occasional nesting along the upper coast. Historical breeding records exist from Jeff Davis and Cameron Counties. This curlew can be found throughout the year at various locations, and in some areas the beginning or ending of migration can be difficult to discern. This species is an uncommon migrant throughout the state with the exception of the eastern third where it is essentially absent. On the High Plains flocks of several hundred or a thousand or more may be encountered. Migration occurs from mid-March to mid-May and mid-July to early November. Long-billed Curlews are rare to locally uncommon summer visitors on the coast and elsewhere within its migratory pathway. Small flocks, sometimes containing up to 50 birds, have been encountered along the Coastal Prairies during the summer.

HUDSONIAN GODWIT *Limosa haemastica* (Linnaeus)

Uncommon to rare spring migrant through the eastern half of the state. Hudsonian Godwits are encountered much more frequently along the Coastal Prairies of the upper and

central coasts than at inland locations. This species has a very short migration window and is mainly encountered between mid-April and mid-May. Hudsonian Godwits are casual spring migrants in the western half of the state, with fewer than ten reports from the Trans-Pecos. Hudsonian Godwits migrate southward along the east coast of North America and as a result are a very rare fall migrant in Texas (accidental away from the coast) with the few records falling between late July and mid-September.

MARBLED GODWIT *Limosa fedoa* (Linnaeus)

Common to uncommon winter resident along the coast. This species is a rare to uncommon migrant throughout the state. Due to a general lack of habitat, this species is very rarely encountered in the Pineywoods or on the Edwards Plateau. Marbled Godwits are rare to uncommon summer visitors along the coast. Migration dates average from late March to early May and from mid-July to mid-November.

RUDDY TURNSTONE *Arenaria interpres* (Linnaeus)

Common migrant and winter resident along the coast. This species is a rare to locally uncommon summer visitor on the coast with most of these individuals remaining in basic plumage. Migrant Ruddy Turnstones are very uncommon at inland locations; this is particularly true in the western half of the state where they are casual. As with so many other shorebird species, the path of migration seems to be most obvious along a corridor through the center of the state. Migration periods extend from late March to late May and from early August to early October.

Review Species

SURFBIRD *Aphriza virgata* (Gmelin)

Casual. There are seven documented records for Texas of this west coast species, and all are from coastal locations. Dates of occurrence range from 16 March to 21 April with the earliest record being the only one not from April. Surfbirds are typically associated with rocky coastlines, but one present from 15 to 21 April 1995 frequented the sand beaches of North Padre Island, Kleberg County (TBRC 1994-67; TPRF 1291).

RED KNOT *Calidris canutus* (Linnaeus)

Uncommon to common migrant along the coast, especially the Upper Texas Coast, and very rare to casual inland, primarily in the eastern half of the state. Red Knots are rare and local winter residents on the coast, as well as very rare summer visitors. Migration occurs between late March and late May and from late August to early November. This species is virtually unrecorded on the Edwards Plateau (Lockwood 2001b) and the South Plains (Kostecke, Floyd, and Stogner 2001) but is casual in the Concho Valley, Trans-Pecos, and Panhandle as well as north-central Texas eastward through the Pineywoods. They are rare inland in the prairies region of the center of the state north to Travis County. Large numbers of this species are often encountered in migration on the Bolivar Peninsula in Galveston County.

SANDERLING *Calidris alba* (Pallas)

Common to abundant migrant and winter resident along the coast. Sanderlings are also rare to uncommon nonbreeding summer visitors along the coast. This species is a rare to locally uncommon migrant inland through the eastern two-thirds of the state and a casual spring and very rare fall migrant farther west. The typical migration period for the Sanderling is between late March and late May and from late July to early November.

SEMIPALMATED SANDPIPER

Calidris pusilla (Linnaeus)

Uncommon to locally common migrant and occasional summer visitor east of the Trans-Pecos. Semipalmated Sandpipers are very uncommon to rare migrants in the Trans-Pecos, although they are unreported from the Big Bend region. Migration dates are from late March to late May and from mid-July to late October. There are no documented records from Texas between early December and late February.

WESTERN SANDPIPER *Calidris mauri* (Cabanis)

Common to abundant migrant along the coast where it is also an uncommon to common winter resident. Migrating

Western Sandpipers are uncommon to locally common inland throughout the state. They are casual to rare as a winter resident in the northern half of the state and the Trans-Pecos while uncommon inland in the remainder of the southern half. This species is an uncommon to rare summer visitor along the coast, becoming very rare inland. Migration is between mid-March and late May and from mid-July to early November.

Review Species

RED-NECKED STINT *Calidris ruficollis* (Pallas)

Accidental. There is one record for Texas of this Asian shorebird. The adult documented in El Paso is one of the very few records from the interior of North America. This species is a rare breeder in western and northern Alaska, and there are numerous records of migrants from both coasts of North America. The species was formerly called Rufous-necked Stint.

17–22 JULY 1996, FORT BLISS SEWAGE PONDS, EL PASO CO.
  (TBRC 1996-94; TPRF 1447)

LEAST SANDPIPER *Calidris minutilla* (Vieillot)

Probably the most common migrant shorebird in Texas. The Least Sandpiper is common to abundant as a migrant statewide and as a winter resident on the coast. They are uncommon to locally common as a winter resident north of the coast to Dallas and Tarrant Counties and west to the Trans-Pecos. The exception is the Panhandle where this species is rare in winter. During the summer, they are a rare to uncommon nonbreeder along the coast and farther inland. Dates of migration are from mid-March to mid-May and between mid-July and mid-November.

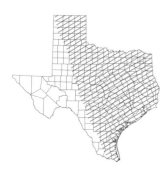

WHITE-RUMPED SANDPIPER
Calidris fuscicollis (Vieillot)

Uncommon to common spring migrant in nearly all areas of the state, except the Trans-Pecos, Edwards Plateau, and South Plains, where it is casual to rare. This species is a late spring migrant compared to other shorebirds with migration beginning in late April and extending through early June. White-rumped Sandpipers are casual to accidental fall migrants with records falling between late July and early November. White-rumped Sandpipers are casual summer visitors on the coast, and these individuals are either very late migrants or injured.

BAIRD'S SANDPIPER *Calidris bairdii* (Coues)

Uncommon to common migrant through most of the state during spring and fall. They are considered rare to locally uncommon in the Pineywoods. Average migration dates range between mid-March and mid-May and from mid-July to mid-October. Baird's Sandpipers winter in South America and are not expected in Texas during winter, although fall migrants have been known to linger well into December.

PECTORAL SANDPIPER *Calidris melanotos* (Vieillot)

Locally common as a migrant statewide, except in the Trans-Pecos, South Plains, and East Texas, where they are rare to uncommon in the spring. Pectoral Sandpipers are more readily found in fall when they are uncommon to common throughout the state with the exception of the Big Bend region where they are considered rare. Migration dates are from early March to late May and from mid-July to mid-November.

Review Species

SHARP-TAILED SANDPIPER
Calidris acuminata (Horsfield)

Accidental. There are two documented records of this species in the state. The breeding range of Sharp-tailed Sandpipers and Pectoral Sandpipers overlaps in Siberia. It has been speculated that Sharp-taileds found in North America are migrating with Pectorals to wintering grounds in South America.

17–18 MAY 1991, ARLINGTON, TARRANT CO.
  (TBRC 1991-56; TPRF 993)
21–22 SEPT. 1996, SAN ANTONIO, BEXAR CO. (TBRC 1996-128)

Review Species

PURPLE SANDPIPER *Calidris maritima* (Brünnich)

Casual winter visitor on the immediate coast, accidental inland. There are 15 documented records of this species from the state with all but two occurring on the coast. All

records fall between 12 November and 28 April, and all but two involve single individuals. Separating winter-plumaged Purple and Rock Sandpipers *(C. ptilocnemis)* may not be possible in the field. The TBRC considers all records from Texas to be of Purple Sandpipers, an East Coast species, until such time as either a Rock Sandpiper, from the West Coast, is documented in or near Texas or field identification criteria are developed that clearly separate the two in basic plumage.

DUNLIN *Calidris alpina* (Linnaeus)

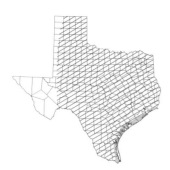

Common to abundant winter resident on the coast and rare inland throughout most of the state. Dunlins are very rare in winter on the High Plains and in the Trans-Pecos. This species is a rare to uncommon migrant through the central part of the state, becoming very rare in the western third of Texas and the Pineywoods. Dunlins are more frequently encountered at inland sites during the fall than in the spring. Average migration dates are between mid-March and late May and from early September to mid-November.

Review Species

CURLEW SANDPIPER *Calidris ferruginea* (Pontoppidan)

Casual. There are nine documented records of this species in Texas. Five of these are from the spring, falling between 28 April and 25 May. Three fall records exist from late August to late November. The other is from mid-summer, a basic-plumaged bird present at Bolivar Flats, Galveston County, from 24 June to 7 July 1994. Four of these birds were found along the Coastal Prairies.

STILT SANDPIPER *Calidris himantopus* (Bonaparte)

Uncommon to locally common migrant statewide. Stilt Sandpipers are rare to uncommon winter residents on the coast, being most common along the lower coast and in the Lower Rio Grande Valley. They are rare in winter inland to central Texas and casual farther north. Migration occurs from late March to late May and from early July to late October. As many as 4,000 Stilt Sandpipers are found each winter at Laguna Atascosa National Wildlife Refuge, Cameron County.

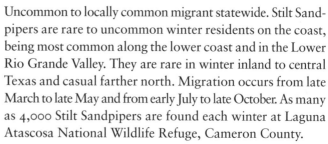

BUFF-BREASTED SANDPIPER
Tryngites subruficollis (Vieillot)

Rare to uncommon migrant in the eastern half of the state and casual farther west. This species is more frequently encountered along the coast than at inland locations and is uncommon to common there during the peak of migration. Buff-breasteds are grassland species and are often found well away from water, much like the Upland Sandpiper. Migration dates range between early April and mid-May and from late July to early October. Market hunting in the late 1800s severely reduced the population of Buff-breasted Sandpipers, which has still not recovered.

Review Species

RUFF *Philomachus pugnax* (Linnaeus)

Very rare migrant and accidental winter visitor. There are 24 documented records of this species in Texas. The vast majority of these sightings are from coastal areas, as well as from Bexar and Travis Counties. Spring migrants have been found between 29 March and 14 May and fall migrants primarily between 25 July and 5 October. A few have lingered as late as early January.

SHORT-BILLED DOWITCHER
Limnodromus griseus (Gmelin)

Uncommon to rare migrant throughout the eastern half of the state. Short-billed Dowitchers are most often encountered along the coast. This species is a very rare to rare migrant through the western half of the state and very rarely seen in the Pineywoods. In general, the status of this species is poorly understood both in terms of seasonal movements and abundance because of identification problems involving the very similar Long-billed Dowitcher. These two species were considered as one until the 1950s (AOU 1957). Compounding the identification problem is the fact that two subspecies of Short-billed Dowitchers are found in the state, *L. g. griseus* and *L. g. hendersoni*. This species is a locally common winter resident along the coast. They are apparently encountered more often in the fall than in the spring, with migration dates ranging from late March to mid-May and from mid-July to mid-October.

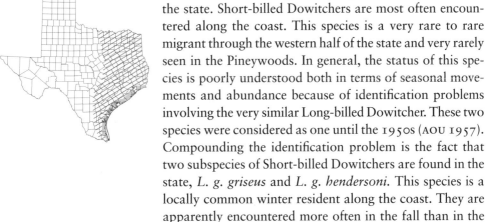

LONG-BILLED DOWITCHER
Limnodromus scolopaceus (Say)

Uncommon to common migrant throughout the state and abundant on the coast. Long-billed Dowitchers are common winter residents along the coast, as well as locally common inland in the southern half of the state. This species becomes increasingly less common northward during the winter and is casual in the Panhandle at that season. Long-billed Dowitchers migrate through Texas between early March and late May and from late July to mid-November. During the spring, a few individuals routinely linger into early June; as a result they can be found during every month of the year. Long-billed Dowitchers outnumber Short-billeds in Texas.

WILSON'S SNIPE *Gallinago delicata* (Ord)

Common migrant throughout the state. This species is a common winter resident in the eastern two-thirds of the state, particularly in the southern half. In the western third of the state, Wilson's Snipe is uncommon to rare during the winter. They are generally present in Texas between mid-September and late April. This species was formerly considered conspecific with *G. gallinago* of Eurasia (Banks et al. 2002). The Old World taxon retains the name Common Snipe.

AMERICAN WOODCOCK *Scolopax minor* Gmelin

Rare to locally common winter resident in the eastern half of the state, becoming rare to very rare farther west. American Woodcocks have been recorded in the state during every month of the year. This species is a rare, but regular, breeder in the eastern third of the state with nesting activities generally occurring between January and April. It is possible, if not probable, that breeding in Texas is more widespread and common than is currently known. Migrant woodcocks typically arrive in late September or early October and depart between mid-February and early March. They are secretive and nocturnal and are usually found in dense woodlands during the day but frequently feed in more open areas at night. Their secretive habits make determining the actual status difficult, and there may be larger numbers present during the winter than records indicate.

WILSON'S PHALAROPE *Phalaropus tricolor* (Vieillot)

Common to abundant migrant across the state. The migration periods fall between late March and late May and from late June to late October. In winter, Wilson's Phalarope is rare to casual inland, primarily in the southern half of the state, with a few reports from as far north as the Panhandle. An amazing concentration of more than 200 was present in Hidalgo County during the 2002–2003 winter. Wilson's Phalarope is also a casual summer resident in the Panhandle but is more common during wet years. The first nesting was discovered in Carson County in 1980 (Seyffert 1985b). There have been five additional breeding records from the Panhandle (Seyffert 2001).

RED-NECKED PHALAROPE

Phalaropus lobatus (Linnaeus)

Uncommon to rare fall migrant throughout the western third of the state. Red-necked Phalaropes are rare to very rare throughout most of the remainder of the state, except for the Edwards Plateau and Pineywoods, where they are unreported. This species is more numerous in fall than in spring, when they are very rare to rare. Red-necked Phalaropes have occasionally been reported from offshore waters during the late summer and fall. Fall migrants are found between late August and mid-October. Spring records are scattered between late April and late May. Up to four Red-necked Phalaropes were at La Sal de Rey, Hidalgo County, during the 2002–2003 winter, providing the first record for that season.

Review Species

RED PHALAROPE *Phalaropus fulicarius* (Linnaeus)

Very rare fall and accidental spring migrant. There are 28 documented records of this species for Texas. Of these, 21 are from the fall, and the dates of occurrence range from 15 July to 17 November. Spring records are between 20 April and 1 June. There is a single winter record of a bird found in Austin, Travis County, in January 1975 (TPRF 167). There are 37 reports of Red Phalaropes from prior to the development of the Review List in 1987 for which there is no documentation on file at Texas A&M University.

Family Laridae: Gulls, Terns, and Allies

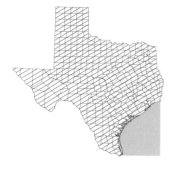

POMARINE JAEGER

Stercorarius pomarinus (Temminck)

Uncommon migrant and winter resident and a rare to very rare summer visitor along the coast and in the Gulf. Pomarine Jaegers have been found in Texas during every month of the year. This species is a rare to very rare migrant inland with more reports during the fall than spring. Pomarine Jaegers are occasionally blown inland by hurricanes. During fall migration, large numbers have been reported from petroleum platforms in the Gulf of Mexico. These jaegers are occasionally seen on beaches and, more frequently, following fishing and shrimping boats that are near shore.

PARASITIC JAEGER

Stercorarius parasiticus (Linnaeus)

Uncommon migrant and winter resident along the coast and in off-shore waters and rare inland. In general, Parasitic Jaegers are less common than Pomarine Jaegers in Texas, particularly inland. Although this species is a very rare summer visitor, they are less likely to be encountered in summer than are Pomarines. Parasitic Jaegers are very rare to casual migrants inland, and, as with the Pomarine Jaeger, there are more reports during the fall than spring. This species is also occasionally blown inland by hurricanes.

Review Species

LONG-TAILED JAEGER

Stercorarius longicaudus Vieillot

Casual migrant with 17 documented records, most falling between 16 August and 5 November. These coincide with the primary fall migration period of this species. Long-tailed Jaeger is typically a late spring migrant, and the four early to mid-June records fit this pattern. There is a single February record for the state, which it is harder to reconcile with the migration pattern, because this species winters in the southern oceans. The majority of fall migrants found in Texas are immature birds.

LAUGHING GULL *Larus atricilla* Linnaeus

Abundant resident along the coast. Two small breeding colonies of Laughing Gulls have become established inland

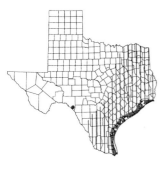

at Falcon Reservoir, Zapata County, and at Lake Amistad, Val Verde County. Otherwise, this species is an uncommon to casual visitor inland throughout the state as far north as the southern Panhandle. Most of these inland records are from the late summer and fall, reflecting postbreeding dispersal. Laughing Gulls have become uncommon late summer and fall visitors to many of the large reservoirs in the eastern half of the state. They are less common inland during winter and spring but are becoming more frequent.

FRANKLIN'S GULL *Larus pipixcan* Wagler

Common to uncommon migrant in all areas of Texas. Franklin's Gull is a rare winter visitor along the coast and to inland reservoirs and landfills, particularly in the eastern two-thirds of the state. Migrating birds pass through between late February and mid-May and from late August to early December, sometimes in very large flocks of 1000 or more individuals. Franklin's Gull is a casual visitor to the Panhandle during the summer and is accidental in other parts of the state at that time of year.

Review Species

LITTLE GULL *Larus minutus* Pallas

Very rare winter visitor to the eastern half of the state. There are 37 documented records of Little Gull for Texas. Interestingly, almost half of the documented sightings from the state are from Dallas and Tarrant Counties. Most records fall between 14 November and 27 February, although there are six for the spring with the latest occurring on 20 April. There are only two records from the western half of the state: one near Lubbock on 9 April 1983 (TBRC 1984-9) and one at Imperial Reservoir, Pecos County, on 10 November 2000 (TBRC 2000-130; TPRF 1904).

Review Species

BLACK-HEADED GULL *Larus ridibundus* Linnaeus

Very rare winter visitor. There are 21 documented records for Texas, almost all from the northeastern quarter of the state. All fall between 26 October and 25 March. There have been two Black-headed Gulls that returned to the same location for several years. One at Cooper Lake, Delta County, was present for five consecutive winters. The most amazing record for this species was of one banded as a juvenile in Finland in 1996 and discovered at the Village

Creek Drying Beds, Tarrant County, in 1998. This individual returned to Village Creek for three consecutive winters.

BONAPARTE'S GULL *Larus philadelphia* (Ord)

Uncommon to common winter resident along the coast and inland on large reservoirs. This species is most common in the eastern two-thirds of the state and is a rare to uncommon migrant and winter visitor in the western third. Fall migrants typically arrive in late October to early November and most depart by early March, although some have lingered as late as May. Bonaparte's Gulls wintering on inland reservoirs can sometimes be found in very large flocks.

Review Species

HEERMANN'S GULL *Larus heermanni* Cassin

Accidental. There are two records of the species in Texas. The first was at Big Lake, Reagan County, in early December 1975 (Maxwell 1977). Heermann's Gulls breed along the west coast of Mexico and locally in southern California but are known for their postbreeding dispersal. They have been found as far east as Michigan, Ohio, and Florida and as far south as Guatemala.

2–4 DEC. 1975, BIG LAKE, REAGAN CO. (TPRF 97)
8 FEB. 1983, MUSTANG ISLAND, NUECES CO.
    (TBRC 1988-137; TPRF 648)

Review Species

BLACK-TAILED GULL *Larus crassirostris* Vieillo

Accidental. There is one documented record of this Asian gull in Texas. A near adult-plumaged bird was discovered at the Brownsville Landfill, Cameron County, in the spring of 1999 (D'Anna et al. 1999). There have been numerous records of Black-tailed Gull from both coasts of North America including one as far south as Belize (Lethaby and Bangma 1998).

11–13 FEB. AND 5–16 MAR. 1999, BROWNSVILLE, CAMERON CO.
    (TBRC 1999-10; TPRF 1745)

Review Species

MEW GULL *Larus canus* Linnaeus

Very rare winter visitor to the state with most sightings from El Paso, Fort Worth, and San Antonio. The status of Mew Gull appears to be changing in Texas. Prior to 1995, there were only five documented records, but to date there are 25. Whether this increase in sightings reflects an actual change in abundance or is simply the result of greater scru-

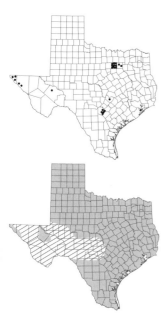

tiny of gulls by observers is debatable. Texas records of Mew Gull fall between 22 November and 16 March and all appear to pertain to the North American subspecies, *L. c. brachyrhynchus.*

RING-BILLED GULL *Larus delawarensis* Ord

Common migrant throughout the state and a common to abundant winter resident along the coast and on inland reservoirs. Fall migrants reach Texas in early September, and spring migrants depart by mid-April. This species is also an uncommon to rare summer visitor throughout their winter range but is not known to nest in the state. The majority of summering individuals are not adults. Ring-billed Gull is the most widespread and common of the white-headed gulls found in Texas in the winter.

CALIFORNIA GULL *Larus californicus* Lawrence

Rare to very rare migrant and winter visitor to the coast and scattered inland locations. This species has been found in increasing numbers in Texas since about 1990 due partly to an increase of observers visiting landfills and other areas with large concentrations of gulls, such as East Beach in Galveston. California Gull has become an annual winter visitor to reservoirs in El Paso and Hudspeth Counties with an increasing number of sightings from other seasons. There were more than 60 accepted records for the state when this species was removed from the Review List in November 1999. Most Texas records fall between late October and early March.

HERRING GULL *Larus argentatus* Pontoppidan

Common migrant and winter resident along the coast. This species is a rare winter resident inland but is uncommon and local on the many reservoirs found in the northeastern quarter of the state. Herring Gulls are uncommon to rare summer visitors along the coast and very rare on inland reservoirs at this season. The vast majority of summering individuals are in first- or second-year plumages, often with very worn and bleached plumage that makes identification difficult. There are two breeding records for the state; a nest with eggs was discovered on a spoil island in the Laguna Madre, Cameron County, on 9 June 1989 (Farmer 1990) and again at the same location in 1990.

THAYER'S GULL *Larus thayeri* Brooks

Rare to very rare winter and spring visitor. The majority of the 53 state records of Thayer's Gull are from the coast, but there have been many inland sightings as well. All fall between 5 November and 21 April. Thayer's Gull was considered accidental in Texas prior to 1990, but since then over 40 sightings have been documented. Two factors may have influenced this increase in recent years. First, Thayer's Gull was previously considered a subspecies of Herring Gull and thus did not attract a great deal of attention. Secondly, a plethora of detailed information was published during the 1990s on how to identify large white-headed gulls. The taxonomic status of this species continues to be debated but now focuses on whether it should be considered conspecific with Iceland Gull, rather than a subspecies of Herring Gull. Heavily worn spring birds are difficult to verify given their similarity to Herring Gulls in the same condition.

ICELAND GULL *Larus glaucoides* Meyer

Accidental. There is one documented record of this species for Texas, a first-winter individual. Plumage variation in Iceland and Thayer's Gulls makes documenting this species exceedingly difficult. Taxonomic uncertainty reflects the similarity in appearance of these two taxa. Some recent studies have suggested that Thayer's and Iceland Gulls should be considered as one species, while others have suggested that the North American population of Iceland Gull, *L. g. kumlieni,* may represent a species separate from the nominate Greenland population (AOU 1998).

15 JAN.–12 FEB. 1977, SOUTH PADRE ISLAND, CAMERON CO.
  (TBRC 1989-245; TPRF 935)

LESSER BLACK-BACKED GULL
Larus fuscus Linnaeus

Rare to locally uncommon winter resident on the coast, becoming very rare inland. There are inland records from all regions of the state except the Edwards Plateau. This species has occurred with greater frequency since 1990. During the winter of 1999–2000, more than 20 separate individuals were located along the coast, including 10 at the Brownsville Landfill, Cameron County. One of the most interesting records involved an individual that wintered at the same location near Port Aransas for 12 years. Wintering Lesser Black-backed Gulls have generally been found from early September to late April. Lesser Black-backed Gull was formerly a Review Species, and there were over 90 documented records when removed from the list in 1997.

Review Species

SLATY-BACKED GULL *Larus schistisagus* Stejneger

Accidental. There is one documented record of a sub-adult Slaty-backed Gull for Texas. This species has been found with increasing frequency in the interior United States since the 1980s and for that reason may have been expected to eventually be found in Texas. However, few would have predicted that the first record of this Asian gull for Texas would have been so far south.

7–22 FEB. 1992, BROWNSVILLE, CAMERON CO.
(TBRC 1992-24; TPRF 1071)

Review Species

YELLOW-FOOTED GULL *Larus livens* Dwight

Accidental. The lone record for Texas was a second-year bird found near Surfside, Brazoria County, in 1998 (Weeks and Patten 2000). This individual represents not only the first record for Texas, but also an unexpected first record for the entire Gulf of Mexico. The entire breeding population of Yellow-footed Gull is found in the Gulf of California, Mexico. Postbreeding dispersal to inland southern California is well known, and wandering individuals have been found as far north as northern Utah and central California and as far south as Oaxaca, Mexico.

9 JULY 1998, SURFSIDE, BRAZORIA CO.
(TBRC 1998-141; TPRF 1743)

Review Species

WESTERN GULL *Larus occidentalis* Audubon

Accidental. There are two records of the species in Texas. Western Gulls are found along the West Coast of North America from southwestern British Columbia to Baja California. Dispersal inland is very rare, although there are records for Arizona and New Mexico.

14 MAY 1986, FORT BLISS, EL PASO CO. (TBRC 1987-3; TPRF 514)
6 APR. 1995, BOCA CHICA, CAMERON CO.
(TBRC 1995-51; TPRF 1495)

GLAUCOUS GULL *Larus hyperboreus* Gunnerus

Rare winter resident along the coast and very rare to casual winter visitor inland with records from all regions of the state except the Edwards Plateau and Trans-Pecos. Glaucous Gull records from Texas fall between late November and early April, with a few individuals lingering as late as mid-May. There is one exceptionally early record from San Luis Pass, Galveston County, on 28 September 1995 (TBRC 1995-154; TPRF 1410). All of the Glaucous Gulls found in Texas have been either first- or second-year birds, except for one third-winter bird at Galveston during the winter of 1996–97. This species was removed from the Review List in 1997; at the time there were over 70 documented records for the state.

Review Species

GREAT BLACK-BACKED GULL

Larus marinus Linnaeus

Very rare winter visitor along the coast. Almost half of the 35 documented records for the state come from the upper coast. Records of Great Black-backed Gull in Texas extend from late September to early May. There is one documented inland record: a third-winter bird was discovered near Longview, Harrison County, on 30 December 1992 and was rediscovered at Lake O' the Pines, Marion County, in early January 1993, where it remained until March.

Review Species

KELP GULL *Larus dominicanus* Lichtenstein

Accidental. There are three records of this primarily southern-hemisphere gull. An adult was discovered at Galveston in January 1996 and remained until April. What appeared to be the same individual returned the following winter. Kelp Gulls have been present in the Mississippi Delta of Louisiana for several years and have hybridized with Herring Gulls. This species has also been documented in Indiana and Maryland. There are additional records from the Yucatan Peninsula (Howell, Correa S., and Garcia B. 1993) and northern Tamaulipas, Mexico (Gee and Edwards 2000).

15 JAN.–5 APR. 1996, GALVESTON, GALVESTON CO.
  (TBRC 1996-17; TPRF 1393)
30 NOV. 1996–21 APR. 1997, GALVESTON, GALVESTON CO.
  (TBRC 1996-180; TPRF 1523)
6 MAY 1996, NORTH PADRE ISLAND, KLEBERG CO.
  (TBRC 1996-88; TPRF 1627)

SABINE'S GULL *Xema sabini* (Sabine)

Rare fall migrant with records from all regions of the state. The majority of migrating Sabine's Gulls have been found in Texas between late August and early November, although there are four additional records of late migrants from late November and December. More unexpected are single documented spring (6 May 1995) and summer (13–15 July 1996) records. Interestingly, both of these records are from McNary Reservoir, Hudspeth County. Sabine's Gull was removed from the Review List in 1999. At that time, there were almost 60 documented records for the state with only five involving adult birds.

BLACK-LEGGED KITTIWAKE

Rissa tridactyla (Linnaeus)

Rare winter visitor along the coast and at scattered inland localities over the eastern half of the state, becoming casual in the western third. Records of Black-legged Kittiwake generally fall between late November and late March with a few from April. The vast majority are first-winter birds. This species was removed from the Review List in 1999; at the time there were approximately 70 documented records. Of those, fewer than ten were from the western third of the state (El Paso, Hudspeth, Midland, Pecos, Randall, and Reeves Counties).

GULL-BILLED TERN *Sterna nilotica* Gmelin

Common resident along the coast, although generally much less numerous in the winter. Gull-billed Terns are normally found in marsh habitats. They are a casual visitor away from the coast with records as far inland as Granger Lake, Williamson County, and Lake Waco, McLennan County. Oberholser (1974) lists sight records from Dallas and Denton Counties, but Pulich (1988) notes that these lack details. Interestingly, there are small resident populations at Falcon Reservoir, Zapata County, and Lake Casa Blanca, Webb County.

CASPIAN TERN *Sterna caspia* Pallas

Common resident along the coast. Caspian Terns are also rare to uncommon migrants and winter visitors to the eastern half of the state away from the coast, and casual migrants in the western half. These migrants originate from breeding populations in central Canada that winter along the Gulf Coast. Migrants can generally be found between late February and late May and from mid-September through October. The few mid-summer inland records may either be postbreeding wanderers from the coast or very early migrants from farther north.

ROYAL TERN *Sterna maxima* Boddaert

Common resident primarily confined to coastal habitats. This species is casual to accidental inland in the eastern half of the state, primarily during the summer and fall. Most inland reports are associated with the passage of tropical storms. Surprisingly, Royal Terns have appeared in north-central and northeastern Texas on at least five occasions (White 2002).

Review Species

ELEGANT TERN *Sterna elegans* Gambel

Accidental. There are three documented records of this species for Texas. Frank Armstrong collected the first bird in 1889 at Corpus Christi, Nueces County. In the Northern Hemisphere, Elegant Terns are found along the west coast of North America with most of the breeding population restricted to the Gulf of California, Mexico.

25 JULY 1889, CORPUS CHRISTI, NUECES CO.
  (BMNH 91-10-20-92; TPRF 1460)
23 DEC. 1985, BALMORHEA LAKE, REEVES CO. (TPRF 397)
4–18 NOV. 2001, GALVESTON, GALVESTON CO.
  (TBRC 2001-134; TPRF 1988)

SANDWICH TERN *Sterna sandvicensis* Latham

Common summer resident and rare to uncommon winter resident along the coast. All inland records of Sandwich Tern in Texas are of birds found after tropical storms. Two were found near Austin, Travis County, on 12 September 1961; another two were located at Falcon Reservoir, Zapata County, on 22 September 1967; and one was in Burleson County on 11 October 1982 (TCWC 11274). More recently, one was at Lake Alcoa, Milam County, on 12 September 1998.

Review Species

ROSEATE TERN *Sterna dougallii* Montagu

Accidental. Texas has two documented records of this species. Oberholser (1974) reported a specimen taken by Frank Armstrong in the spring of 1901. The TBRC had been un-

able to determine where it was housed until 1996 (Royal Ontario Museum 39704). Oberholser also listed two other specimens, but their locations are still unknown. The closest breeding colonies to Texas are found in the Florida Keys. Separating Roseate Terns from the more common Forster's and Common Terns is an identification challenge that has made documenting this species difficult.

10 APR. 1901, CORPUS CHRISTI, NUECES CO.
  (TBRC 1996-111; TPRF 1535)
25 JUNE 1995, COOPER LAKE, DELTA CO. (TBRC 1995-92)

COMMON TERN *Sterna hirundo* Linnaeus

Common fall and uncommon spring migrant along the coast and offshore, rare to casual inland. Fall migrants generally outnumber those found in spring, both on the coast and inland. Common Tern is a rare winter resident on the coast and a casual visitor to inland reservoirs. Small numbers of basic-plumaged birds are found in summer, primarily along the coast. There are numerous reports of breeding colonies along the coast from the 1880s to the 1930s. Dresser (1865) reported the species as an abundant nester in Galveston Bay in 1864 while Pemberton (1922) reported thousands of individuals in Cameron County in 1921. The veracity of these reports has often been questioned, in part because of the large numbers of nesting pairs reported and the dearth of nesting records since that time. It may be that Forster's Terns were mistaken for Common Terns in these reports.

Review Species

ARCTIC TERN *Sterna paradisaea* Pontoppidan

Accidental. Texas has five documented records of this species: two spring and three fall migrants. Arctic Tern is likely to occur as a very rare migrant, particularly during the late spring, in the Gulf of Mexico (Lee and Cardiff 1993). Separating Arctic from Common Terns is very difficult; sight records, including one photograph taken prior to 1996, were insufficient to document the species.

21 SEPT. 1996, OFF PORT O'CONNOR, CALHOUN CO.
  (TBRC 1996-119)
5–7 JUNE 1997, MCNARY RESERVOIR, HUDSPETH CO.
  (TBRC 1997-98; TPRF 1614)
26 JULY 1997, OFF PORT O'CONNOR, CALHOUN CO.
  (TBRC 1997-117; TPRF 1636)
18 OCT. 2001, LAKE WORTH, TARRANT CO.
  (TBRC 2002-17; TPRF 2060)
27 MAY 2002, EL PASO, EL PASO CO. (TBRC 2002-64)

FORSTER'S TERN *Sterna forsteri* Nuttall

Common resident along the coast and common to uncommon migrant in nearly all parts of Texas. Forster's Terns are also locally common winter residents on inland lakes and reservoirs east of the Pecos River except on the High Plains. In the Trans-Pecos, they are casual winter visitors. This species has been found nesting in small numbers at Choke Canyon Reservoir, Live Oak/McMullen Counties, and at Lake Amistad, Val Verde County. Forster's Tern is the most common species of tern found wintering on inland reservoirs statewide. Along the coast, this species is found in much higher numbers during winter than in summer.

LEAST TERN *Sterna antillarum* (Lesson)

Common summer resident along the coast and rare to locally uncommon at scattered inland locations. Least Terns are uncommon to rare migrants in the eastern two-thirds of the state, becoming increasingly rare westward. They are also a very rare winter resident along the coast. The two breeding populations, one coastal and the other inland, represent separate subspecies. The Interior Least Tern, *S. a. athalassos,* is listed as an Endangered Species and known to breed along the Red River to Hall County, along the Canadian River to Roberts County, locally in north-central Texas, and at reservoirs around San Angelo, Tom Green County; Lake Amistad, Val Verde County; and Falcon Reservoir, Zapata County. Least Tern may also nest at Choke Canyon Reservoir, Live Oak/McMullen Counties, but the subspecies involved has not been determined. There are isolated breeding records from reservoirs at various other locations across the state, perhaps most frequently in northeast Texas.

BRIDLED TERN *Sterna anaethetus* Scopoli

Uncommon to rare summer and fall visitor in offshore waters. Prior to 1988 there were no records of this pelagic tern for the state. The first Bridled Terns were associated with the passage of Hurricane Frances. Since that time, deepwater pelagic trips have revealed that this species is more common and regular than previously thought. The highest number of individuals observed on a single trip was more than 200 off Port O'Connor, Calhoun County, on 28 June 1997. Despite the regular occurrence along the Continental Shelf in the Gulf of Mexico, Bridled Terns are still a very rare to casual visitor along the coast. This species remained on the Review List until 1997.

SOOTY TERN *Sterna fuscata* Linnaeus

Rare and local summer resident along the central and lower coasts and uncommon to rare visitor to offshore waters in late summer and fall. Sooty Terns nest in small numbers on islands in the Laguna Madre and previously nested in Galveston County (Meitzen 1963). This species has occasionally been found along the coast loafing in tern colonies or on the beach. Larger numbers are routinely found along the immediate coast following hurricanes and tropical storms. These disturbances have pushed Sooty Terns far inland, with records from as far west as Brewster and Jeff Davis Counties and as far north as Cooper Lake, Delta County.

BLACK TERN *Chlidonias niger* (Linnaeus)

Uncommon to common migrant in all parts of the state including offshore waters, at times abundant along the coast. Spring migrants begin to appear in late March to early April and can be found into late May. Fall migrants are present from early July through early October. This species is locally uncommon during the summer on the coast, and rare to very rare at inland locations. However, these summering birds do not breed despite the fact that small numbers are in alternate plumage. Black Tern is a very rare winter visitor along the coast and casual inland along the Coastal Prairies.

Review Species

BROWN NODDY *Anous stolidus* (Linnaeus)

Casual summer visitor to offshore waters and the coast. Texas has seven documented records, and all occur between 27 April and 18 September. The closest breeding colonies of Brown Noddies can be found on islands off the Yucatan Peninsula, Mexico, and the Dry Tortugas, Florida.

BLACK NODDY *Anous minutus* Boie

Accidental visitor to the state, with three documented records. All are from the spring and summer, as would be expected since this species winters at more tropical latitudes. A single individual was seen at opposite ends of the Bolivar Peninsula, Galveston County, during the spring of 1998. Photos confirmed that only one individual was involved. Separating Black from Brown Noddies requires detailed study of both plumage and bill structure. The identification of the 1975 record has recently been questioned and will be more thoroughly evaluated.

22 JUNE 1975, NORTH PADRE ISLAND, NUECES CO. (TPRF 77)
15 APR. AND 1 MAY 1998, GALVESTON CO.
  (TBRC 1998-63; TPRF 1692)
27 JULY 1998, ST. JOSE ISLAND, ARANSAS CO.
  (TBRC 1998-100; TPRF 1693)

BLACK SKIMMER *Rynchops niger* Linnaeus

Locally common resident along the coast. Black Skimmer is a vagrant inland, occurring with greater regularity within 100 miles of the coast. This species has been found as far inland as the Dallas–Fort Worth area and Cooper Lake, Delta County, to the north and as far inland as Balmorhea Lake, Reeves County, and Midland County to the west. Dispersal far away from the coast is largely limited to summer and early fall and is often associated with the passage of a hurricane or strong tropical storm. There are a few spring inland records, as well.

ORDER COLUMBIFORMES

Family Columbidae: Pigeons and Doves

ROCK PIGEON *Columba livia* Gmelin

Common resident throughout the state, primarily in urban areas. Rock Pigeons were introduced from Europe to Nova Scotia in the early 1600s and quickly spread westward. In Texas, this feral species has become an established resident around human environs and is uncommon to rare in remote rural areas. Natural populations of Rock Pigeons nest on cliffs, which explains their presence in areas with tall buildings that mimic their natural habitat. Formerly known as Rock Dove.

RED-BILLED PIGEON *Patagioenas flavirostris* Wagler

Locally uncommon to rare summer resident in the western Lower Rio Grande Valley. Red-billed Pigeons are found primarily in close association with the Rio Grande. The center of abundance for this species in Texas is Hidalgo and Starr Counties. Red-billeds have been found upriver to northern Webb and southern Maverick Counties, where they are rare to locally uncommon. There are several reports of this species away from the known range, particularly along the lower coast north to Victoria County. One of these is documented, a single bird at Corpus Christi, Nueces County, from 3 to 5 March 1988 (TPRF 615). There is also a documented sight record in the Hill Country from Kerr County on 12 October 2002. Red-billed Pigeons are rare and very local winter residents within the breeding range.

BAND-TAILED PIGEON *Patagioenas fasciata* Say

Common to uncommon summer and irregular winter resident at the higher elevations of the Davis and Chisos Mountains. This species is a rare, and possibly declining, summer resident in the Guadalupe Mountains. Band-tailed Pigeons are very rare visitors, primarily in the fall, to the lowlands of the Trans-Pecos, and casual visitors east of the Pecos River. There are ten records from the Panhandle and South Plains and four from the western Edwards Plateau. Most of these are from the fall and early winter, but a single spring and two summer records are among them. This species is also a fall vagrant to the Coastal Prairies, with records from Aransas, Chambers, and Galveston Counties.

EURASIAN COLLARED-DOVE
Streptopelia decaocto (Frivaldszky)

Locally common in urban areas throughout the state, although perhaps most prevalent along the coast. This species was first reported in Texas in March 1995 and by 1996 had reached the northern High Plains in Randall County. They became established breeders on the upper coast by 1999. Since then, populations have become established in many areas of the state, even as far west as Fabens, El Paso County, and north to Dallam County. Eurasian Collared-Doves have been reported in over 80 percent of the counties in the state, including all those along the Coastal Prairies. This species has the potential to be found at any location but is less frequently encountered in rural areas. (See Ringed Turtle-Dove account in appendix B.)

WHITE-WINGED DOVE *Zenaida asiatica* (Linnaeus)

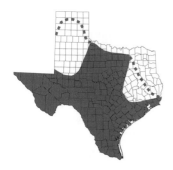

Common to locally abundant summer resident throughout the southern half of the state. The population of White-winged Doves in Texas is undergoing a rapid range expansion. This dove is now resident north to Dallas and Tarrant Counties, east to Jefferson County. The highest density of White-wingeds in the state is found within the city limits of San Antonio, where over one-half million are estimated to be resident. Breeding populations have become established in suburban areas as far north as Amarillo, Potter/Randall Counties, and Denton, Denton County. White-wingeds depart from rural areas in the northern portions of their Texas range in winter. However, they are beginning to winter in increasing numbers in urban areas as far north as the Panhandle.

MOURNING DOVE *Zenaida macroura* (Linnaeus)

Common to abundant summer and winter resident throughout the state. Large numbers of Mourning Doves from outside the state replace the summer resident populations during the winter. This species is the most abundant game bird in North America (Tomlinson et al. 1994).

PASSENGER PIGEON *Ectopistes migratorius* (Linnaeus)

Extinct. The Passenger Pigeon was once a regular fall and winter resident in the northeastern quarter of Texas. Occasionally, large numbers would invade the state, and birds could be found as far west as the Rolling Plains and western Edwards Plateau. Although primarily a winter resident, there are several reports of nesting in the state. The only specimen of this species from Texas is a single egg collected near Mobile, Tyler County, on 3 May 1877. Large numbers of Passenger Pigeons were reported from Texas until the early 1880s when the population declined abruptly (Casto 2001). Oberholser (1974) considered a report from upper Galveston Bay from March 1900 as the last reliable report of its presence. The Passenger Pigeon is thought to have once been the most common bird in North America.

INCA DOVE *Columbina inca* (Lesson)

Common resident in the southern two-thirds of the state, becoming uncommon and local farther north and in the Pineywoods. As with the White-winged Dove, this species is expanding its range northward and eastward. Small breeding populations have been found as far north as Amarillo, Potter/Randall Counties, and single breeding attempts have been documented in other Panhandle communities. Inca Doves are much more frequently encountered in cities and towns than in rural areas.

COMMON GROUND-DOVE

Columbina passerina (Linnaeus)

Uncommon to locally common resident in the South Texas Brush Country, Coastal Prairies, and southern Trans-Pecos along the Rio Grande, but uncommon to rare away from the river. They are uncommon and local summer residents along the southern edge of the Edwards Plateau. This species is locally uncommon to rare along the upper coast east to the Texas-Louisiana border. Common Ground-Doves occur casually at all seasons north of the breeding range, although fall records are more numerous. These records are from virtually all areas of the state including the northernmost reaches.

Review Species

RUDDY GROUND-DOVE

Columbina talpacoti (Temminck)

Casual visitor to the Lower Rio Grande Valley, the Big Bend region, and El Paso County. Texas has 12 documented records of Ruddy Ground-Dove. Documented records from the Lower Rio Grande Valley belong to the bright rufous subspecies *C. t. rufipennis* of eastern Mexico. The individuals thus far documented in the Trans-Pecos appear to belong to the pallid western subspecies, *C. t. eluta* (TPRF 870 et al.); however, there are no specimens from west Texas to confirm this identification. A record from Brooks County represents the only one for the South Texas Brush Country north of the Lower Rio Grande Valley. All records fall between 18 October and 5 May.

WHITE-TIPPED DOVE *Leptotila verreauxi* Bonaparte

Common resident in the Lower Rio Grande Valley. White-tipped Doves are uncommon and local north through the South Texas Brush Country to Dimmit, McMullen, and

Refugio Counties. This species is slowly expanding its range northward. In the west, White-tipped Doves were first encountered in LaSalle and Dimmit Counties in the late 1980s and are now a casual visitor as far north as southern Val Verde County. Along the coast, they have been found on several occasions as far north as Calhoun County since 1999. There are three records from the Edwards Plateau, one from the Devils River in central Val Verde County (TPRF 220), and single individuals from Comal and Real Counties. Two summer reports have been made from Big Bend National Park, Brewster County.

Review Species

RUDDY QUAIL-DOVE *Geotrygon montana* (Linnaeus)

Accidental. Texas has one record of this tropical dove. There are six documented records for the United States, and this was the first from outside of Florida. Ruddy Quail-Doves are uncommon to rare residents in northeastern Mexico as far north as southern Tamaulipas.

2–6 MAR. 1996, BENTSEN–RIO GRANDE VALLEY SP, HIDALGO CO. (TBRC 1996-28; TPRF 1468)

ORDER PSITTACIFORMES

Family Psittacidae: Parakeets and Parrots

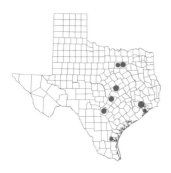

MONK PARAKEET *Myiopsitta monachus* (Boddaert)

This relatively drab parakeet is native to southern South America and has been introduced to the United States. It is a very locally common resident in a number of metropolitan areas, including Austin, Dallas, Galveston, Houston, San Antonio, and Temple. The origin of most of these populations is presumed to be escaped cage birds, although a small number of Monk Parakeets was intentionally released in Austin in the early 1980s. This is the only member of its family to construct communal stick nests. Monk Parakeets are common in the pet trade, and some sightings may be of local escapees.

CAROLINA PARAKEET
Conuropsis carolinensis (Linnaeus)

Extinct. Apparently this species was once resident along the Red River Valley west to Montague County. The only report of breeding for Texas comes from Red River County (Oberholser 1974). Carolina Parakeets were irregular nonbreeding summer wanderers southwest to Brown County in the Rolling Plains (Bent 1940). During the fall and winter, these native parakeets were reported from across the eastern third of the state, west to Colorado and Nueces Counties. The last report of the species in the state was a bird killed in Bowie County around 1897 (Oberholser 1974).

GREEN PARAKEET *Aratinga holochlora* (Sclater)

Uncommon to locally common resident of the Lower Rio Grande Valley. Green Parakeets are found primarily in urban areas and were first reported in the state in 1960 (Oberholser 1974). Populations are now well established and appear to be increasing. There has been considerable debate about the origin of these birds, and it is plausible that some arrived as a result of displacement due to extensive habitat loss in adjacent northeastern Mexico. Escapees cannot be ruled out, although the species has been regarded as an undesirable caged bird (Oberholser 1974). Green Parakeet has been reported north to Corpus Christi, Nueces County, and Kingsville, Kleberg County.

RED-CROWNED PARROT
Amazona viridigenalis (Cassin)

Red-crowned Parrots have been in the Lower Rio Grande Valley since the early 1970s (Neck 1986; J. Arvin pers. comm.). In recent years, flocks containing from 70 to 200 or more birds have been regularly seen in Brownsville, Harlingen, McAllen, and elsewhere in the Lower Rio Grande Valley. Breeding occurs, and the population appears to be stable or increasing. Like the Green Parakeet, this species is fairly rare to locally uncommon and declining in adjacent Mexico, where habitat loss has been extensive. The increasing presence of this parrot in Texas has sparked debate about likely origin, and, as with the Green Parakeet, it is thought possible that some arrived as a result of displacement due to habitat loss. Local escapees are likely responsible for some of the Red-crowneds in the Valley as well. The origin of any individual or flock is indeterminable. Scattered reports exist from Austin, Corpus Christi, and San Marcos, Hays County, which seem less likely to be of wild origin.

ORDER CUCULIFORMES

Family Cuculidae: Cuckoos and Allies

BLACK-BILLED CUCKOO
Coccyzus erythropthalmus (Wilson)

Rare spring and rare to very rare fall migrant in the eastern half of the state. Black-billed Cuckoos are most frequently encountered in woodlots and other stop-over habitats along the Coastal Prairies, where they can be locally uncommon. These birds occur regularly throughout the eastern half of the South Texas Brush Country and east of the Balcones Escarpment. Black-billed Cuckoos are very rare to casual migrants west to the central Trans-Pecos. Migration typically occurs from mid-April to late May and from mid-July to early November. The only nesting reports for the state are from north-central Texas in the 1880s and from Live Oak County in 1977 (Fischer 1979). Pulich (1988) and others have questioned these reported nestings.

YELLOW-BILLED CUCKOO
Coccyzus americanus (Linnaeus)

Common migrant and summer resident throughout most of the state. Yellow-billed Cuckoos are uncommon and local in the western Trans-Pecos and are accidental winter visitors along the coast. Migration is typically from early April to late May (mid-May to mid-June in the Trans-Pecos) and from mid-August to mid-October, with a few individuals lingering into late November.

Review Species

MANGROVE CUCKOO *Coccyzus minor* (Gmelin)

Casual. There are nine documented records of this species in the state. All have been of the buff-throated subspecies, *C. m. continentalis,* found in Mexico. All are from near the coast, except for one from the Lower Rio Grande Valley at Santa Ana National Wildlife Refuge, Hidalgo County. Coastal records come from Brazoria, Cameron, Galveston, Harris, Matagorda, and Nueces Counties. Most records are from between April and August, but two are from December. Mangrove Cuckoo was first documented in the state in Galveston, Galveston County, on 30 December 1964.

Review Species

DARK-BILLED CUCKOO
Coccyzus melacoryphus Vieillot

Accidental. There is a single documented record of this South American species for Texas. An adult Dark-billed Cuckoo was delivered to a wildlife rehabilitator in Hidalgo County on 10 February 1986. It is not known exactly where the bird was found, but it is thought to have come from Hidalgo County. The bird later died and was placed into the avian collection at Louisiana State University. Dark-billed Cuckoos are long-distance austral migrants that have also been documented as vagrants north to Clipperton Island (off the west coast of Mexico), Grenada, and Panama.

10 FEB. 1986, HIDALGO CO. (TBRC 1995-115; TPRF 1600)

GREATER ROADRUNNER
Geococcyx californianus (Lesson)

Common to locally uncommon resident throughout the state, except the Pineywoods and northeastern sector, where they are rare to locally uncommon. Greater Roadrunners breed from early March to early October. They are also highly territorial, with males defending the same area for years.

GROOVE-BILLED ANI *Crotophaga sulcirostris* Swainson

Common summer resident in the Lower Rio Grande Valley west to Webb County. Groove-billed Anis are locally uncommon to rare north through the South Texas Brush Country to Bexar, Gonzales, and Val Verde Counties. They are rare visitors along the Rio Grande west to Brewster County during the spring and summer. This species has occurred in virtually all areas of the state as a summer vagrant. There are isolated nesting records from as far north as Tom Green and Lubbock Counties (Maxwell 1980). Groove-billed Anis are uncommon fall and winter visitors in the eastern Lower Rio Grande Valley and along the coast, especially on barrier islands, north to Jefferson County. Breeding occurs from May to mid-September (Oberholser 1974). Though the species can be found throughout the year, there is a significant withdrawal from the state during the winter, at which time the species becomes rare and local away from the coast.

ORDER STRIGIFORMES

Family Tytonidae: Barn Owls

BARN OWL *Tyto alba* (Scopoli)

Rare to locally common resident throughout most of the state. Barn Owls are generally rare and local in the forested parts of the Pineywoods and above 5,000 feet in the mountains of the Trans-Pecos. Barn Owls are found in open habitats and tend to avoid closed-canopy forests. They are cavity nesters and, as their name implies, have adapted to take advantage of nonnatural structures.

Family Strigidae: Typical Owls

FLAMMULATED OWL *Otus flammeolus* (Kaup)

Uncommon to rare summer resident in the Chisos, Davis, and Guadalupe Mountains. Flammulated Owls are migratory, although the winter range of the species is poorly known. Migrants have been found at various locations throughout the Trans-Pecos, and the migration route encompasses the western third of the state east to Crosby, Lubbock, and Midland Counties. The spring migration period extends from late March to early May, while that of the fall is from late September through mid-November. Migrating Flammulated Owls have been found as far east as the upper and central coasts, with records from Galveston, Jefferson, and Nueces Counties. An unexpected record involved one photographed over 50 miles from shore on a petroleum platform off Calhoun County on 10 October 1999 (TPRF 1812). Since then two others have been found on platforms in the Gulf.

WESTERN SCREECH-OWL
Megascops kennicottii (Elliot)

Common to uncommon resident in the Trans-Pecos and western Edwards Plateau. They are inexplicably rare and local in El Paso and Hudspeth Counties but are uncommon residents east to western Kerr County on the Edwards Plateau and Tom Green County in the Concho Valley. There is only one confirmed record for the Texas Panhandle

(Seyffert 2001), even though this owl is resident in the western Oklahoma Panhandle. Western Screech-Owl has not been reported from the South Plains (Kostecke, Floyd, and Stogner 2001). Western Screech-Owls are found in a variety of habitats in the Trans-Pecos and primarily occupy mesquite and live oak savannahs, as well as other upland habitats, on the Edwards Plateau.

EASTERN SCREECH-OWL *Megascops asio* (Linnaeus)

Common resident throughout the eastern three-quarters of the state. Eastern Screech-Owls have a less continuous distribution on the High Plains, occupying riparian corridors and urban areas with numerous trees. This owl is resident, at least locally, as far west as the Pecos River drainage. They possibly range farther west along the Rio Grande, but the extent of this range is currently open to speculation. Eastern Screech-Owl was an uncommon resident as far west as southern Brewster County until at least the early 1970s. Since that time, scattered records have come from Brewster, El Paso, Hudspeth, and Jeff Davis Counties but with no indication of resident populations.

GREAT HORNED OWL *Bubo virginianus* (Gmelin)

Common resident throughout the state except in the Pineywoods where they are uncommon. The Great Horned Owl is possibly most common in the arid habitats of the Trans-Pecos where it is one of the dominant avian predators. This species is one of the more adaptable owls in the United States when it comes to habitat use. In Texas, they are found in open woodlands, desert scrublands, and riparian corridors. The only habitat not routinely used is dense closed-canopy forest.

Review Species

SNOWY OWL *Bubo scandiacus* (Linnaeus)

Accidental. Texas has four records of this arctic species, three of which are specimens. The most recent was an apparently healthy bird discovered during the spring of 2002. There have been several records from Oklahoma, including a number from the winter of 1974–75. A Snowy Owl was found dead near Waco, McLennan County, on 31 December 1974, but the location of the specimen is unknown. Snowy Owls are known to move southward in

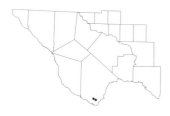

large numbers when food resources become scarce in their normal wintering areas, and Texas observers should be aware of the possibility of this species appearing again.

1900 (NO EXACT DATE), WACO, MCLENNAN CO.
   (IN PRIVATE COLLECTION)
1934 (NO EXACT DATE), DALLAS CO. (DALLAS MNH)
15–16 FEB. 1955, LAKE WICHITA, ARCHER CO. (TCWC 11916)
22 MAR.–2 APR. 2002, TYE, TAYLOR CO.
   (TBRC 2002-34; TPRF 1990))

Review Species

NORTHERN PYGMY-OWL *Glaucidium gnoma* Wagler

Accidental. There are two documented records for the state, both from the Chisos Mountains in Big Bend National Park, Brewster County. There are more than a dozen undocumented reports from the mountains of the Trans-Pecos, most of them of heard-only birds. Some of these reports may be valid, although confusion with Northern Saw-whet Owl may account for others. A recent study has suggested that the Northern Pygmy-Owl should be split into two species, *G. californicum* of the western United States and *G. gnoma* of the interior of Mexico southward (Heidrich, Koenig, and Wink 1995). The individuals found in Texas are thought to belong to *G. gnoma*. There are 11 reports of Northern Pygmy-Owls from prior to the development of the Review List in 1987 for which there is no documentation on file at Texas A&M University.

12 AUG. 1982, BOOT SPRING, BIG BEND NP, BREWSTER CO.
   (TPRF 278)
25 APR. 1993, CHISOS MOUNTAINS, BIG BEND NP, BREWSTER CO.
   (TBRC 1993-73)

FERRUGINOUS PYGMY-OWL

Glaucidium brasilianum (Gmelin)

Uncommon and local resident on the Coastal Sand Plain. This species is also a rare resident in Starr County and very rare and local elsewhere in the Lower Rio Grande Valley. There are recent documented records from Laguna Vista, Cameron County, and Bentsen–Rio Grande Valley State Park, Hidalgo County. The largest population of Ferruginous Pygmy-Owls in Texas is found in the open live oak woodlands of Kenedy County and eastern Brooks County. Smaller populations exist in mesquite savannas elsewhere in Brooks County, and habitat is available for dispersal between these populations and those found in the Valley (G. Proudfoot, pers. comm.). A sight record from Rio Grande Village, Brewster County, in Big Bend National Park on 9 April 1999 (TBRC 1999-87) is the only one for the Trans-Pecos.

ELF OWL *Micrathene whitneyi* (Cooper)

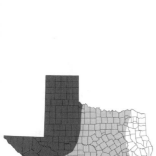

Uncommon to locally common summer resident from the southern Trans-Pecos eastward onto the western Edwards Plateau, and in the Lower Rio Grande Valley. This species was found on the southwestern Edwards Plateau in the late 1980s. In 2002, nesting was documented in Irion County, expanding the known range farther north. Elf Owls are also a rare summer resident in the Guadalupe Mountains and, possibly, in the Sierra Diablo, Culberson/Hudspeth Counties. This owl is a rare winter resident in the Lower Rio Grande Valley. There is an apparent break in its distribution along the Rio Grande from southern Kinney County through Webb County. The lack of records may be the result of insufficient survey efforts.

BURROWING OWL *Athene cunicularia* (Molina)

Uncommon to common summer resident and uncommon to rare winter resident in the western half of the state, east to Wilbarger County. Burrowing Owl is a rare to very rare migrant and winter visitor farther east and south to the prairies along the coast. This species was formerly much more common and widespread in Texas, including areas away from traditional breeding sites. Conversion of prairie habitats to agriculture and the decline in populations of Black-tailed Prairie Dogs *(Cynomys ludovicianus)* have caused a substantial decline in the number of resident owls. Simmons (1925) reported that Burrowing Owl was an uncommon and local breeding species as far southeast as Travis County.

Review Species

MOTTLED OWL *Ciccaba virgata* (Cassin)

Accidental. There is one record for Texas, the only one for the United States. This lone record consists of a road-killed individual (Lasley, Sexton, and Hillsman 1988). Mottled Owls are found in northern Nuevo Leon, Mexico, within 75 miles of the Rio Grande.

23 SEPT. 1983, BENTSEN–RIO GRANDE VALLEY SP, HIDALGO CO. (TPRF 377)

SPOTTED OWL *Strix occidentalis* (Xántus de Vesey)

Rare and local resident in wooded canyons in the Guadalupe and Davis Mountains of the Trans-Pecos. This species has been known from the Guadalupe Mountains since the early 1900s, but only a small number of pairs have been found. They have been reported from only three locations in the Davis Mountains (Bryan and Karges 2001) but may be more widespread than these few records indicate. Spotted Owls, presumably wandering from populations in southern New Mexico, have also been documented during the fall and winter in El Paso County.

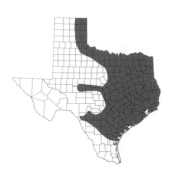

BARRED OWL *Strix varia* Barton

Uncommon to common resident in the eastern two-thirds of the state. Barred Owls are found as far west as the eastern Panhandle and eastern Val Verde County and as far south as Nueces County. Barred Owls occupy forests throughout the eastern third of the state but are restricted to riparian corridors on the Edwards Plateau, the eastern Panhandle, and the Coastal Prairies. Two Barred Owls were collected in Cameron County in May 1900. These specimens represent the only documented records from south of the Nueces River. Thornton (1951) heard a Barred Owl in the Pecos River drainage in July 1949, but whether this indicated residency or merely a wandering individual is unknown.

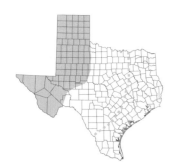

LONG-EARED OWL *Asio otus* (Linnaeus)

Uncommon migrant and winter resident in the Panhandle, rare to locally uncommon migrant and winter resident on the South Plains and westward through the Trans-Pecos. This species is rare and unpredictable during winter in the remainder of the state, with the exception of the Pineywoods where it is typically absent. A few Long-eared Owls have been found as far south as the Lower Rio Grande Valley. Long-eared Owls are well known for communal winter roosts, which can sometimes contain as many as 40 individuals. They formerly nested sporadically in Texas, but such records have been scarce in recent years. The last reported nesting occurred at Buffalo Lake National Wildlife Refuge, Randall County, in 1996.

Review Species

STYGIAN OWL *Asio stygius* (Wagler)

Accidental. Two records of this tropical owl exist for Texas and the United States. The first was of one photographed at Bentsen–Rio Grande Valley State Park, Hidalgo County, in 1994 (Cooksey 1998). Another Stygian Owl was discovered at the same location in 1996 (Wright and Wright 1997). The first record did not come to light until after the discovery of the second bird. This species is not known to occur within 500 miles of Texas, but Stygian Owl is a widespread and very poorly understood species and may occur much closer to Texas than is currently known.

9 DEC. 1994, BENTSEN–RIO GRANDE VALLEY SP, HIDALGO CO.
    (TBRC 1998-46; TPRF 1705)
26 DEC. 1996, BENTSEN–RIO GRANDE VALLEY SP, HIDALGO CO.
    (TBRC 1997-4; TPRF 1527)

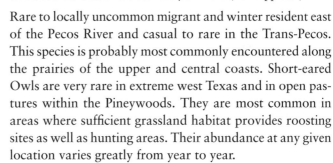

SHORT-EARED OWL *Asio flammeus* (Pontoppidan)

Rare to locally uncommon migrant and winter resident east of the Pecos River and casual to rare in the Trans-Pecos. This species is probably most commonly encountered along the prairies of the upper and central coasts. Short-eared Owls are very rare in extreme west Texas and in open pastures within the Pineywoods. They are most common in areas where sufficient grassland habitat provides roosting sites as well as hunting areas. Their abundance at any given location varies greatly from year to year.

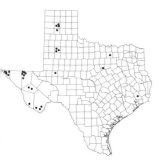

Review Species

NORTHERN SAW-WHET OWL

Aegolius acadicus (Gmelin)

Very rare summer resident in the Guadalupe Mountains (Newman 1974) and, possibly, in the Davis Mountains (Bryan and Karges 2001) of the Trans-Pecos. A single summer record exists from the Chisos Mountains in 1997 (TBRC 1997-86). Northern Saw-whet Owl is a casual migrant and winter visitor elsewhere in the state. Except for single birds in Denton, Liberty, and Somervell Counties, all other documented records are from the Trans-Pecos and High Plains. There are 27 documented records for the state.

ORDER CAPRIMULGIFORMES

Family Caprimulgidae: Nighthawks and Nightjars

LESSER NIGHTHAWK
Chordeiles acutipennis (Hermann)

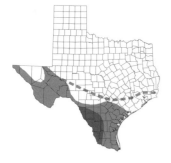

Common to uncommon migrant and summer resident from El Paso County across much of the Trans-Pecos to the South Texas Brush Country. Lesser Nighthawk is a rare migrant and summer visitor to the southern Edwards Plateau and is found north on the Coastal Prairies to Calhoun County. This species is a very rare to rare migrant to the upper coast, and vagrants have been found as far north as Bailey and Lubbock Counties. Migration falls between early April and mid-May and from early August to late October. Lesser Nighthawks are a locally uncommon winter resident in the western half of the South Texas Brush Country.

COMMON NIGHTHAWK *Chordeiles minor* (Forster)

Uncommon to common migrant and summer resident throughout the state, except in the Pineywoods where it is a common migrant and rare summer resident. This species occasionally overwinters in the southern half of the state, primarily in or near urban areas where it is rare to very rare. Typical migration occurs between early April and late May and again from early August to late October.

COMMON PAURAQUE *Nyctidromus albicollis* (Gmelin)

Common resident in the South Texas Brush Country north to southern Maverick County in the west and Atascosa and Wilson Counties in the east. Common Pauraques are rare north along the coast to Calhoun County and along the Rio Grande to northern Maverick County, although the status there is unclear. Pauraques are vagrants north to Bastrop and Grimes Counties.

COMMON POORWILL
Phalaenoptilus nuttallii (Audubon)

Common to uncommon summer resident in the western two-thirds of the state. Common Poorwills are uncommon migrants and uncommon to rare summer residents on the

38. Whooping Cranes *(Grus americana)* were once widespread along the Texas coast. Today, the entire natural population of this Endangered species spends each winter in a small area of the central coast. While they feed on a variety of plants and animals on their wintering grounds, small crabs and wolfberry *(Lycium* sp.) seem to be especially relished. *Photograph by Greg W. Lasley.*

39. This Collared Plover *(Charadrius collaris)* was a very unexpected visitor to the National Fish Hatchery in Uvalde during early May 1992. This small plover had been expected to occur in Texas eventually, but most observers would have predicted the first U.S. record to come from the coast. *Photograph by Willie Sekula.*

40. Although Wilson's Plover *(Charadrius wilsonia)* is often considered to be a strictly coastal breeder in Texas, recent finds indicate they can also be found nesting well inland. This species has recently been documented breeding on saline ponds as far inland as eastern Brooks County in South Texas. *Photograph by Brush Freeman.*

41. Mountain Plover *(Charadrius montanus)* populations have seriously declined across their range and are candidates for the Endangered species list. Unlike other *Charadrius* species in North America, they are a grassland species and are virtually never seen in wetlands.   *Photograph by Greg W. Lasley.*

42. Ornithological accounts from the late 1800s suggest that Northern Jacana *(Jacana spinosa)* was a rare resident in the Lower Rio Grande Valley. A small population was also present at Maner Lake, Brazoria County, during the 1970s. Since then this species has been a very rare visitor to the state. This immature bird was near Seadrift, Calhoun County, from 10 December 1992 to 22 April 1993. *Photograph by Greg W. Lasley.*

43. Wandering Tattler *(Heteroscelus incanus)* has occurred in Texas on one occasion. This species typically winters on rocky shorelines along the Pacific Coast and was therefore an unexpected vagrant to Texas. The Texas record is from Galveston in the spring of 1992. *Photograph by Martin Reid.*

44. This Eskimo Curlew *(Numenius borealis)* was one of two present on Galveston Island in March 1962. These may be the only Eskimo Curlews ever photographed in the wild and are the last thoroughly documented in Texas or anywhere else. *Photograph by Don Bleitz/TPRF.*

45. The Hudsonian Godwit *(Limosa haemastica)* has an elliptical migration route that brings them through Texas on the journey northward and along the Atlantic seaboard in the fall. As a result, late summer and fall records of this species in Texas are very rare.
Photograph by Brush Freeman.

46. Although wintering Purple Sandpipers *(Calidris maritima)* are primarily found along rocky shorelines along the Atlantic Coast, they are casual visitors along the Gulf Coast. There are even scattered inland records including two in Texas. This individual was photographed at Freeport, Brazoria County, on 17 December 1990.
Photograph by Greg W. Lasley.

47. Buff-breasted Sandpipers *(Tryngites subruficollis)* frequent short-grass prairies and fields during migration, although they are also seen along the edges of water impoundments. This attractive shorebird primarily migrates through the Great Plains in the center of the continent.
Photograph by Mark W. Lockwood.

48. The primary migration paths of the Red Phalarope *(Phalaropus fulicaria)* take them just offshore along the east and west coasts of North America to wintering grounds off South America. A few migrants are found in the interior, most often in fall. This immature bird was at Muleshoe National Wildlife Refuge, Bailey County, on 18 September 1982.   *Photograph by Cliff Stogner.*

49. The Black-tailed Gull *(Larus crassirostris)* is an Asian species that has occurred in North America with increasing frequency since the early 1990s. This individual was at Brownsville, Cameron County, intermittently from mid-February through mid-March 1999. *Photograph by Jimmy McHaney.*

50. Lesser Black-backed Gull *(Larus fuscus)* was once considered a very rare visitor to Texas, but that is no longer the case. This species is now found annually in the state, with most sightings coming from along the coast. *Photograph by Mark W. Lockwood.*

51. Although some observers predicted that Slaty-backed Gull *(Larus schistisagus)* would eventually be found in Texas, few would have guessed it would appear at the southern tip. This subadult was photographed at Brownsville, Cameron County, on 15 February 1992.   *Photograph by Martin Reid.*

52. Kelp Gulls *(Larus dominicanus)* are found primarily in the southern hemisphere. Since the early 1990s, this species has occurred several times along the Gulf of Mexico, as well as in the Caribbean and elsewhere in North America. This individual was found on North Padre Island, Kleberg County, on 6 May 1996 and represents the third accepted state record. *Photograph by Willie Sekula.*

53. Among the discoveries in the state in the 1990s was the regular occurrence of Bridled Terns *(Sterna anaethetus)*. They are often found well offshore with Sooty Terns, foraging along floating lines of sargassum or feeding with other pelagic species over schools of tuna and other fish near the surface. This individual, one of the first to be documented in Texas, was found near Port Aransas, Nueces County, on 17 September 1988. *Photograph by Tony Amos.*

54. The Brown Noddy *(Anous stolidus)* is a bird of tropical waters and is extremely rare in Texas. Its flight is strong and swift, resembling that of a Common Nighthawk, and its call is somewhat similar to that of a crow. This species is long lived, and recaptured birds from banding efforts have been found to be 21 to 25 years old. This individual was photographed on an oil platform off Kenedy County on 27 April 2000. *Photograph by Alan Wormington.*

55. Although widespread throughout the Neotropics and common in northeastern Mexico, the Red-billed Pigeon *(Patagioenas flavirostris)* barely enters the United States along the Rio Grande in South Texas. Their presence in Texas is continually under threat due to changes in their preferred riparian habitats. *Photograph by Steve Bentsen.*

56. Ruddy Ground-Doves *(Columbina talpacoti)* have appeared in Texas in the Lower Rio Grande Valley and in the Trans-Pecos. This male was photographed at Lajitas, Brewster County, on 9 March 1990 and appears to belong to the drab western subspecies, *C. t. eluta.*
Photograph by Mark W. Lockwood.

57. White-tipped Doves *(Leptotila verreauxi)* are more often heard than seen. They are primarily ground-dwelling birds and, despite their size, can be rather difficult to see given their wary nature and affinity for dense brush.
Photograph by Steve Bentsen.

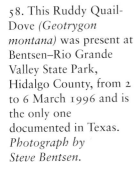

58. This Ruddy Quail-Dove *(Geotrygon montana)* was present at Bentsen–Rio Grande Valley State Park, Hidalgo County, from 2 to 6 March 1996 and is the only one documented in Texas.
Photograph by Steve Bentsen.

59. The origin of Texas populations of Green Parakeet *(Aratinga holochlora)* and 60. *(right)* Red-crowned Parrot *(Amazona viridigenalis)* has been much debated. It is certainly possible, if not probable, that some of these birds arrived naturally from populations in northeastern Mexico.
Photographs by Steve Bentsen (parakeet) and Mark W. Lockwood (parrot).

61. Groove-billed Anis *(Crotophaga sulcirostris)* are common in the South Texas Brush Country during the hot summer months. They are known for a communal nesting behavior in which 2 to 6 females often lay eggs in a single nest with the adults sharing nest duties.   *Photograph by Steve Bentsen.*

62. Snowy Owl *(Bubo scandiacus)* has been documented only four times in Texas. This individual was the most recent and the first to be documented in 47 years. It was photographed near Abilene, Taylor County, on 23 March 2002. *Photograph by Jimmy McHaney.*

63. Ferruginous Pygmy-Owl *(Glaucidium brasilianum)* is a denizen of the oak mottes of the Coastal Sand Plain. They were formerly more widespread through the Lower Rio Grande Valley, but conversion of native woodlands to agriculture has virtually extirpated this tiny owl.   *Photograph by Mark W. Lockwood.*

64. The Elf Owl *(Micrathene whitneyi)*, as its name implies, is the smallest owl in the United States. It was not discovered until the late 1980s that this species occurred on the western Edwards Plateau. This individual was photographed at Kickapoo Cavern State Park, Kinney County, on 12 June 2002.
Photograph by Mark W. Lockwood.

65. One of the most unexpected birds to be documented in Texas has to be Stygian Owl *(Asio stygius)*. For both of the Texas records, observers were lucky enough to find the birds on their day roosts. This individual was the second found in Texas and was photographed at Bentsen–Rio Grande Valley State Park, Hidalgo County, on 26 December 1996. *Photograph by Jim Culbertson.*

66. The South Texas Brush Country is the northern apex of the range of the Common Pauraque *(Nyctidromus albicollis)*. This species often pursues insects by swiftly chasing them on foot with its relatively (for a caprimulgid) long legs. *Photograph by Steve Bentsen.*

67. Green Violet-ear *(Colibri thalassinus)* is a widespread and common species throughout Mexico and southward to Bolivia. In Texas, this species has been documented annually since 1994, and there are now more than 41 documented records for the state. This one was at Sandy Creek, Travis County, from 16 June through 8 July 1995.   *Photograph by Greg W. Lasley.*

68. The first seven documented records of Green-breasted Mango *(Anthracothorax prevostii)* from Texas were all birds in immature plumage. Although the first individual was found in 1988, it was not until February 2001 that an adult was documented. This immature bird was at Corpus Christi, Nueces County, from 6 to 27 January 1992 and was the second to be documented in the state. *Photograph by Greg W. Lasley.*

69. Broad-billed Hummingbird *(Cynanthus latirostris)* was once considered a very rare to casual visitor to Texas. Since 1992, there have been a remarkable number of occurrences, particularly in the Trans-Pecos during the spring and summer. *Photograph by Kelly B. Bryan.*

70. White-eared Hummingbird *(Hylocharis leucotis)* is an accidental visitor to Texas, with most of the records from the mountains of the Trans-Pecos, the Davis Mountains in particular. This immature male provided the ninth record for the state when it visited the Davis Mountains from 31 July to 23 August 1997.   *Photograph by Greg W. Lasley.*

71. Hundreds of Buff-bellied Hummingbirds *(Amazilia yucatanensis)* can frequently be found in the oak woodlands of the Coastal Sand Plain during the early fall. They appear to feed primarily on Turk's Cap *(Malvaviscus drummondii)* and small insects as they make their way southward for the winter. *Photograph by Greg W. Lasley.*

72. The Lucifer Hummingbird *(Calothorax lucifer)* has long been considered a specialty of Big Bend National Park, but in recent years, this species has been found to be a regular visitor to the Davis Mountains and adjacent areas to the north. It has also been found on the Edwards Plateau on a number of occasions, including this male that was photographed in Gillespie County between 14 and 23 May 2000. *Photograph by Heidi Schulz.*

High Plains and northern Rolling Plains. The eastern edge of this species' range is poorly defined, but birds are present in low numbers east to Bastrop, Bosque, Goliad, and Starr Counties. This nightjar has been reported during migration east to Dallas, Galveston, and Navarro Counties. Common Poorwills are rare to locally uncommon winter residents in the southern third of the summer range and have been recorded in late fall north to the Panhandle and west to El Paso County. Determining the winter status is complicated by the fact that they are only active on warm nights.

CHUCK-WILL'S-WIDOW
Caprimulgus carolinensis Gmelin

Uncommon migrant and summer resident in the eastern two-thirds of the state, west to the eastern Rolling Plains and Edwards Plateau. They are found west to Kinney and Edwards Counties of the Edwards Plateau. Summer residents are found south to DeWitt and Karnes Counties and rarely south to Refugio County. Migrants have been found as far west as Val Verde County and on the High Plains. In the northeastern Panhandle, there is evidence of possible nesting, particularly in the Canadian River drainage. Migration occurs between early April and early May and from mid-August to early October.

WHIP-POOR-WILL *Caprimulgus vociferus* Wilson

Common summer resident at upper elevations in the mountains of the Trans-Pecos. Whip-poor-wills are rare to uncommon migrants in the eastern half of the state west to the central Edwards Plateau, and casual migrants farther west to the High Plains and western Edwards Plateau. They are very rare winter visitors along the coast with one documented record inland from Trinity County. Two distinctive subspecies are found in the United States, and both occur in Texas. The eastern subspecies, *C. v. vociferus*, is found during migration in the eastern two-thirds of the state. The western subspecies, *C. v. arizonae*, is a summer resident in the Trans-Pecos. The two subspecies are easily distinguished by their vocalizations and may represent separate species. Migration periods range from late March to mid-May and from late August to late October for both subspecies. They are quite vocal at dusk and dawn during spring migration.

ORDER APODIFORMES

Family Apodidae: Swifts

Review Species

WHITE-COLLARED SWIFT
Streptoprocne zonaris (Shaw)

Accidental. Texas has four documented records of this tropical swift. The second of these provided the second specimen for the United States (Lasley 1984) as well. Since then, two others have been supported with photographs, the first ever taken of this species in the United States (Eubanks and Morgan 1989). All Texas records are from along or near the coast. Considering the wide variety of habitats this species uses in northeastern Mexico, observers should be aware of the potential for this large swift to occur in other areas of the state.

4 DEC. 1974, ROCKPORT, ARANSAS CO. (TBRC 1988-38)
8 MAR. 1983, NORTH PADRE ISLAND, KLEBERG CO.
  (TCWC 11177)
20 DEC. 1987, FREEPORT, BRAZORIA CO.
  (TBRC 1988-144; TPRF 555)
18 MAY 1997, BROWNSVILLE, CAMERON CO.
  (TBRC 1997-101; TPRF 1666)

CHIMNEY SWIFT *Chaetura pelagica* (Linnaeus)

Common migrant and summer resident east of the Trans-Pecos. In the Trans-Pecos, Chimney Swifts are rare spring migrants and early summer visitors to Pecos, Reeves County, and are casual migrants and sporadic summer residents in Alpine, Brewster County, and Fort Davis, Jeff Davis County (Peterson and Zimmer 1998). Chimney Swifts are rare, but increasing, during the summer months in the Lower Rio Grande Valley. Spring migrants appear in Texas as early as early March, although they are not common until late March or early April for most of the state. Summer residents and fall migrants are present until mid-October with a few lingering into early November. Chimney Swifts winter in South America, and mid-winter *Chaetura* swifts should be carefully documented since Vaux's Swift *(C. vauxi)* has been recorded in Louisiana during that season, although not in Texas.

WHITE-THROATED SWIFT
Aeronautes saxatalis (Woodhouse)

Common summer resident and locally uncommon winter resident in the Trans-Pecos, east to central Val Verde County (Maxwell 1980). Small numbers of this species winter irregularly at Palo Duro Canyon State Park, Randall County, and at Caprock Canyons State Park, Briscoe County, in the Panhandle (Seyffert 1984, 2001). White-throated Swifts are very rare to casual migrants in the western Panhandle and have wandered eastward during the fall to the Edwards Plateau and the central coast, even once in winter to Brazos County.

Family Trochilidae: Hummingbirds

Review Species

GREEN VIOLET-EAR *Colibri thalassinus* (Swainson)

Very rare spring and summer visitor to the eastern two-thirds of the state. Most of the Green Violet-ear records for Texas are from the eastern half of the Edwards Plateau, the Lower Rio Grande Valley, and along the coast. There are two records from the Pineywoods and single records from north-central Texas and the Trans-Pecos. Green Violet-ears have occurred between 14 April and 3 October, but the majority are seen from mid-May through July. There are 41 documented records of this species for Texas.

Review Species

GREEN-BREASTED MANGO
Anthracothorax prevostii (Lesson)

Casual visitor to the Lower Rio Grande Valley and the central coast. The first record for the state occurred at Brownsville, Cameron County, from 14 to 23 September 1988 (TBRC 1988-272; TPRF 773). Since then there have been 11 others, and most of these records are of immature birds. Separating immature plumaged Green-breasted from the primarily South American Black-throated Mango *(A. nigricollis)* is extremely difficult. Careful in-hand examination of one at Corpus Christi, Nueces County, which was present from 6 to 27 January 1992, confirmed that it was a Green-breasted Mango. The TBRC considers all records of *Anthracothorax* species to be of Green-breasted Mango until such time as another species is documented in or near Texas.

BROAD-BILLED HUMMINGBIRD
Cynanthus latirostris Swainson

Rare to very rare visitor, primarily during the spring and fall, in the Trans-Pecos. Broad-billed Hummingbirds are casual to very rare winter visitors to El Paso County. Elsewhere in the state, this species is a casual visitor with records from all seasons. There are 54 documented records of this species for Texas, with almost half from the Trans-Pecos. Broad-billed Hummingbird is reported to have been a very rare summer resident in Brewster County during the 1930s. This is based on a report by Quillin (1935) of a nest with two eggs found on 17 May 1934. Van Tyne and Sutton (1937) knew of no other reports from the county. This species was removed from the Review List in 2003.

Review Species

WHITE-EARED HUMMINGBIRD
Hylocharis leucotis (Vieillot)

Casual visitor to the Trans-Pecos, accidental on the Edwards Plateau and in the Lower Rio Grande Valley. There are twelve documented records from the Trans-Pecos, most of them from the Davis Mountains. Other Trans-Pecos records exist from the Chisos and Guadalupe Mountains and from El Paso County. Yearly from 1993 through 1995, at least one White-eared Hummingbird was present during the summer at the Davis Mountains Resort, Jeff Davis County. Since then, there have been only three others from that location. The two sightings documented outside the Trans-Pecos likely represent postbreeding dispersal. One was present in Starr County from 14 to 16 July 1990 (TBRC 1991-76; TPRF 973) and another was in Fredericksburg, Gillespie County, from 31 July to 4 August 2000 (TBRC 2000-73; TPRF 1921).

Review Species

BERYLLINE HUMMINGBIRD
Amazilia beryllina (Deppe)

Accidental. The four documented records for the state are all from the Trans-Pecos. Interestingly, three of these come from the same location in the Davis Mountains. The first three records are all from late summer and probably involve postbreeding wanderers. The most recent record refers to a male that spent the summer in the Davis Mountains. It was first seen coming to feeders in late May, and presumably the same bird returned in June and July.

18 AUG. 1991, CHISOS MTNS., BREWSTER CO. (TBRC 1991-121)
17 AUG.–4 SEPT. 1997, DAVIS MTNS., JEFF DAVIS CO.
  (TBRC 1997-137; TPRF 1661)
3 AND 8 AUG. 1999, DAVIS MTNS., JEFF DAVIS CO.
  (TBRC 1999-80; TPRF 1922)
25 MAY, 4 JUNE, AND 12 JULY 2000, DAVIS MTNS., JEFF DAVIS CO.
  (TBRC 2000-53; TPRF 1923)

BUFF-BELLIED HUMMINGBIRD

Amazilia yucatanensis (Cabot)

Uncommon to locally common summer resident in the Lower Rio Grande Valley and along the coast north to Victoria County. This species appears to be expanding its range northward up the coast and inland into south-central Texas. In recent years, there have been numerous records, primarily during spring and summer, from as far east as the Louisiana border and inland to Bastrop and Washington Counties. Most Buff-bellied Hummingbirds retreat southward during the winter and are rare to uncommon and very local at feeders and ornamental plantings in the Lower Rio Grande Valley and along the coast as far north as Calhoun County. There are scattered winter records farther north along the coast and inland to Austin and Travis Counties.

Review Species

VIOLET-CROWNED HUMMINGBIRD

Amazilia violiceps (Gould)

Accidental. Texas has seven documented records of this species. The first was at El Paso from 2 to 14 December 1987 (TBRC 1988-83; TPRF 594). Violet-crowned Hummingbirds have been found at widely scattered locations, including such unexpected places as Lake Jackson, Brazoria County, on the Upper Texas Coast and Weslaco, Hidalgo County, in the Lower Rio Grande Valley. The longest-staying individual was recorded in El Paso from 6 November 2001 to 16 February 2002 (TBRC 2001-135; TPRF 1996). Most of the other records are of individuals present for only one or two days. Records occur between October and June.

BLUE-THROATED HUMMINGBIRD

Lampornis clemenciae (Lesson)

Uncommon to rare summer resident in the Chisos Mountains of Big Bend National Park. This species is a rare, and

possibly irregular, summer visitor to the Davis and Guadalupe Mountains. There is a breeding record from the Guadalupe Mountains but none from the Davis Mountains. Blue-throated Hummingbirds usually arrive on the breeding grounds in mid-April and are present through September. This hummingbird is a casual spring and fall migrant elsewhere in the Trans-Pecos. Blue-throated Hummingbirds have been reported during late summer and early fall, a few of which include documentation, at scattered locations from the South Plains, Edwards Plateau, Bastrop, and Midland Counties, as well as the upper and central coasts and the Lower Rio Grande Valley. There is also a documented mid-winter record at Mission, Hidalgo County, from 2 to 13 February 1996 (TPRF 1349).

MAGNIFICENT HUMMINGBIRD
Eugenes fulgens (Swainson)

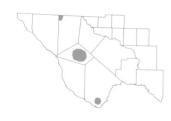

Uncommon and local summer resident in the Davis Mountains and rare in the Guadalupe Mountains. Magnificent Hummingbird is a rare summer visitor to the Chisos Mountains of the Trans-Pecos. Breeding birds arrive in early April and remain into early October. This species has been reported from low elevations in the Trans-Pecos west to El Paso. A single documented record comes from east of the Pecos River involving a female at Hebbronville, Jim Hogg County, from 15 to 21 July 2001 (TPRF 1961). Another report of Magnificent Hummingbird from Bexar County from 24 to 26 May 1959 has been widely cited (Oberholser 1974; TOS 1995). Examination of the material provided to the editor of Audubon Field Notes in 1959 appears to point towards Green Violet-ear. If true, this bird may have been the very first Green Violet-ear found in the United States.

LUCIFER HUMMINGBIRD
Calothorax lucifer (Swainson)

Locally common summer resident in the Chisos Mountains of the Trans-Pecos. They are rare and local during the summer in the Davis Mountains, and scattered records exist from the Chinati and Glass Mountains and the Sierra Vieja of that region, although breeding has not been confirmed from any of these locations. Breeding birds are present from early March and have lingered as late as early November

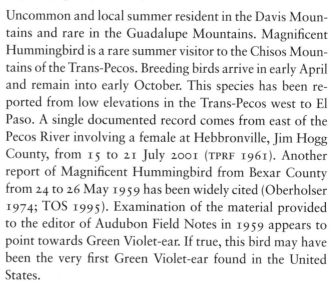

(Wauer 1996). Elsewhere in the Trans-Pecos, this species has been noted in the Guadalupe Mountains and in El Paso County. There are seven records from the Edwards Plateau, five of which involve postbreeding wanderers (Lockwood 2001b). One spring record from the South Texas Brush Country consists of a male in Kenedy County on 11 April 1999.

RUBY-THROATED HUMMINGBIRD
Archilochus colubris (Linnaeus)

Common summer resident in the eastern half of Texas, west to the edge of the Edwards Plateau, and south to Victoria County on the Coastal Prairies. Ruby-throateds are common to abundant migrants across the eastern third of the state and uncommon spring and common fall migrants farther west through the Edwards Plateau and South Texas Brush Country. They are rare to uncommon migrants on the High Plains and casual spring and rare fall migrants in the Trans-Pecos. Ruby-throateds are present in Texas from early March through mid-November. They are very rare winter visitors along the coast and casual inland primarily in the eastern half of the state.

BLACK-CHINNED HUMMINGBIRD
Archilochus alexandri (Bourcier and Mulsant)

Common to locally abundant summer resident in the western two-thirds of the state. Black-chinned Hummingbirds are most common as breeding birds in the Trans-Pecos and Edwards Plateau. The eastern edge of the breeding range extends from the western edge of the Blackland Prairies in Dallas and Bell Counties, south and east to Goliad County. Black-chinned Hummingbirds are uncommon to rare summer residents south of the Balcones Escarpment to the Lower Rio Grande Valley. In migration, this species is found much farther east, although it is rare in the Pineywoods. Black-chinned Hummingbirds are present in Texas from early March through early November. They are rare in winter along the coast, mainly at feeders, and rare to very rare inland as far north as the Panhandle.

ANNA'S HUMMINGBIRD *Calypte anna* (Lesson)

Uncommon to rare fall migrant and winter resident in the western and central Trans-Pecos. Migrants generally begin

to arrive in mid-September. This western hummingbird is a rare to very rare and irregular visitor, most often in late fall, to the remainder of the state. Anna's Hummingbird is a very rare winter resident outside of the Trans-Pecos mostly along the coast, but individuals have wintered as far north as Lubbock and Randall Counties on the High Plains. Texas has two breeding records: one from Jeff Davis County in 1976 (TPRF 101; Schmidt 1976) and another in El Paso County in 2000.

Review Species

COSTA'S HUMMINGBIRD *Calypte costae* (Bourcier)

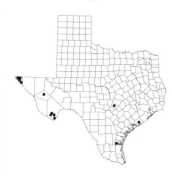

Casual visitor to the Trans-Pecos and accidental farther east. There are nine documented records from the Trans-Pecos scattered from late September to mid-March. A record of up to seven individuals present at a single location in El Paso County between 28 October 1994 and 12 December 1995 stands out as particularly noteworthy. All other records of Costa's Hummingbirds involve single individuals. Three records come from east of the Pecos River, with single birds at San Marcos, Hays County, from 6 February to 2 March 1974, Kingsville, Kleberg County, from 21 to 24 January 1988, and Matagorda, Matagorda County, from 17 to 21 December 2001. An adult male Costa's present near Fort Davis from 10 June to 1 September 2001 provides the only summer record.

CALLIOPE HUMMINGBIRD *Stellula calliope* (Gould)

Casual spring and uncommon fall migrant in the western half of the Trans-Pecos and rare fall migrant east through the High Plains and Concho Valley, becoming casual farther east. Most records of Calliope Hummingbird away from the Trans-Pecos are from the fall. Males pass through the state between mid-July and early August, followed by females and young of the year from mid-August to mid-September, irregularly to early November. There are scattered records of Calliope Hummingbirds lingering through the winter at feeders, most often in El Paso County and along the coast but some from other inland locations as well.

BROAD-TAILED HUMMINGBIRD
Selasphorus platycercus (Swainson)

Uncommon to locally common summer resident in the Chisos, Davis, and Guadalupe Mountains of the Trans-

Pecos. They are common to uncommon migrants through the remainder of the Trans-Pecos. Broad-tailed Hummingbirds are rare spring and uncommon fall migrants on the High Plains and Edwards Plateau, becoming less common farther east. Fall migrants are present primarily between mid-August and mid-October. Broad-tailed Hummingbirds are rare and local winter residents in El Paso County, and many instances of individuals lingering through the winter at feeders throughout the state have been documented.

RUFOUS HUMMINGBIRD *Selasphorus rufus* (Gmelin)

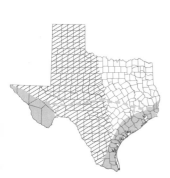

Rare spring and common fall migrant in the Trans-Pecos. Rufous Hummingbird is an uncommon to common fall migrant on the High Plains and western Rolling Plains, becoming locally uncommon to rare farther east. Fall migrants are present primarily between mid-July and early October. Rufous Hummingbirds follow an elliptical migratory path, passing through Texas in the fall and returning up the west coast of North America in spring. They are rare to locally uncommon winter residents on the coast and in the Lower Rio Grande Valley and are found locally inland throughout the southern half of the state, including the Trans-Pecos. They also linger through the winter at feeders farther north. Migrants found in Texas during the spring may be individuals that wintered along the Gulf Coast.

Review Species

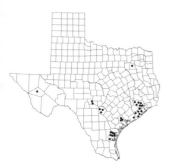

ALLEN'S HUMMINGBIRD *Selasphorus sasin* (Lesson)

Very rare fall migrant and winter visitor to the state. Fall migrants arrive as early as mid-July, and wintering individuals typically depart by early March. Recent banding efforts along the upper and central coasts suggest that this species is a rare, but regular, winter resident as is the case in southern Louisiana. The difficulty in separating Allen's and subadult Rufous Hummingbirds has obscured the status of this species within the state. Documenting the occurrence of Allen's Hummingbird requires examining the shape of retrix 2 and measuring retrix 5 (the outermost tail feather) to eliminate Rufous Hummingbird (Stiles 1972; McKenzie and Robbins 1999). The situation is further confused by the possibility that fully adult Rufous Hummingbirds may have green backs on very rare occasions. Recent studies suggest that adult male *Selasphorus* hummingbirds that appear to be Allen's with fully developed gorgets and adult tail feathers are indeed Allen's (B. Sargent, pers. comm.). Care must be taken to eliminate male Rufous Hummingbirds that have not acquired rufous feathers on their backs. There are 30 accepted records for this species in the state.

ORDER TROGONIFORMES

Family Trogonidae: Trogons

Review Species

ELEGANT TROGON *Trogon elegans* Gould

Accidental. Texas has five documented records of this species. All pertain to single birds from Brewster and Hidalgo Counties. Records from the west are from forested canyons while those in the Lower Rio Grande Valley have been from subtropical woodlands. To date, records are from all seasons and no pattern of occurrence is discernible. The subspecies present in Mexico and the southwestern United States was previously known as the Coppery-tailed Trogon *(T. e. ambiguous).*

14 SEPT. 1977, BENTSEN–RIO GRANDE VALLEY SP, HIDALGO CO.
 (TPRF 132)
25–31 JAN. 1990, DELTA LAKE, HIDALGO CO.
 (TBRC 1990-19; TPRF 857)
29 APR. 1993, BIG BEND NP, BREWSTER CO. (TBRC 1993-114)
28 NOV. 1995–8 JAN. 1996, BIG BEND NP, BREWSTER CO.
 (TBRC 1996-52)
16 JUNE 1996, BIG BEND NP, BREWSTER CO. (TBRC 1996-83)

ORDER CORACIIFORMES

Family Alcedinidae: Kingfishers

RINGED KINGFISHER *Ceryle torquata* (Linnaeus)

Locally common resident from the Lower Rio Grande Valley west to Webb County. Ringed Kingfishers are uncommon and local north along the Rio Grande and its tributaries to Val Verde and Kinney Counties. Beginning in the 1990s, this species was reported with increasing frequency farther north on the Edwards Plateau, particularly along the Nueces and

Guadalupe Rivers, and was even documented nesting along the Nueces River, Uvalde County, in 2001. Wandering Ringed Kingfishers are casual north to Bastrop, Mason, and Llano Counties. Recently, they have also occurred with greater frequency on the central coast, particularly between Victoria and Kleberg Counties. Vagrants have been found as far west as Pecos County and on the Upper Texas Coast to Fort Bend County. There are documented records from Oklahoma and Louisiana, demonstrating the potential for this species to appear anywhere in Texas.

BELTED KINGFISHER *Ceryle alcyon* (Linnaeus)

Uncommon to locally common winter resident throughout the state. Wintering birds are present from late August to early May. Belted Kingfishers are uncommon and local summer residents across the northern third of the state. They are rare to very rare and local in summer in the remainder of the state, east of the Trans-Pecos.

GREEN KINGFISHER *Chloroceryle americana* (Gmelin)

Uncommon resident from the Edwards Plateau south to the Lower Rio Grande Valley. Green Kingfishers are found north along the Coastal Prairies to Victoria and Jackson Counties. They are rare along the Rio Grande to Brewster County and along the lower Pecos River drainage. Green Kingfishers are rare to locally uncommon east to Bastrop County where nesting records exist. They have occurred as vagrants during the summer north to Randall County in the Panhandle and east to Washington County. This species is very sensitive to cold weather. During colder than normal winters, northern populations retreat well to the south and often do not return for several years.

ORDER PICIFORMES

Family Picidae: Woodpeckers

LEWIS'S WOODPECKER *Melanerpes lewis* (Gray)

Irregular and very rare migrant and winter visitor to the western two-thirds of the state. The majority are from the

Trans-Pecos, although there are scattered records eastward to Dallas County. Lewis's Woodpeckers documented in the South Texas Brush County during the winters of 2000–2001 and 2001–2002 are among the southernmost records known for this species. These woodpeckers have shown an irruptive pattern of occurrence with individuals appearing as early as October and lingering into spring. All of the documented records fall between late August and mid-May. This species was removed from the Review List in 2002; at the time there were 59 documented records. There are 33 reports of Lewis's Woodpeckers from prior to the development of the Review List in 1987 for which there is no documentation on file at Texas A&M University.

RED-HEADED WOODPECKER
Melanerpes erythrocephalus (Linnaeus)

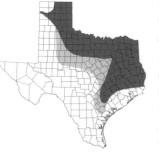

Locally common to rare summer resident in riparian habitats from the western Panhandle eastward across north-central Texas. Red-headed Woodpecker is an uncommon resident throughout the Pineywoods, becoming rare to locally uncommon westward through the Post Oak Savannah region. They are rare and irregular postbreeding wanderers and winter visitors west and south of the breeding range. Red-headed Woodpeckers are irruptive during winter on the southern Rolling Plains and Edwards Plateau, sometimes occurring in large numbers. Farther west into the Trans-Pecos, this woodpecker is a casual visitor with records from all seasons (Peterson and Zimmer 1998). Red-headed Woodpeckers have declined significantly in recent decades.

ACORN WOODPECKER
Melanerpes formicivorus (Swainson)

Common resident in the Chinati, Chisos, Davis, and Del Norte Mountains of the Trans-Pecos but uncommon and more local in the Guadalupe Mountains. A small population exists in Bandera, Kerr, and Real Counties on the central Edwards Plateau. Sightings in this area have dropped dramatically since about 1985, and the status of this population is uncertain (Lockwood 2001b). Away from the breeding range, Acorn Woodpeckers are very rare and irregular visitors from fall through spring as far north on the High Plains and western Rolling Plains as Potter and Randall Counties. Wandering Acorn Woodpeckers have also been documented east to the central (Aransas County) and upper (Harris County) coasts and south to the Lower Rio Grande Valley (Hidalgo County).

GOLDEN-FRONTED WOODPECKER

Melanerpes aurifrons (Wagler)

Common resident in the South Texas Brush Country north through the Edwards Plateau and western Rolling Plains to the south-central Panhandle. Golden-fronted Woodpeckers are also found in riparian habitats in the southern Trans-Pecos, west to Presidio County. This species is a casual, primarily winter, visitor eastward to Parker, Hill, and Bastrop Counties and a rare visitor during the winter on the High Plains as far west as Oldham County and on the northern Rolling Plains to Hemphill County. Golden-fronted Woodpeckers have wandered as far east as Brazos Bend State Park, Brazoria County, where one was found on 15 January 1994. During the last century, this species has expanded its range in Texas west to the central Trans-Pecos and northward to the southern Panhandle (Husak and Maxwell 2000).

RED-BELLIED WOODPECKER

Melanerpes carolinus (Linnaeus)

Common to abundant resident in the eastern third of the state, west to the eastern edge of the Rolling Plains and Edwards Plateau. Red-bellied Woodpeckers can be found south along the coast to Refugio County. They are fairly common residents in the eastern Panhandle and along the Canadian River drainage west to Oldham County, where they are rare. Red-bellieds are very rare to rare wanderers to the remainder of the Panhandle and to the eastern South Plains. On the Edwards Plateau, this species is a rare resident in riparian forests along the Colorado River system as far west as San Saba County. Vagrants have been noted as far west as Midland County and south along the coast to Cameron and Hidalgo Counties in the Lower Rio Grande Valley.

WILLIAMSON'S SAPSUCKER

Sphyrapicus thyroideus (Cassin)

Rare to locally uncommon winter resident in the upper elevations of the Davis and Guadalupe Mountains in the Trans-Pecos, where they arrive as early as mid-October and

usually remain into March. Williamson's Sapsucker is also a rare to very rare migrant and winter visitor to the remainder of the Trans-Pecos and eastward onto the High Plains. This species is a casual winter visitor to the western Edwards Plateau (Lockwood 2001b). Williamson's Sapsuckers have been documented east of the Edwards Plateau in Bastrop, Brazoria, Brazos, and eastern Travis Counties.

YELLOW-BELLIED SAPSUCKER
Sphyrapicus varius (Linnaeus)

Uncommon to locally common migrant and winter resident throughout most of the state, except west of the central mountain ranges of the Trans-Pecos, where they are rare. Yellow-bellied Sapsuckers arrive in early October and remain through March, with a few lingering into April. There are, however, a small number of records of individuals remaining as late as early May. This species often shares habitat with the closely related Red-naped Sapsucker where their ranges overlap.

RED-NAPED SAPSUCKER *Sphyrapicus nuchalis* Baird

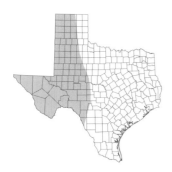

Rare to uncommon migrant and winter resident in the Trans-Pecos. Red-naped Sapsucker is a rare to very rare migrant through the High Plains and western Rolling Plains south to the Edwards Plateau. Away from the Trans-Pecos, this species is less common as a winter resident than as a migrant. Fall migrants typically begin arriving in late September. Winter residents and spring migrants have generally departed the state by early March, with a few individuals lingering into late April. Red-naped Sapsuckers have been found east to Brazos, Grimes, and Galveston Counties and south to the Lower Rio Grande Valley. This species may be a very rare and irregular summer resident in the Guadalupe Mountains of the Trans-Pecos where Newman (1974) collected an adult female in breeding condition in the "Bowl" on 3 June 1971. No evidence of breeding activity has been noted since that time.

Review Species

RED-BREASTED SAPSUCKER
Sphyrapicus ruber (Gmelin)

Accidental. Texas has two records of Red-breasted Sapsucker. The first record was of an adult, and close examination of the photos suggested that the bird belonged to

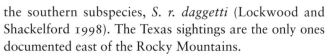

the southern subspecies, *S. r. daggetti* (Lockwood and Shackelford 1998). The Texas sightings are the only ones documented east of the Rocky Mountains.

27 FEB. 1996, MCGREGOR, MCLENNAN CO.
  (TBRC 1996-175; TPRF 1586)
3 DEC 2000, BIG BEND RANCH SP, PRESIDIO CO. (TBRC 2001-30)

LADDER-BACKED WOODPECKER
Picoides scalaris (Wagler)

Common to uncommon resident throughout the western two-thirds of the state. Ladder-backed Woodpeckers can be found east to Dallas, Limestone, Bastrop, and Matagorda Counties. This species is a vagrant farther east to Brazos County and north along the Coastal Prairies to Harris and Waller Counties. There are no documented records from northeast Texas or the Pineywoods.

DOWNY WOODPECKER *Picoides pubescens* (Linnaeus)

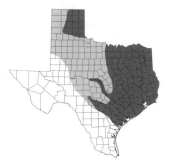

Common to uncommon resident in the eastern half of the state as far west as the eastern edge of the Rolling Plains and Edwards Plateau, and south to the Guadalupe River delta. On the Edwards Plateau they are resident only along the Colorado, Guadalupe, and Medina River drainages. These small woodpeckers are rare to uncommon residents in the Panhandle as far west as Potter and Randall Counties, and they are rare migrants and winter residents in the remainder of the Panhandle, the Rolling Plains, and the eastern Edwards Plateau. This species is a casual visitor farther west to the Trans-Pecos, with records from the Guadalupe and Davis Mountains and El Paso County. A single winter record exists from the Lower Rio Grande Valley in Starr County.

HAIRY WOODPECKER *Picoides villosus* (Linnaeus)

Uncommon to locally common resident in the eastern third of Texas, west to Tarrant and Bastrop Counties where they are rare and local. This species is also present at higher elevations in the Guadalupe Mountains of the Trans-Pecos and in the eastern Panhandle including the Canadian River drainage as far west as Potter County. Hairy Woodpeckers are rare and irregular migrants and winter visitors elsewhere on the High Plains and the eastern Edwards Plateau. They are casual winter visitors away from the Guadalupe Mountains in the Trans-Pecos and have wandered as far south as the Nueces River drainage along the Coastal Prairies.

RED-COCKADED WOODPECKER

Picoides borealis (Vieillot)

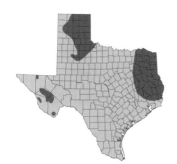

Rare to locally uncommon resident in open pine forests in the southern half of the Pineywoods. This species apparently ranged considerably farther west and north until the early 1900s. Eggs were collected in Lavaca (in 1912) and Lee (in 1883) Counties (Oberholser 1974). Red-cockaded Woodpecker is a habitat specialist and requires intensive fire management of the pine forests that it occupies. They live in family groups of up to ten individuals. The population present in the Sam Houston National Forest is one of the largest remaining. The U.S. Fish and Wildlife Service lists this species as Endangered.

NORTHERN FLICKER *Colaptes auratus* (Linnaeus)

Common to uncommon summer resident in the Panhandle and South Plains and at mid- and upper elevations in the mountains of the Trans-Pecos. Northern Flicker is an uncommon to rare summer resident in the Pineywoods, found primarily in towns and cities. They are rare to very rare in woodland habitats on the Coastal Prairies along the upper coast. This species is a common winter resident throughout the northern two-thirds of the state, becoming rare in the southern South Texas Brush Country and very rare in the Lower Rio Grande Valley. This taxon was previously considered two species, and both forms occur in Texas along with hybrids.

"YELLOW-SHAFTED" FLICKER

The breeding populations in Texas outside the Trans-Pecos belong to this group. Yellow-shafted Flickers are present in winter as far west as the central High Plains and eastern Edwards Plateau, south to the Lower Rio Grande Valley. They are also rare and irregular winter visitors west through the Trans-Pecos. At that season it is not uncommon to encounter hybrids in the western half of the state.

"RED-SHAFTED" FLICKER

Breeding populations in the Trans-Pecos belong to this subspecies group. Red-shafted Flickers are found in winter throughout the western two-thirds of the state, becoming increasingly less common eastward. They are casual in the Pineywoods.

PILEATED WOODPECKER
Dryocopus pileatus (Linnaeus)

Uncommon to locally common resident in the Pineywoods and Post Oak Savannahs. Pileated Woodpeckers are found west to Karnes, Travis, and Wise Counties. Vagrants have been found west to San Saba and Kerr Counties on the Edwards Plateau and to Eastland and Young Counties in north-central Texas. There are a few scattered records from along the central coast south of Lavaca Bay to Aransas County. In recent years, they have been found regularly in very small numbers in the Guadalupe River delta, Calhoun and Refugio Counties.

Review Species

IVORY-BILLED WOODPECKER
Campephilus principalis (Linnaeus)

The Ivory-billed Woodpecker has been extirpated from Texas and, possibly, from the continental United States. The last reliable record for this species in North America dates from 1945. Ivory-billed Woodpeckers were formerly residents in the eastern third of the state, west to the bottomlands of the Trinity River and along the coast to the Brazos River. Only three well-documented records exist for Texas, although there have been 45 other published reports from the state (Shackelford 1998).

3 MAY 1885, NECHES RIVER, JASPER CO.
(MILWAUKEE PUBLIC MUSEUM 338)
C. 1900, BOIS D'ARC ISLAND (TRINITY RIVER), DALLAS CO.
(DALLAS MNH 6216)
26 NOV. 1904, TARKINGTON, LIBERTY CO.
(USNM 195199 AND 195200)

ORDER PASSERIFORMES

Family Tyrannidae: Tyrant Flycatchers

NORTHERN BEARDLESS-TYRANNULET
Camptostoma imberbe Sclater

Rare to locally uncommon resident in the Lower Rio Grande Valley, northward through the Coastal Sand Plain. Northern Beardless-Tyrannulet appears to be increasing in abundance in the Lower Rio Grande Valley. There is a single report from farther north of one in Goliad County on 27

May 1995. There have been two unexpected records from Presidio County in the Trans-Pecos, one at a remote spring in the foothills of the Chinati Mountains on 28 July 2001 (TPRF 1963) and another observed near Ruidoso on 21 January 2002.

GREENISH ELAENIA *Myiopagis viridicata* (Vieillot)

Accidental. There is one record for the United States of this tropical flycatcher (Morgan and Feltner 1985). The northern populations of Greenish Elaenia range from southern Tamaulipas, Mexico, south to Panama. The disjunct populations in southern South America are long-distance austral migrants. This individual could potentially have come from either population.

20–23 MAY 1984, HIGH ISLAND, GALVESTON CO.
  (TBRC 1998-289; TPRF 330)

TUFTED FLYCATCHER

Mitrephanes phaeocercus (Sclater)

Accidental. There are two records of this tropical flycatcher for the state. The first was discovered at Rio Grande Village, Big Bend National Park, Brewster County, in 1991. This record was also the first for the United States (Zimmer and Bryan 1993). Tufted Flycatchers are found as far north as southern Tamaulipas, Mexico.

3 NOV. 1991–17 JAN. 1992, RIO GRANDE VILLAGE, BREWSTER CO.
  (TBRC 1991-132; TPRF 1000)
2–6 APR. 1993, 25 MI. WEST OF FORT STOCKTON, PECOS CO.
  (TBRC 1993-41; TPRF 1149)

OLIVE-SIDED FLYCATCHER

Contopus cooperi (Nuttall)

Uncommon to rare migrant throughout the state. Migrants are present in Texas between late April and early June and from early August to mid-October. Olive-sided Flycatchers are uncommon summer residents at upper elevations of the Guadalupe Mountains in the Trans-Pecos. This species is rare and irregular during the summer in the Davis Mountains, but nesting has not been observed (Peterson et al. 1991).

GREATER PEWEE *Contopus pertinax* Cabanis and Heine

Casual visitor to the Trans-Pecos and accidental elsewhere. There are 11 documented records for the state, the first quite

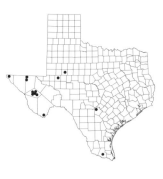

unexpectedly found at Big Spring, Howard County, from 22 October to 17 November 1984 (TPRF 329). Trans-Pecos records include one from the Chisos Mountains, two from the Guadalupe Mountains, one from El Paso County, and five from the Davis Mountains. Three Greater Pewees were present at one location in the Davis Mountains during the summer of 2002 where nesting was documented, providing a first breeding record for Texas (TBRC 2002-76). One was present in Hidalgo County from 12 December 2002 to 19 March 2003 (TBRC 2002-123). The two additional documented records involve single birds at San Antonio, Bexar County, on 7 April 1991 (TBRC 1991-62), and Midland, Midland County, 30 April 1998 (TBRC 1998-78).

WESTERN WOOD-PEWEE *Contopus sordidulus* Sclater

Rare to locally common summer resident in the mountains of the central and northern Trans-Pecos. Numerous summer sightings have come from the northern Panhandle, although nesting has not been observed (Seyffert 2001). Western Wood-Pewee is a common to uncommon migrant through the High Plains, western Rolling Plains, and Trans-Pecos. Curiously, this species has rarely been detected on the Edwards Plateau. Western Wood-Pewees are probably overlooked in this region because of the presence of Eastern Wood-Pewees. Migrants have been documented east to north-central Texas, the upper coast, and the Lower Rio Grande Valley. Migrant Western Wood-Pewees are present in Texas generally between late April and late May and from early August to early October.

EASTERN WOOD-PEWEE *Contopus virens* (Linnaeus)

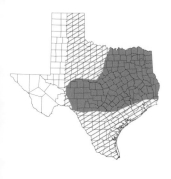

Common to uncommon and local summer resident in eastern Texas, west to the eastern edge of the Rolling Plains and throughout the Edwards Plateau. This species is a local breeder as far west as the Pecos River and its tributaries. Eastern Wood-Pewees are common to uncommon migrants in the eastern two-thirds of the state and a rare migrant on the High Plains, the western edge of the Edwards Plateau, and the Trans-Pecos. The difficulty in separating these migrants from the more common Western Wood-Pewee in the western third of the state clouds the status of this species. Migrant Eastern Wood-Pewees are present in Texas between mid-April and late May and from early August to mid-November.

YELLOW-BELLIED FLYCATCHER
Empidonax flaviventris (Baird and Baird)

Uncommon to common migrant in the eastern half of the state. Yellow-bellied Flycatchers are rare migrants through the eastern Rolling Plains and eastern Edwards Plateau. This species is a casual migrant farther west with records from the western Edwards Plateau (Kinney County), Concho Valley (Tom Green County), and Trans-Pecos (Brewster and Jeff Davis Counties). The migration periods for Yellow-bellied Flycatcher are between late April and late May and from mid-August to mid-October.

ACADIAN FLYCATCHER *Empidonax virescens* (Vieillot)

Common migrant and summer resident in the eastern third of the state. Acadian Flycatcher is also a locally uncommon summer resident on the Edwards Plateau west to the Devils River drainage, Val Verde County, where they are rare and local. An isolated report of a nest with eggs came from Santa Ana National Wildlife Refuge, Hidalgo County, in 1940. Migrants are very rarely encountered away from known breeding areas west of the Balcones Escarpment. Acadian Flycatchers arrive in Texas in late March and are present into late October.

ALDER FLYCATCHER *Empidonax alnorum* Brewster

Uncommon to common migrant in the eastern third of the state. Alder Flycatchers are known to occur west to the eastern Edwards Plateau but are undocumented farther west. Migrants are found between very late April and early June and from late July to early October. The status of Alder Flycatcher, particularly in the western half of the state, is obscured by the presence of its sibling species, the Willow Flycatcher. These two species were formerly considered conspecific under the name Traill's Flycatcher. Alder Flycatchers can be safely identified in the field by voice only.

WILLOW FLYCATCHER *Empidonax traillii* (Audubon)

Uncommon to rare migrant throughout the state. Willow Flycatcher was formerly considered conspecific with the

Alder Flycatcher. Since the two taxa were recognized, Willow Flycatcher was thought to be the more common. However, recent evidence, including banding data, shows that Willow Flycatcher is less common than Alder in the eastern half of the state. The migration period of the two species is basically the same, with birds present between very late April and early June and from late July to early October. Willow Flycatcher was formerly a summer resident in the central and western Trans-Pecos. The last nesting record for the Southwestern Willow Flycatcher *(E. t. extimus)* in Texas, now listed as Endangered, occurred in the 1890s in Brewster County.

LEAST FLYCATCHER
Empidonax minimus (Baird and Baird)

Common to uncommon migrant throughout most of the state. Least Flycatchers are common migrants west to the eastern third of the Trans-Pecos, becoming rare to very uncommon farther west. In the Trans-Pecos, this species is much more common as a fall than as a spring migrant and can be common as far west as the Davis Mountains. Migrant Least Flycatchers are present in the state between mid-April and early June and from late July through October. This species is a rare to very rare winter resident in the Lower Rio Grande Valley and along the coast, with a few scattered winter records from inland locations.

HAMMOND'S FLYCATCHER
Empidonax hammondii (Xántus de Vesey)

Uncommon migrant through the western half of the Trans-Pecos, becoming rare farther east. Hammond's Flycatcher is also a casual to very rare migrant through the western High Plains south to the Concho Valley. This species is generally more common in fall than in spring. The migration period extends from mid-April to late May and early August through October. This species is a very rare winter visitor in the Trans-Pecos with records from Brewster, Culberson, El Paso, and Presidio Counties. There is also a documented winter record from Bastrop State Park, Bastrop County, from 16 to 18 February 1987.

GRAY FLYCATCHER *Empidonax wrightii* Baird

Locally common summer resident in the Davis Mountains. This population was discovered in 1989 and breeding was documented in 1991 (Peterson et al. 1991). Gray Flycatchers are an uncommon to rare migrant in the western Trans-Pecos and are rare to casual farther east in the region and on the High Plains. Migrants are present from mid-April to late May and from mid-August through early October. Gray Flycatcher is a rare and local winter resident along the Rio Grande in Brewster and Presidio Counties. Winter records exist outside that region from Bailey, Karnes, and Nueces Counties.

DUSKY FLYCATCHER *Empidonax oberholseri* Phillips

Common migrant through the western half of the Trans-Pecos and a rare migrant through the remainder of the Trans-Pecos. This flycatcher has been reported with increasing frequency from the western High Plains during migration. Migrants are present between mid-April and late May and from early August to early October. Dusky Flycatcher is a rare and very local summer resident at the highest elevations of the Davis Mountains (Bryan and Karges 2001). This species probably nested in the Guadalupe Mountains in 1972 (Newman 1974) and possibly at other times, but the first documented nesting record for Texas came from the Davis Mountains in 2000 (TPRF 1809). Dusky Flycatchers are rare to locally uncommon winter residents along the Rio Grande in the southern Trans-Pecos.

CORDILLERAN FLYCATCHER
Empidonax occidentalis Nelson

Locally uncommon to rare summer resident in the Chisos, Davis, and Guadalupe Mountains of the Trans-Pecos. Cordilleran Flycatcher is an uncommon to rare migrant throughout the remainder of the Trans-Pecos and on the western High Plains. This species may be a very rare migrant through the western Rolling Plains and Edwards Plateau, but documentation of its occurrence is lacking. Cordilleran Flycatcher was formerly considered conspecific with the Pacific-slope Flycatcher *(E. difficilis)* under the name Western Flycatcher. These two species are impossible to visually differentiate in the field; therefore the actual status of these species as migrants through Texas is unknown.

There are vocal differences, but the diagnostic calls are very rarely given during migration. There are many reports of "Western" Flycatchers from the eastern two-thirds of the state, but few include documentation.

Review Species

BUFF-BREASTED FLYCATCHER
Empidonax fulvifrons (Giraud)

The status of Buff-breasted Flycatcher in Texas is difficult to assess. The first record for the state was a male discovered on the Davis Mountains Preserve, Jeff Davis County, on 3 May 1999 (Horvath and Karges 2000). This bird was relocated in mid-June near the original location, and during subsequent observations a female and nest were discovered. The pair successfully raised young and remained until 28 August (TBRC 1999-48; TPRF 1799). A pair of Buff-breasted Fly-catchers occupied the same territory during the summer from 2000 through 2003. The earliest spring arrival date is 23 April and the latest fall date is 28 September. It seems likely that more than one pair of flycatchers could be present, but despite intensive searches, no others have been located.

BLACK PHOEBE *Sayornis nigricans* (Swainson)

Locally uncommon to rare resident in the Trans-Pecos, the southwestern Edwards Plateau, and southward near the Rio Grande to the central Lower Rio Grande Valley. Black Phoe-bes are closely tied to rivers and other bodies of water and as such have a very discontinuous range. This species is a rare to very rare winter visitor to the remainder of the Edwards Plateau and to the South Plains. Populations in the Trans-Pecos fluctuate during the winter, becoming less common in the mountains and more common in El Paso and Hudspeth Counties. Black Phoebes are casual visitors to the Panhandle from April to December and the central coast and South Texas Brush Country away from the Rio Grande during the fall and winter. Vagrants have been docu-mented from north-central Texas and the upper coast.

EASTERN PHOEBE *Sayornis phoebe* (Latham)

Uncommon to common summer resident in the northern two-thirds of the state, except in the eastern half of the Panhandle and the Central Brazos Valley where they are local. Eastern Phoebe is generally absent from the Trans-Pecos during the summer. This species is a common migrant

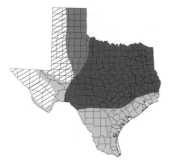

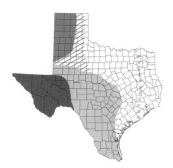

in the eastern two-thirds of the state, becoming increasingly less common westward to the extreme western Trans-Pecos, where they are rare. They are common winter residents over the eastern two-thirds of the state but generally absent from the High Plains south to the northwestern Edwards Plateau. This flycatcher is also a rare to very rare winter resident in the eastern half of the Trans- Pecos, primarily along the Rio Grande.

SAY'S PHOEBE *Sayornis saya* (Bonaparte)

Common to uncommon resident in the Trans-Pecos and east to Upton County and an uncommon summer resident in the western two-thirds of the Panhandle, becoming rare south through the South Plains. Say's Phoebe is an uncommon to rare winter resident in the western Edwards Plateau. They are also rare to very rare migrants and winter visitors through the Rolling Plains and uncommon during these seasons in the South Texas Brush Country. This species is a very rare, but regular, winter visitor east to the central coast and the Blackland Prairies region from north-central Texas south to Williamson County. Vagrants have found their way as far east as northeast Texas (White 2002) and the upper coast.

VERMILION FLYCATCHER
Pyrocephalus rubinus (Boddaert)

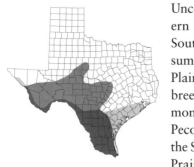

Uncommon to common summer resident across the southern Trans-Pecos east through the Edwards Plateau and South Texas Brush Country. Vermilion Flycatchers are rare summer visitors throughout the High Plains and Rolling Plains east through north-central Texas with a few isolated breeding records (Sexton 1999). This species is an uncommon winter resident along the Rio Grande in the Trans-Pecos from western Hudspeth County eastward through the South Texas Brush Country and north along the Coastal Prairies. They regularly wander eastward during the fall as far as the Pineywoods. Vermilion Flycatchers often remain through the early winter at a given locality.

Review Species

DUSKY-CAPPED FLYCATCHER
Myiarchus tuberculifer (d'Orbigny and Lafresnaye)

Very rare summer visitor to the Davis and Chisos Mountains of the Trans-Pecos. Prior to 1991, Texas had only

two documented records of this species. Since 1996, Dusky-capped Flycatchers have been almost annual visitors to the upper elevations of the Davis Mountains. The first breeding record for Texas was documented in the Chisos Mountains during the summer of 2000. This species has since been found nesting in the Davis Mountains. Away from these two mountain ranges there are single records from El Paso (11 May 1891) and Midland (3 September 1994) Counties. There are also two records from the Lower Rio Grande Valley from the winter of 2000–2001. The birds documented in the Lower Rio Grande Valley are the only records for the United States of the subspecies from northeastern Mexico, *M. t. lawrencei;* all others belong to *M. t. olivascens.* To date, Texas has 22 documented records of Dusky-capped Flycatcher.

ASH-THROATED FLYCATCHER
Myiarchus cinerascens (Lawrence)

Common to uncommon summer resident in the western half of the state. Ash-throated Flycatchers are found east through the Rolling Plains and the Edwards Plateau and south through the South Texas Brush Country. They are rare migrants east through the Blackland Prairies, Post Oak Savannah, and Coastal Prairies. Returning Ash-throated Flycatchers arrive in Texas in mid-March. The breeding population begins to disperse in late July, but fall migrants are present until late September. This species is rare to locally uncommon in winter along the Rio Grande in the southern Trans-Pecos, in the southern third of the state, and along the coast. There are isolated winter records inland including one from as far north as north-central Texas.

GREAT CRESTED FLYCATCHER
Myiarchus crinitus (Linnaeus)

Common to uncommon summer resident in the eastern half of the state westward through the eastern Panhandle and the western Edwards Plateau. The southern edge of the breeding range of this species in Texas is bounded by the Nueces River drainage on the central coast. Great Crested Flycatchers are common migrants in the eastern half of the state, west to the central Edwards Plateau. Farther west, this species becomes increasingly rare as a migrant and is casual during fall in the Trans-Pecos. Great Crested Flycatchers arrive in Texas by mid-March and are present into late October. This flycatcher is casual in winter along the Coastal Prairies and in the South Texas Brush Country. Most winter records are from December and could represent lingering migrants.

BROWN-CRESTED FLYCATCHER
Myiarchus tyrannulus (Müller)

Common summer resident in the Lower Rio Grande Valley. Brown-crested Flycatchers are uncommon to rare summer residents north through the South Texas Brush Country to the southern edge of the Edwards Plateau. The northern extent of the breeding range is along riparian corridors in Terrell and Val Verde Counties in the west and Gonzales and Victoria Counties in the east. They are rare summer residents along the Rio Grande west to Brewster County. This species has also been found with increasing frequency in the southern Post Oak Savannah and Blackland Prairie regions north to Fayette and Travis Counties, suggesting they may breed farther north than previously thought. Brown-crested Flycatcher is also a very rare to casual summer visitor to El Paso County in far west Texas. In winter, the species is very rare to casual on the Coastal Prairies north to Bastrop, Brazoria, and Galveston Counties.

GREAT KISKADEE *Pitangus sulphuratus* (Linnaeus)

Locally common resident in the Lower Rio Grande Valley. Great Kiskadee is an uncommon and local resident north along the Rio Grande and its tributaries to southern Val Verde County. This species is also an uncommon and local summer resident north along the coast to Nueces County and very local to Calhoun County. Kiskadees nested farther up the coast in Baytown, Chambers County, in 2002. There are isolated Great Kiskadee records from almost all areas of the state. They have wandered at all seasons, although primarily in spring, as far north as the South Plains and north-central Texas and west to Big Bend National Park, Brewster County, and Imperial Reservoir, Pecos County. The only regions of the state where this species has not been reported are the Panhandle and the Pineywoods.

Review Species

SULPHUR-BELLIED FLYCATCHER
Myiodynastes luteiventris Sclater

Casual visitor to the state. Texas has 13 documented records of Sulphur-bellied Flycatcher. This species nested on the Santa Margarita Ranch, Starr County, in 1975 and 1976 and was seen in the same area on one occasion during the summer of 1977. Since that time, two additional records of single birds have come from the Lower Rio Grande Valley: one near Falcon Dam, Starr County, on 29 May 2000 and another on South Padre Island, Cameron County, from 5 to 7 April 2001. There is one record from the Trans-Pecos while the remaining records are from along the coast, including two from Galveston County. All reports of Sulphur-bellied Flycatcher require detailed notes and preferably close photography to eliminate the similar Streaked Flycatcher, *M. maculates*. Streaked Flycatcher has not been documented in the United States but is a potential vagrant to Texas due to its migratory nature and the close proximity of its northernmost summer range. There are 15 reports of Sulphur-bellied Flycatchers from prior to the development of the Review List in 1987 for which there is no documentation on file at Texas A&M University.

Review Species

PIRATIC FLYCATCHER *Legatus leucophaius* (Vieillot)

Accidental. Texas has two documented records of this tropical flycatcher. The only other records of Piratic Flycatcher for the United States come from Florida and New Mexico. Both of the latter records were initially identified as Variegated Flycatcher *(Empidonomus varius)*, which is very similar and has wandered to North America previously.

4 APR. 1998, RIO GRANDE VILLAGE, BREWSTER CO.
  (TBRC 1998-60; TPRF 1685)
21–22 OCT. 2000, OFF NORTH PADRE ISLAND, KENEDY CO.
  (TBRC 2000-126; TPRF 1933)

TROPICAL KINGBIRD *Tyrannus melancholicus* Vieillot

Uncommon and local resident in the Lower Rio Grande Valley. The status of Tropical Kingbird in Texas changed dramatically during the 1990s. Prior to 1991, only a single documented record existed for the state, a specimen collected on 5 December 1909 near Brownsville, Cameron County. Since 1991, this species has become a permanent

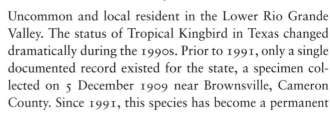

resident in Cameron and Hidalgo Counties. A few scattered sightings come from farther up the Rio Grande in Starr County. Since 1997, Tropical Kingbirds have consistently nested at Cottonwood Campground in Big Bend National Park, Brewster County. Breeding pairs have also been found near Marathon, Brewster County, in 1999 and Midland County in 2001. Silent Couch's/Tropical Kingbirds have been found with increasing regularity along the coast, as well as various inland locations across the state. Tropical Kingbirds have been conclusively identified by voice along the Coastal Prairies on four occasions, twice in Galveston County and once each in Kenedy and Nueces Counties.

COUCH'S KINGBIRD *Tyrannus couchii* Baird

Common to uncommon summer resident in the Lower Rio Grande Valley. Couch's Kingbirds are locally uncommon northward through the South Texas Brush Country to southern Val Verde County and along the coast to Calhoun County. There are also isolated breeding records north to Bexar and Travis Counties. Couch's Kingbirds are very rare visitors to the upper coast in fall and winter, although the frequency has increased in recent years. Silent Couch's/Tropical Kingbirds have been found at various inland locations across the state. Vocalizing individuals definitively identified as Couch's have been found on the Edwards Plateau and in the southern Trans-Pecos. The northernmost documented records come from Lubbock County from 7 to 23 September 2000 and Fort Worth, Tarrant County, on 2 September 2001. Couch's Kingbirds withdraw southward from the northern portions of their range during winter and are uncommon to rare, though irregular, during this season in the Lower Rio Grande Valley. During mild winters, they may be found as far north as the central coast.

CASSIN'S KINGBIRD *Tyrannus vociferans* Swainson

Uncommon to locally common summer resident in mid- and upper elevations of the central Trans-Pecos from the Guadalupe Mountains south through the Davis and Chinati Mountains. Migrants arrive in early April and most depart by early October, with a few lingering into November. Elsewhere in the state, a pair of Cassin's Kingbirds was discovered breeding in the northwestern corner of the Panhandle in 1983. There have been other summer sightings from Dallam County, but additional nestings have not been confirmed. Cassin's Kingbird is an uncommon to rare migrant throughout the remainder of the Trans-Pecos and through the western High Plains. Occasionally, migrants have been reported from as far east as Travis and Lee Counties and along the upper coast. Cassin's Kingbird is a casual winter visitor to the South Texas Brush Country and the southernmost portion of the Trans-Pecos.

Review Species

THICK-BILLED KINGBIRD

Tyrannus crassirostris Swainson

Casual to accidental visitor to the state with 15 documented records, many of which pertain to returning pairs in Big Bend National Park. Thick-billed Kingbird was first documented in Texas in the Chisos Basin of Big Bend National Park, Brewster County, on 21 June 1967 (Wauer 1967). One was again encountered at Big Bend National Park during the summer of 1985. Between 1985 and 1991, Thick-billed Kingbirds were summer residents at Rio Grande Village (seven documented records) and Cottonwood Campground (four documented records). They bred successfully at Cottonwood Campground from 1988 through 1991. Since then, only two additional sightings have come from southern Brewster County and one from southern Presidio County. Away from Big Bend, there are unexpected records of single birds from Palo Duro Canyon, Randall County, on 30 October 1998 (TBRC 1998-144; TPRF 1744), and the Davis Mountains on 17 May 2003 (TBRC 2003-42).

WESTERN KINGBIRD *Tyrannus verticalis* Say

Common to uncommon summer resident in the western two-thirds of the state. In the eastern third, Western Kingbirds are uncommon to locally common summer residents in the Post Oak Savannahs but generally absent from the Pineywoods. In the Trans-Pecos, Western Kingbirds are generally absent from the mid- and upper elevations of the mountain ranges. This species is a common to uncommon migrant throughout the state west of the Pineywoods, where very rare. Western Kingbirds arrive on the breeding grounds in early to mid-April. In the eastern half of the state the breeding population disperses by late July and early August and is rare into September. This species is a common to uncommon migrant through the western half of the state from August through mid-September. Lingering fall migrants have been noted as late as mid-October and very rarely into November.

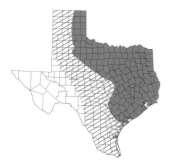

EASTERN KINGBIRD *Tyrannus tyrannus* (Linnaeus)

Common to locally uncommon summer resident in the eastern third of the state as far west as the central Panhandle and the eastern edge of the Edwards Plateau. This species is a common to uncommon migrant through the eastern two-thirds of the state, becoming abundant along the upper and central coasts. These kingbirds frequently congregate along the coast in large flocks, sometimes numbering in the thousands. Eastern Kingbird is a rare migrant in the eastern Trans-Pecos and very rare to casual in the western half. The migration periods are between late March and mid-May and mid-August to early October, with a few stragglers present into early November.

Review Species

GRAY KINGBIRD *Tyrannus dominicensis* (Gmelin)

Accidental. There are five documented records of this kingbird for the state. All have been, as expected, in very close proximity to the coast. Gray Kingbirds are summer residents along the eastern Gulf Coast to southern Alabama and islands off the coast of Mississippi.

31 AUG. 1951, ROCKPORT, ARANSAS CO. (TBRC 1988-218)
24 APR. 1974, GALVESTON, GALVESTON CO. (TPRF 323)
23 MAY–1 JUNE 1992, CORPUS CHRISTI, NUECES CO.
  (TBRC 1992-74; TPRF 1082)
10 OCT. 2001, QUINTANA, BRAZORIA CO. (TBRC 2001-126)
18 MAY 2002, SOUTH PADRE ISLAND, CAMERON CO.
  (TBRC 2002-61)

SCISSOR-TAILED FLYCATCHER
Tyrannus forficatus (Gmelin)

Common to locally abundant summer resident throughout the eastern three-quarters of the state, including the eastern third of the Panhandle. Scissor-tailed Flycatchers are locally uncommon in the eastern Trans-Pecos and western Panhandle. In the Trans-Pecos, they are very local west to Balmorhea, Reeves County, and casual migrants and summer visitors farther west. Spring migrants and residents arrive in southernmost Texas in late February and are present throughout the state by early April. Summer residents and migrants are present well into November, and a few linger through December, particularly along the coast. There are many records of birds overwintering at scattered locations throughout much of the state, but they are most commonly encountered along the coast and the southern-most parts. Interestingly, a small number of Scissor-taileds regularly overwinter in the vicinity of Choke Canyon Reservoir in McMullen and Live Oak Counties.

Review Species

FORK-TAILED FLYCATCHER *Tyrannus savana* Vieillot

Casual visitor to the state with records from the fall, winter, and spring. There are 13 documented records of Fork-tailed Flycatcher for Texas, and all but three are from along the Coastal Prairies. Those three records include two from Travis County, one involving two birds, and another on a petroleum platform off North Padre Island, Kenedy County. Records of this species for the United States are generally believed to belong to the South American subspecies *T. s. savana*. These birds are austral migrants that over-shoot their normal wintering ground in northern South America or have undergone a reverse migration. There are two, or possibly three, December records from the lower coast that appear to belong to the subspecies found in Mexico, *T. s. monachus* (Lockwood 1997).

Genera *incertae sedis*

The following genera, along with five others from the neotropics, present a taxonomic challenge. The AOU *(1998) lists them as* incertae sedis, *to acknowledge that they are related to tyrant flycatchers but are of uncertain affinities. In the past, these species have been placed in the Tyrannidae.*

Review Species

ROSE-THROATED BECARD

Pachyramphus aglaiae (Lafresnaye)

Very rare and irregular visitor to the Lower Rio Grande Valley, primarily Hidalgo County. Rose-throated Becards were formerly a rare and local resident in the Lower Rio Grande Valley, limited to Cameron and Hidalgo Counties. Since the mid-1970s, there have been 20 documented records for the state, the majority between early December and mid-March. Since 1980, very few summer records exist, and the only nesting attempts (all unsuccessful) occurred at Anzalduas County Park and Santa Ana National Wildlife Refuge, Hidalgo County. Three records come from outside the Lower Rio Grande Valley. Single individuals were documented near Fort Davis, Jeff Davis County, on 18 July 1973 (Runnells 1975); near Rockport, Aransas County, on 10 January 1990, and on the King Ranch, Kenedy County, on 20 January 1992. The 27 reports of Rose-throated Becards from prior to the development of the Review List in 1987 have no documentation on file at Texas A&M University.

Review Species

MASKED TITYRA *Tityra semifasciata* (Spix)

Accidental. The one record of this species for the state is also the only record for the United States. Masked Tityra occurs as close as central Tamaulipas in northeastern Mexico, where they occupy humid and semiarid forest edges in lowlands up to 2500 meters in elevation (Howell and Webb 1995).

17 FEB.–10 MAR. 1990, BENTSEN–RIO GRANDE VALLEY SP, HIDALGO CO. (TBRC 1990-33; TPRF 860)

Family Laniidae: Shrikes

LOGGERHEAD SHRIKE *Lanius ludovicianus* Linnaeus

Rare to locally common resident throughout the state, except for portions of the South Texas Brush Country and the southwestern Edwards Plateau, where they are largely absent during the summer. Loggerhead Shrikes are more common as migrants throughout the state. In many areas, the local resident populations increase in the winter with an influx of birds from farther north. This is particularly true on the Coastal Prairies.

NORTHERN SHRIKE *Lanius excubitor* Linnaeus

Rare to very rare winter resident in the Panhandle and casual on the South Plains. Northern Shrikes are casual to accidental visitors on the Rolling Plains away from the Panhandle, as well as in many other areas of the state. There are three records from north-central Texas (Palo Pinto and Wichita Counties) and one from Irion County in the Concho

73. Although Elegant Trogon *(Trogon elegans)* is a common resident in the mountains of northeastern Mexico, this spectacular bird has rarely wandered into Texas. This adult female was at Delta Lake, Hidalgo County, from 25 to 31 January 1990 and provided the second record for the state. *Photograph by Jim Flynn.*

74. Ringed Kingfishers *(Ceryle torquata)* are denizens of rivers and resacas of south Texas, becoming increasingly rare north into Central Texas. This species often flies at surprisingly high altitudes, unlike the other two species in Texas. It also favors higher perches from which it makes long dives into the water in pursuit of small fish. *Photograph by Steve Bentsen.*

75. Green Kingfisher *(Chloroceryle americana)* is a tiny kingfisher of wooded streams and ponds. The perches from which they forage are rarely higher than 5 or 6 feet above the water's surface. *Photograph by Tim Cooper.*

76. The Lewis's Woodpecker *(Melanerpes lewis)* is well known for flycatching, and this behavior is one of the most specialized for any woodpecker in the world. This highly migratory species is a casual to very rare visitor to Texas. This adult was present at Choke Canyon, McMullen County, from 27 November to 17 December 2000 and is the southernmost thus far found in the state. *Photograph by John C. Arvin.*

77. Golden-fronted Woodpecker's *(Melanerpes aurifrons)* range in the United States is confined to Texas and a small portion of southwestern Oklahoma. This woodpecker is most common in mesquite savannahs but can be found in other open woodland habitats as well. They forage more frequently on the ground than the closely related Red-bellied Woodpecker. *Photograph by Tim Cooper.*

78. The Endangered Red-cockaded Woodpecker *(Picoides borealis)* is a habitat specialist requiring large tracts of open pine forest with a grassy under-story. Recent research suggests that the species continues to slowly decline despite careful habitat management. The largest population in the state is found in the Sam Houston National Forest of East Texas. *Photograph by Greg W. Lasley.*

79. Northern Beardless-Tyrannulet *(Camptostoma imberbe)* is the smallest flycatcher found in the United States, though its song is surprisingly loud and completely different from the songs of the similar-appearing *Empidonax* species found in the state. *Photograph by Brian E. Small.*

80. The Greenish Elaenia *(Myiopagis viridicata)*, which appeared at High Island in 1984, stunned the birding community. The typical range of this tropical species extends no further north than southern Tamaulipas, Mexico. *Photograph by Ted Eubanks.*

81. There are two well-documented occurrences of Tufted Flycatcher *(Mitrephanes phaeocercus)* for the United States, and both are from Texas. This handsome flycatcher is found in the Mexican highlands just south of the border. *Photograph by Mary Gustafson.*

82. Not many years ago, Buff-breasted Flycatcher *(Empidonax fulvifrons)* was anticipated as a vagrant that would eventually be found in the state. Investigations of the avifauna of the upper elevations of the Davis Mountains that began in 1999 resulted in the discovery of a breeding pair that has returned each summer since.
Photograph by Greg W. Lasley.

83. Brown-crested Flycatchers *(Myiarchus tyrannulus)* found in Texas belong to the subspecies *M. t. cooperi* and are smaller than *M. t. magister* found in southern Arizona. Texas birds are closer in size and structure to Ash-throated Flycatcher, making field identification more challenging. As a result, familiarity with these species' vocalizations becomes more important.
Photograph by Greg W. Lasley.

84. Great Kiskadees *(Pitangus sulphuratus)* are most often found near water and are a conspicuous and vocal component of the avifauna of South Texas.
Photograph by Tim Cooper.

85. Although Sulphur-bellied Flycatcher *(Myiodynastes luteiventris)* is only a casual visitor to Texas, they have appeared as far east as the Upper Texas Coast. There was a resident pair in Starr County for several years in the 1970s.
Photograph by Steve Bentsen.

86. Though Piratic Flycatcher *(Legatus leucophaius)* has been documented twice in Texas, only a handful of fortunate observers has had the pleasure of seeing them here. This individual was found on an oil platform in the Gulf off Kenedy County on 21 October 2000.
Photograph by Alan Wormington.

87. Couch's Kingbird *(Tyrannus couchii)* can safely be separated from the very closely related Tropical Kingbird only by its vocalizations. Most Couch's Kingbirds withdraw from Texas during the winter, while Tropical Kingbirds are permanent residents.   *Photograph by Steve Bentsen.*

88. In the United States, Scissor-tailed Flycatchers *(Tyrannus forficatus)* are found from Texas north through the southern Great Plains to southeastern Nebraska. This elegant bird is a common summer resident in open habitats throughout most of Texas.
Photograph by Tim Cooper.

89. Rose-throated Becards *(Pachyramphus aglaiae)* have had a history of sporadic occurrence in the Lower Rio Grande Valley and were more regular breeders in the 1970s. There has not been a successful nesting in Texas since then, but there have been unsuccessful attempts and even a few instances where unmated birds built nests. *Photograph by Mark W. Lockwood.*

90. Masked Tityra *(Tityra semifasciata)* is common in southern Tamaulipas, but despite its close proximity, there is only one U.S. record. Accordingly, the find of this bird in 1990 drew excited crowds of birders from all over the country. *Photograph by Greg W. Lasley.*

91. The Black-capped Vireo *(Vireo atricapilla)* is one of two Endangered songbirds found in Texas. This vireo often nests in loose colonies and favors open shrubland habitats. Intensive cowbird management is underway in many areas to help protect this species. *Photograph by Mark W. Lockwood.*

92. Despite its rather drab plumage, the Gray Vireo *(Vireo vicinior)* is much sought after by birders. The arid juniper and oak habitat of this species is often in fairly rugged terrain that, combined with the very large areas the territorial males defend, can often make Gray Vireos difficult to find. *Photograph by Kelly B. Bryan.*

93. Yellow-green Vireos *(Vireo flavoviridis)* are reported almost annually from the Lower Rio Grande Valley. These reports have often involved what appeared to be territorial males, but confirmed breeding has often been very difficult to document. This individual was one of a pair that successfully nested at Laguna Atascosa National Wildlife Refuge in 1989. *Photograph by Mike Krzywonski.*

94. There is one record of Yucatan Vireo *(Vireo magister)* for the United States. This species is typically found only on the Yucatan Peninsula of Mexico and is thought to be sedentary. Therefore, it was quite an unexpected visitor to Texas. *Photograph by Don Cunningham/VIREO.*

95. Green Jay *(Cyanocorax yncas)* is a common and colorful resident of the wooded areas of South Texas. The bright greens and blues of their plumage serve them well as they blend into the foliage.   *Photograph by Tim Cooper.*

96. The tiny U.S. population of Brown Jays *(Cyanocorax morio)*, consisting on average of fewer than a dozen birds, exists only in the Lower Rio Grande Valley. This population moves freely back and forth across the Rio Grande between Starr County and Mexico.   *Photograph by Mark W. Lockwood.*

97. The population of Mexican Jay *(Aphelocoma ultramarina)* in Texas is restricted to the Chisos Mountains of the Big Bend region. There are very few instances where they have been found elsewhere in the state.   *Photograph by Mark W. Lockwood.*

98. Like Brown Jay, the Tamaulipas Crow *(Corvus imparatus)* is represented in the United States only by a handful of individuals restricted to the southernmost tip of Texas. After the initial discovery of this species in Texas in 1968 numbers grew until several hundred wintered each year at the Brownsville Sanitary Landfill. However, the population has declined precipitously over the last decade, and in recent years only 2 to 6 birds per year have been noted.
Photograph by Mark W. Lockwood.

99. The range of the Cave Swallow *(Petrochelidon fulva)* has spread rapidly across the state in the past 20 years. This species was once found only in natural caves and sinkholes but now utilizes man-made structures as nesting habitat. They can be found as far north as the Oklahoma border and are one of the most common breeding swallows in many areas of the state where it was absent less than two decades ago.
Photograph by Mark W. Lockwood.

100. Black-crested Titmouse *(Baeolophus atricistatus)* replaces the closely related Tufted Titmouse in the more arid western half of the state. It is smaller than Tufted, and some authors divide the Texas population into at least three distinct subspecies. *Photograph by Steve Bentsen.*

101. Black-tailed Gnatcatcher *(Polioptila melanura)* is by weight the smallest passerine found in Texas. Unlike its cousin the Blue-gray Gnatcatcher, its preferred habitat is desert scrub and brushy sides of canyons and ravines from the Tran-Pecos southeastward through the western South Texas Brush Country. *Photograph by Mark W. Lockwood.*

102. Clay-colored Robin *(Turdus grayi)* is a tropical species that has been found with increasing frequency in the Lower Rio Grande Valley in recent years. While reported as early as 1940, the first documented record of this species in Texas did not occur until 1959. Clay-colored Robins are now year-round residents with breeding confirmed in many locations.
Photograph by Greg W. Lasley.

103. The White-throated Robin *(Turdus assimilis)* is a tropical species that has visited the Lower Rio Grande Valley on three occasions. Surprisingly, for two of these records there were two individuals present. This one was photographed at Bentsen–Rio Grande Valley State Park on 27 March 1998.
Photograph by Mark W. Lockwood.

104. Prior to the 1990s, there were only two documented records of Rufous-backed Robin *(Turdus rufopalliatus)* for Texas. Since 1992 there have been nine records, including three from the South Texas Brush Country. This individual was at Sarita, Kenedy County, for the first two weeks of February 2000. *Photograph by Jimmy McHaney.*

105. Varied Thrush *(Ixoreus naevius)* is a casual winter visitor to the state from northwestern North America. Although it was first reported as early as 1935, the first documented record is from 1978. This beautiful male was at Davis Mountains State Park, Jeff Davis County, from 8 to 27 March 1992. *Photograph by Jim Flynn.*

106. Aztec Thrush *(Ridgwayia pinicola)* is a denizen of the mountains of western Mexico and has been documented in Texas on four occasions. Surprisingly, two of these records are from the central coast, including this individual that was at Corpus Christi, Nueces County, on 18 May 1996.
Photograph by Steve Bentsen.

107. The Long-billed Thrasher *(Toxostoma longirostre)* is a common component of the avifauna of the South Texas Brush Country. They are somewhat shy and retiring in nature and are more often heard than seen.   *Photograph by Tim Cooper.*

108. During the late winter and early spring, Crissal Thrashers *(Toxostoma crissale)* often sing from exposed perches within their desert scrub habitat. During the rest of the year, they are very shy and often extremely difficult to find to the disappointment of many who seek them. *Photograph by Kelly B. Bryan.*

Valley. Another three records exist from the Trans-Pecos (Culberson and El Paso Counties). Northern Shrikes are seldom found in the Panhandle prior to mid-November, and most depart in February.

Family Vireonidae: Vireos

WHITE-EYED VIREO *Vireo griseus* (Boddaert)

Common to uncommon migrant throughout the eastern two-thirds of the state. Farther west, White-eyed Vireo is a very rare spring and casual fall migrant to Lubbock, Midland, Potter, and Randall Counties and the eastern Trans-Pecos. This species is also a common to locally abundant summer resident through the eastern two-thirds of the state west to the central Edwards Plateau. They are uncommon and somewhat local westward through the Concho Valley and western Edwards Plateau to the Devils River drainage, Val Verde County, and more local along the Rio Grande and Pecos River in Terrell County. This species is a locally uncommon to rare winter resident from the southern Pineywoods westward to the Balcones Escarpment and uncommon to common south of the Edwards Plateau. Recent observations indicate that they are also locally uncommon winter residents along the Devils River in Val Verde County.

BELL'S VIREO *Vireo bellii* Audubon

Locally common summer resident in the Trans-Pecos and eastward to the eastern Edwards Plateau. Bells' Vireo is a rare to very rare, and for the most part local, summer resident eastward through the Pineywoods, north to the eastern Panhandle, and south through the South Texas Brush Country. There are scattered summer records from the eastern Panhandle, but evidence of nesting is generally lacking (Seyffert 2001). Bell's Vireo is a rare to uncommon migrant through most of the state. They are very rare winter visitors in the Lower Rio Grande Valley, and there is one documented winter record from El Paso County. The population of Bell's Vireos has declined in Texas over the past two decades. This is particularly evident in the eastern half of the state where it is now a rare and local breeder. Brood parasitism by Brown-headed Cowbirds *(Molothrus ater)* likely plays an important role in this decline.

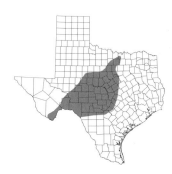

BLACK-CAPPED VIREO *Vireo atricapilla* Woodhouse

Rare to locally uncommon summer resident from Brewster County eastward across the Edwards Plateau and north to Taylor and Palo Pinto Counties. A small population of Black-capped Vireos has recently been discovered in Montague County. The stronghold for the species in Texas appears to be on the southwestern Edwards Plateau. Black-capped Vireos are rarely reported during migration, but a few reports have come from outside the breeding range. Most notable are individuals found in Cameron, Jeff Davis, Kleberg, Midland, Presidio, and Starr Counties. There is an additional report of nesting Black-capped Vireos from Bastrop County, including the collection of the eggs (Singley 1887). The location of the specimens, if they still exist, is unknown, and there is no other evidence of this species occurring in Bastrop County. Nesting birds arrive on the breeding grounds in late March and early April, and most depart by early September. This species is a habitat specialist that requires open shrublands where foliage is present down to ground level. Heavy browsing by livestock or deer changes the structure of the vegetation making habitat unsuitable for nesting. Management of Brown-headed Cowbirds *(Molothrus ater)* plays an important role in the protection of this Endangered Species.

GRAY VIREO *Vireo vicinior* Coues

Uncommon to rare, but local, summer resident from the southern Trans-Pecos east to the western Edwards Plateau. They are local nesters in the Guadalupe Mountains but are absent from the Davis Mountains, except as migrants. Gray Vireo is a rare winter resident in southern Brewster and Presidio Counties and may occur in Terrell County as a winter visitor. Vagrants have been found in Coke, El Paso, Kerr, and Randall Counties. This species appears to have greatly expanded its range in Texas in the past 30 years (Bryan and Lockwood 2000). The first record from east of the Pecos River was obtained in 1974 (Pulich and Parrot 1977). It wasn't until the mid-1980s that Gray Vireos were discovered to be locally uncommon on the southwestern Edwards Plateau.

YELLOW-THROATED VIREO *Vireo flavifrons* Vieillot

Common to uncommon summer resident in the eastern third of the state north of the Coastal Prairies. Yellow-throated

Vireos reach the western edge of their range in Texas in the riparian woodlands that line the rivers of the Edwards Plateau. They nest as far west as the Devils River, Val Verde County, and very locally along the Pecos River drainage. Yellow-throated Vireo is also a rare summer resident in riparian habitats along the Concho River as far west as Tom Green County (Maxwell 1979). South of the Edwards Plateau, they occupy riparian woodlands of the Nueces, Frio, and Sabinal Rivers. This species is an uncommon migrant through the eastern half of the state, becoming increasingly rare westward. They are casual to very rare in winter in the Lower Rio Grande Valley.

PLUMBEOUS VIREO *Vireo plumbeus* Coues

Common summer resident in the Davis and Guadalupe Mountains of the central Trans-Pecos and rare and local summer resident in the Chisos Mountains. Plumbeous Vireo is a common migrant throughout the Trans-Pecos and an uncommon to rare migrant east through the High Plains and western Edwards Plateau. This species is a rare winter visitor throughout the Trans-Pecos. Migrants and winter visitors have been found along the coast with scattered records inland. Plumbeous Vireo is one of three species that were formerly treated as subspecies of the Solitary Vireo *(V. solitarius)*.

CASSIN'S VIREO *Vireo cassinii* Xántus de Vasey

Uncommon to rare migrant through the western half of the Trans-Pecos, becoming very rare to casual farther east. Cassin's Vireo is more common during fall migration and has been found with regularity east to the western High Plains. This species is apparently a very rare winter visitor to the state. There is a specimen from Big Bend National Park, Brewster County, and several reports from the Trans-Pecos, Lower Rio Grande Valley, and along the coast. Cassin's Vireo is part of the Solitary Vireo complex. Observers should be aware of the similarity between Cassin's and other members of this complex and the identification challenge these similar species represent (Heindel 1996).

BLUE-HEADED VIREO *Vireo solitarius* (Wilson)

Common to uncommon migrant east of the Pecos River, becoming a rare to casual migrant in the Trans-Pecos. Blue-

headed Vireo is an uncommon winter resident in much of the eastern two-thirds of the state. Spring migrants are present from late March to mid-May. Returning autumn migrants arrive as early as late August but typically are not present until after mid-September. This species is the most likely member of the Solitary Vireo complex to be encountered east of the Pecos River.

HUTTON'S VIREO *Vireo huttoni* Cassin

Locally common summer and uncommon winter resident in the Davis and Chisos Mountains of the Trans-Pecos. Hutton's Vireos are very rare in the Trans-Pecos away from the breeding range, with four records from El Paso County. Scattered summer and winter records exist for the Guadalupe Mountains, where nesting has been confirmed. A pair of Hutton's Vireos was discovered nesting in Real County in 1990 (Lasley and Gee 1991), providing the first record for the Edwards Plateau. Interestingly, this species has been found with increasing frequency at all seasons on the plateau since the spring of 1999. Two were found east of the Balcones Escarpment in Bastrop County between 25 February and 10 March 2001. This unexpected increase in sightings suggests that Hutton's Vireo could be a very low-density resident on the Edwards Plateau.

WARBLING VIREO *Vireo gilvus* (Vieillot)

Uncommon to rare summer resident in the Davis and Guadalupe Mountains and sporadic nester in the Chisos Mountains of the Trans-Pecos. This vireo is also an uncommon to rare summer resident from the eastern Panhandle east, very locally, across north-central Texas. There are also isolated breeding records south to Travis County. Warbling Vireo is an uncommon to common migrant throughout the state and as such is encountered between mid-April and early June and from late August to early October. In the Trans-Pecos migrants are found as early as the end of July. Recent studies have shown that there are two distinctive groups within the Warbling Vireo (AOU 1998). It has been suggested that these two groups should be recognized as distinct species, Eastern *(V. gilvus)* and Western *(V. swainsonii)* Warbling-Vireos. These two groups differ morphologically, vocally, genetically, and ecologically.

If split in the future, breeding populations in the Trans-Pecos would be included in the Western Warbling-Vireo whereas breeding populations found elsewhere in the state would fall under the Eastern Warbling-Vireo.

PHILADELPHIA VIREO *Vireo philadelphicus* (Cassin)

Uncommon spring and rare fall migrant in the eastern third of the state. This species is most commonly encountered along the coast. Migrants have been reported from all areas of the state but are rare to very rare west of the Blackland Prairies. Spring migrants pass through Texas between early April and late May with the peak of migration from late April to early May. Fall migrants are present from late August through October.

RED-EYED VIREO *Vireo olivaceus* (Linnaeus)

Common to uncommon summer resident in the eastern half of the state. This species reaches the western edge of its breeding range in Texas in the riparian woodlands that line the rivers of the Edwards Plateau. The San Antonio River in Victoria County on the central coast marks the southern extent of the breeding range. During migration, Red-eyed Vireos can be found in all areas of the state but are rare in the western half. Spring migrants first appear in early March and fall migrants may linger until late October.

Review Species

YELLOW-GREEN VIREO *Vireo flavoviridis* (Cassin)

Casual spring migrant to the coast and very rare summer resident in the Lower Rio Grande Valley. There are 38 documented records for the state. The only recent successful nesting records are from Laguna Atascosa National Wildlife Refuge, Cameron County, during the summers of 1988 and 1989. Documented records of this species have increased dramatically since 1997. Records of migrants found away from the Lower Rio Grande Valley fall between 15 April and 28 May. Isolated summer records come from Brewster and Travis Counties. Despite the rarity of this species, Yellow-green Vireos are often reported without supporting documentation. The 38 reports of Yellow-green Vireos from prior to the development of the Review List in 1987 have no documentation on file at Texas A&M University.

BLACK-WHISKERED VIREO *Vireo altiloquus* (Vieillot)

Casual spring and accidental fall visitor along the upper and central coasts. Texas has 19 documented records of this species with 11 from Galveston County. Most records are from the spring and presumably represent spring migrants that over-shoot the western edge of their regular breeding range along the eastern Gulf Coast. These sightings range from early April to late May, and most birds remained for only one or two days. The two accepted fall records come from High Island, Galveston County, with two individuals present from 20 August to 2 October 1989 (TBRC 1989-195) and a single bird there from 23 to 24 August 1991 (TBRC 1991-112).

YUCATAN VIREO *Vireo magister* (Lawrence)

Accidental. The only record for Texas was a single bird near Gilchrist, Galveston County, discovered in the spring of 1984. This unexpected first record for the United States (Morgan et al. 1985) remains the only record from north of the Yucatan Peninsula, Mexico.

28 APR.–27 MAY 1984, GILCHRIST, GALVESTON CO. (TPRF 318)

Family Corvidae: Jays and Crows

STELLER'S JAY *Cyanocitta stelleri* (Gmelin)

Locally common resident of the Davis and Guadalupe Mountains of the Trans-Pecos and an irregular winter visitor to El Paso County. Winter invasions occasionally occur in the remainder of the Trans-Pecos and, on rare occasions, include the South Plains and Panhandle. Stray Steller's Jays reached the western Edwards Plateau during such an invasion in the winter of 1972–73. Breeding populations in the Trans-Pecos are found above 5,000 feet, although they occasionally descend to lower elevations in the fall and winter.

BLUE JAY *Cyanocitta cristata* (Linnaeus)

Common resident in the eastern half of the state, west to the western Edwards Plateau, Permian Basin, and eastern High Plains, and west along the Canadian River drainage to Hartley County. In the western third of this range, particularly in the High Plains and Edwards Plateau, Blue Jays

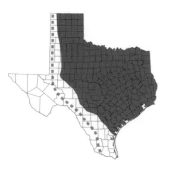

are largely restricted to urban areas and are found elsewhere primarily during migration and winter irruptions. This species is a regular winter visitor in the northwestern Trans-Pecos to Pecos, Reeves County, and occurs irregularly to Brewster, El Paso, and Jeff Davis Counties. Blue Jays are very rare south of the Nueces River, although a nesting pair was discovered in Hidalgo County in 1999 (Brush 2000). In some years, massive migrations are noted throughout the state, with loose flocks of up to 4,000 birds reported from the eastern third of the state.

GREEN JAY *Cyanocorax yncas* (Boddaert)

Common to uncommon resident from the Lower Rio Grande Valley north to Live Oak, Bee, and southern Maverick Counties. Green Jays have been found with increasing regularity during the winter north of their breeding range to southern Val Verde, Kinney, and Uvalde Counties. These winter incursions may be the prelude to a range expansion northward. Wandering individuals have been reported just north of the normal range to Bexar, Victoria, and Calhoun Counties, while vagrants have been found in Brazos, Johnson, and Midland Counties.

BROWN JAY *Cyanocorax morio* (Wagler)

Brown Jays maintain a very precarious foothold in Texas and the United States. These jays were formerly uncommon and local residents along the Rio Grande in Starr County, between Rio Grande City and San Ygnacio. Only a small population persists, reportedly fewer than 12 individuals, centered around the villages of Chapeño and Salineño. Observations of these birds show that they frequently cross to and from Mexico. While it is unknown whether this species continues to breed in the United States, immature Brown Jays are routinely seen within this small population. There is also a specimen and egg set from Cameron County (Hubbard and Niles 1975).

WESTERN SCRUB-JAY

Aphelocoma californica (Vigors)

Common resident on the Edwards Plateau west through the mountains of the central Trans-Pecos north of the Big Bend region. Western Scrub-Jays are rare to locally uncommon residents in the canyonlands of the southern Pan-

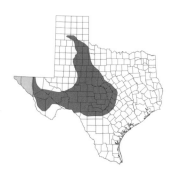

handle, south through the western Rolling Plains. This species is irruptive and irregular elsewhere in the Trans-Pecos, Rolling Plains, and High Plains. Scrub-Jays are very rare to casual visitors east of the Balcones Escarpment and in recent decades appear to be declining in portions of the easternmost Edwards Plateau, possibly due to habitat loss within the greater Austin and San Antonio areas. An incursion of Western Scrub-Jays into the northern South Texas Brush Country in the fall of 1994 was unprecedented.

MEXICAN JAY *Aphelocoma ultramarina* (Bonaparte)

Common resident of the Chisos Mountains of Big Bend National Park. Mexican Jays very rarely wander into the surrounding lowlands, and only two documented records exist away from Big Bend National Park. One was collected near Alpine, Brewster County, on 24 March 1935, and another was discovered in El Paso County on 24 and 25 January 2001. The El Paso record is also notable in that it represents the first Texas occurrence of *A. u. arizonae,* which is typically found in southeastern Arizona and southwestern New Mexico. The Mexican Jays in the Chisos Mountains belong to the subspecies *A. u. couchii.* This species was formerly called Gray-breasted Jay.

PINYON JAY *Gymnorhinus cyanocephalus* Wied

Pinyon Jay is a highly irruptive species to Texas, typically during the fall and winter. Such incursions occurred regularly through the 1970s and 1980s, but more than a decade passed before another large irruption took place in the winter of 2000–2001. These irruptions often involved large flocks and are usually confined to the Trans-Pecos but can occur on the High Plains. A few individuals may linger into the summer, but nesting activities have never been reported.

Review Species

CLARK'S NUTCRACKER
Nucifraga columbiana (Wilson)

Very rare to casual winter visitor to the Trans-Pecos, High Plains, and western Rolling Plains. Texas has 21 documented records of Clark's Nutcracker. Most reports involve winter incursions that typically coincide with influxes of Steller's or Pinyon Jays. One such event took place during the fall and winter of 2000–2001 when small numbers of

Clark's Nutcrackers were present in the Trans-Pecos. There is also a remarkable record from the Upper Texas Coast from the fall of 2000. The largest incursion took place during the fall and winter of 1972–73 in the Panhandle, South Plains, and Trans-Pecos. During this invasion, more than 30 were reported from the Panhandle alone (Seyffert 2001). The only summer records for the state involve two specimens collected on 1 June 1969 in the Guadalupe Mountains, Culberson County, and six birds that lingered in the Davis Mountains until 19 June 2003. There are 20 reports of Clark's Nutcrackers from prior to the development of the Review List in 1987 for which there is no documentation on file at Texas A&M University.

Review Species

BLACK-BILLED MAGPIE *Pica hudsonia* (Sabine)

Accidental. Texas has but four documented records, despite the fact that magpies occur regularly in the Oklahoma Panhandle and northeastern New Mexico. Three of these records are from the extreme northern Panhandle, while the fourth is from El Paso County. All are from early winter to early spring with dates ranging from 5 December to 4 April. Black-billed Magpies have also been found well to the east in Dallas, Hays, and Travis Counties, but questions of natural origin have precluded them from being accepted by the TBRC. There are over a dozen undocumented reports, primarily from the Panhandle, of this species prior to the formation of the TBRC.

27 DEC. 1983, TEXLINE, DALLAM CO. (TBRC 1984-11)
4–6 AND 17 FEB. 1990, EL PASO, EL PASO CO.
  (TBRC 1990-28; TPRF 890)
5 DEC. 1997–16 JAN. 1998, NEAR GRUVER, HANSFORD CO.
  (TBRC 1998-5)
5 DEC. 1999–4 APR. 2000, NEAR GRUVER, HANSFORD CO.
  (TBRC 1999-106; TPRF 1855)

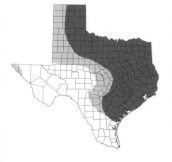

AMERICAN CROW *Corvus brachyrhynchos* Brehm

Common to abundant resident in the eastern half of the state west to the central Panhandle and to the eastern edge of the Edwards Plateau. American Crows are found on the central coast south to Victoria and Refugio Counties. They are rare to locally uncommon migrants and winter visitors to the remainder of the High Plains, western Rolling Plains, eastern Edwards Plateau, and eastern parts of the South Texas Brush Country. American Crows are also common to uncommon and local winter visitors in El Paso and Hudspeth Counties. Large numbers of this species move into Texas from states to the north to increase the overall Texas populations during the winter. Formerly, flocks of many thousands were noted in agricultural areas, especially coming to and from roost sites; however, such flocks are seldom noted today.

Review Species

TAMAULIPAS CROW *Corvus imparatus* Peters

Very rare to casual visitor to southern Cameron County, primarily in the vicinity of the Brownsville Sanitary Landfill. Although formerly a common winter resident and very rare summer resident, this species now barely maintains a toehold in Texas. A single pair nested in Cameron County in 2001 and represented the total known number of individuals in the United States, although six were present in 2002. This species was first reported in 1968 and documented by specimens in 1972. In the fall of 2000, the TBRC voted to place Tamaulipas Crow on the Review List in an effort to maintain a record of its presence in the state. This species was formerly called Mexican Crow and was considered conspecific with Sinaloa Crow, *C. sinaloae*.

FISH CROW *Corvus ossifragus* Wilson

Uncommon resident along the Sabine River north to Newton County and in northeast Texas along the Red River drainage west to Delta and Fannin Counties (White 2000). Fish Crows have expanded their range during summer westward along the Sulphur River to Delta and Hopkins Counties. In southeast Texas, they are common residents in Jefferson and Orange Counties and rare visitors to Galveston, Harris, and Walker Counties. In northeast Texas, wandering individuals have been noted in Gregg, Hunt, Marion, Rains, Rusk, and Wood Counties. Strecker (1912) did not include this species in his statewide checklist.

CHIHUAHUAN RAVEN *Corvus cryptoleucus* Couch

Uncommon to common resident in the western half of the state from the Panhandle south to the northwestern Edwards Plateau, and from Dimmit and LaSalle Counties in the South Texas Brush Country south to the Lower Rio Grande Valley. On the remainder of the western Edwards Plateau this raven is a common migrant with a few scat-

tered nesting records southeast to Kerr County. In the Trans-Pecos, these ravens are primarily migrants through the Guadalupe Mountains and from the Davis Mountains southward to southern Brewster and Presidio Counties. Chihuahuan Ravens have declined in recent decades from Wichita County southward through Throckmorton County, where they are now rare to locally uncommon summer residents. They are particularly common during the winter in the South Texas Brush Country and Lower Rio Grande Valley. This species is also a casual visitor east to Aransas, Caldwell, Hays, and Nueces Counties, with reports from the upper coast from Galveston and Jefferson Counties. In the fall, they typically stage in large concentrations prior to moving to their wintering grounds. This species was formerly known as White-necked Raven.

COMMON RAVEN *Corvus corax* Linneaus

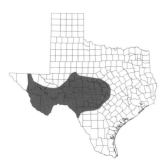

Uncommon to common resident in the mountains of the Trans-Pecos and east through the Edwards Plateau. This species is a rare winter and casual summer visitor to the High Plains. Vagrant Common Ravens have been noted in the Rolling Plains, South Texas Brush Country, and Blackland Prairies. Perhaps the most unexpected record was one discovered at Galveston in November 1998. Almost all reports of the species east of its normal range are from the winter.

Family Alaudidae: Larks

HORNED LARK *Eremophila alpestris* (Linnaeus)

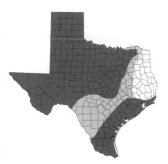

Common to uncommon resident in the Trans-Pecos, from the Panhandle south to the Concho Valley, and along the coast, although much more widespread in winter. Horned Larks are also rare to locally uncommon summer residents across the eastern Rolling Plains to northeast Texas south to Williamson County, as well as on the northern Edwards Plateau. This species is a locally common migrant and winter resident in central Texas, primarily in the Blackland Prairies and Post Oak Savannahs, south to Guadalupe County, where they often associate with longspur flocks. Horned Larks have recently been confirmed as breeding in northeast Texas and are very rare and local in the Pineywoods. Overall distribution in the state is rather patchy, so breeding in many regions is localized. This is especially true in the central third of the state, including most of the Edwards Plateau.

Family Hirundinidae: Martins and Swallows

PURPLE MARTIN *Progne subis* (Linnaeus)

Common to uncommon summer resident in most of the state east of the Pecos River. Purple Martins are rare and local on the western High Plains but absent from the westernmost portion of the Panhandle. This species is a very rare to casual migrant in the Trans-Pecos. Purple Martins are common to locally abundant migrants in the eastern two-thirds of the state, especially in the fall when they congregate in enormous roosts, often consisting of many thousands of birds. In spring, migration and arrival dates range from early January to mid-April and in fall from early July to early October. Migrants linger on rare occasions into the early winter along the coast and in the Lower Rio Grande Valley.

GRAY-BREASTED MARTIN *Progne chalybea* (Gmelin)

Review Species

Accidental. Texas has two documented records of this species. Both are from the 1880s and represented by specimens. The population of Gray-breasted Martins in northeastern Mexico is migratory, and this species might be expected to occur again. However, the similarity to female Purple Martins makes identification in the field very difficult.

25 APR. 1880, RIO GRANDE CITY, STARR CO. (AMNH 89806)
18 MAY 1889, HIDALGO, HIDALGO CO. (AMNH 84808)

TREE SWALLOW *Tachycineta bicolor* (Vieillot)

Common migrant throughout the state, often locally abundant along the coast. Tree Swallows are rare to uncommon winter residents in the southern half of the state, especially along the coast, while very rare and irregular from the Trans-Pecos eastward through the Concho Valley and Edwards Plateau. This species is a rare to locally uncommon summer resident in northeast Texas, with isolated breeding records south to Bell, McLennan, and Nacogdoches Counties. Farther west, nesting has been documented in Hemphill County in the northeastern Panhandle. This swallow formerly bred as far south as Bexar and Jackson Counties.

Typical migration periods are from mid-February to mid-May and from early August to mid-November.

VIOLET-GREEN SWALLOW
Tachycineta thalassina (Swainson)

Uncommon to common summer resident in the mountains of the Trans-Pecos. Violet-green Swallows are common migrants in the central and western Trans-Pecos, becoming rare in the eastern third of the region. This species is a very rare migrant elsewhere in the state with the majority of reports occurring in the fall. Migration falls between mid-March and mid-May and from early September to early October. Violet-green Swallow is a very rare winter visitor in the Trans-Pecos, usually occurring along the Rio Grande.

NORTHERN ROUGH-WINGED SWALLOW
Stelgidopteryx serripennis (Audubon)

Rare to locally uncommon summer resident in most of the state. This species is a common migrant throughout, occurring between mid-March and early May and from early August to late October. Rough-winged Swallows are rare to uncommon winter residents in the southern third of the state, including southern Brewster and Presidio Counties in the Trans-Pecos, and casual elsewhere.

BANK SWALLOW *Riparia riparia* (Linnaeus)

Locally uncommon summer resident along the Rio Grande from Cameron to Terrell County. There are scattered breeding records from the Edwards Plateau, east to Bell and Hays Counties and possibly northward. Bank Swallows are common to uncommon migrants throughout the state with migration dates falling between late March and early May and from mid-August to mid-October. They are accidental along the coast and in the Lower Rio Grande Valley during the winter.

CLIFF SWALLOW *Petrochelidon pyrrhonota* Vieillot

Common to locally abundant summer resident throughout the state. Cliff Swallows may be the most common breeding swallow in Texas, now nesting commonly in areas where they were formerly rare or absent. They are uncommon to abundant migrants throughout the state. Migrants pass through between mid-March and mid-May and early

August to late October. Cave Swallows may displace Cliffs locally in the southern half of the state.

CAVE SWALLOW *Petrochelidon fulva* Vieillot

Cave Swallows have greatly expanded their range during the past 15 to 20 years. This species once nested only in limestone caves but now uses a variety of man-made structures. They are common to locally abundant summer residents in the southern half of the state, north through the Edwards Plateau to the southern Rolling Plains and west through the Trans-Pecos. Cave Swallows are uncommon to locally common eastward through the southern Post Oak Savannahs. This species is rare to very rare, but increasing, through north-central Texas north to near the Red River. They are rare and local during the summer on the upper coast to Jefferson County. Cave Swallows are rare to uncommon in the southern third of the state in winter north to Bexar and Val Verde Counties, rarely to Bell and Williamson Counties. Migration ranges from early February to mid-April and from mid-August to late October.

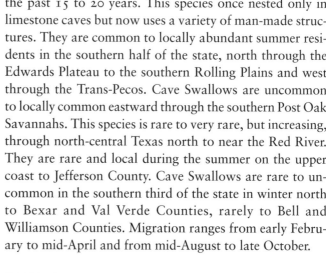

BARN SWALLOW *Hirundo rustica* Linneaus

Rare to common summer resident in every region of the state. Barn Swallows are common to abundant migrants throughout. Migrants pass through Texas between mid-March and mid-May and from mid-August to late October. They are rare to very rare winter stragglers along the coast and in the South Texas Brush Country, very rare north and east of the Balcones Escarpment to about McLennan County. These individuals linger into the early winter but rarely actually overwinter.

Family Paridae: Chickadees and Titmice

CAROLINA CHICKADEE *Poecile carolinensis* (Audubon)

Common resident in the eastern half of the state west through the eastern Rolling Plains and west-central Edwards Plateau, south to about Nueces County on the Coastal Bend. This species is uncommon to common in the eastern Panhandle and along the Canadian River valley as far west as Hartley County. Carolina Chickadees are very rare visitors south and west of their breeding range. The southernmost record is from within a few hundred yards of the Rio Grande in southern Cameron County. Carolina Chickadees are endemic of the southeastern United States and have never been documented in Mexico.

Review Species

BLACK-CAPPED CHICKADEE
Poecile atricapillus (Linneaus)

Accidental. Texas has only one documented record. Black-capped Chickadees were reported from the northeastern quarter of the state on several occasions between 1880 and 1920, and one was supposedly collected from Navarro County in 1880, but the location of this specimen is not known by the TBRC. This species has been confirmed in the western Oklahoma Panhandle, and observers should be alert to its possible occurrence in the Texas Panhandle.

10 APR. 1881, EL PASO CO. (TBRC 1995-35; TPRF 1327)

MOUNTAIN CHICKADEE *Poecile gambeli* (Ridgway)

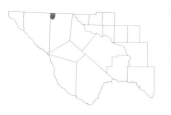

Locally common to uncommon resident in the higher elevations of the Davis and Guadalupe Mountains of the Trans-Pecos. Some Mountain Chickadees move to lower elevations within these ranges during the winter, including into desert scrublands surrounding the Guadalupe Mountains. This species is an uncommon and irregular fall and rare winter visitor to the western Trans-Pecos, particularly in El Paso County. Mountain Chickadee is a casual fall and winter visitor to the western Panhandle and northwestern South Plains.

JUNIPER TITMOUSE *Baeolophus ridgwayi* (Richmond)

Locally uncommon resident in the foothills of the Guadalupe Mountains, and possibly in the Delaware Mountains, in the Trans-Pecos. Juniper Titmouse is accidental in other areas of the western Trans-Pecos and western Panhandle. During the winter of 2000–2001, this species was found in El Paso, Dallam, Jeff Davis, and Potter Counties. Although Juniper Titmouse was known to occur in the Guadalupe Mountains for decades, the first breeding record was not confirmed until 1973. Juniper Titmouse was formerly known as Plain Titmouse and considered conspecific with the Oak Titmouse *(B. inornatus)*.

TUFTED TITMOUSE *Baeolophus bicolor* (Linnaeus)

Common resident of the eastern third of the state. This species is found west to the eastern edge of the Rolling Plains, the Balcones Escarpment, and south to Refugio County on the central coast. Tufted and Black-crested Titmice were formerly considered conspecific (AOU 1998). There is a narrow region where the ranges of these species overlap, forming a hybrid zone that extends from western north-central Texas southward, just east of the Balcones Escarpment to the central coast. While the two groups are genetically distinct (AOU 1998), they interbreed freely in this area, and hybrids outnumber either of the parental species. The hybrid zone appears to be about 15 to 25 miles in width. The appearance of hybrid offspring is variable, but most have a chestnut patch on the forehead.

BLACK-CRESTED TITMOUSE
Baeolophus atricristatus Cassin

Common resident in the western two-thirds of the state. Black-crested Titmouse is found from the Lower Rio Grande Valley northward through the Edwards Plateau to the northern Rolling Plains. The eastern edge of the range extends from along the San Antonio River on the central coast northward to just east of the Balcones Escarpment and on to Clay County on the Red River. This species has a more localized distribution in the Trans-Pecos, including much of the Stockton Plateau and the Davis, Del Norte, Chisos, and Chinati Mountains. This titmouse is an irregular visitor to the High Plains and the Guadalupe Mountains. Hybrids with the Tufted Titmouse are common in a narrow zone of overlap (see Tufted Titmouse account). Black-crested Titmice are typically smaller than their eastern counterpart.

Family Remizidae: Verdin

VERDIN *Auriparus flaviceps* (Sundevall)

Uncommon to common resident from the Lower Rio Grande Valley north to Briscoe County in the southeastern Panhandle and west through the Trans-Pecos. Verdins are found along the coast as far north as western Calhoun County. The eastern edge of their range roughly follows a line from western Calhoun County to Travis County north to Clay County. Vagrants have been reported from Bastrop County (Oberholser 1974), and, until fairly recently, Verdins were residents in Palo Duro Canyon in Randall County.

Family Aegithalidae: Bushtits

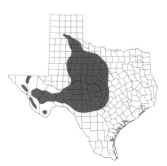

BUSHTIT *Psaltriparus minimus* (Townsend)

Uncommon to common resident from the southern Panhandle south through the Edwards Plateau and west into the Trans-Pecos. This species formerly occurred east to Dallas County (Pulich 1988). In the Trans-Pecos, Bushtits can be locally abundant, occurring in all areas containing oak-juniper habitat west to eastern Hudspeth County. There is one nesting record from Hemphill County in the northeastern Panhandle, and a stray was found in Dallam County in the northwestern Panhandle. Populations in the Trans-Pecos, and to a lesser extent on the Edwards Plateau, exhibit polymorphism. First-year males frequently have black auriculars and were formerly considered a separate species, the Black-eared Bushtit.

Family Sittidae: Nuthatches

RED-BREASTED NUTHATCH
Sitta canadensis Linnaeus

This species is highly irruptive in fall and winter throughout the state, although it seldom reaches the southern South Texas Brush Country. In some years, virtually no reports are received, while in others the species is fairly common. Red-breasted Nuthatches are generally a rare and irregular winter visitor to the Trans-Pecos, except at upper elevations in the Guadalupe Mountains where they are uncommon. Nesting was documented in the Guadalupe Mountains in 1994 and 2003, indicating possible low-density summer residency.

WHITE-BREASTED NUTHATCH
Sitta carolinensis Latham

Common to uncommon resident in the Chisos, Davis, and Guadalupe Mountains of the Trans-Pecos. White-breasted Nuthatch is also a locally uncommon resident in northeast

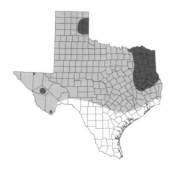

Texas, becoming rare to locally uncommon in the central and southern Pineywoods, as well as the eastern Panhandle. This species is very rare and local in the Post Oak Savannah south to Gonzales and Travis Counties. They were formerly summer residents across north-central Texas. There are isolated historical breeding records from Tom Green and Kerr Counties. White-breasted Nuthatches are rare to very rare migrants and winter visitors to the northern half of the state away from the areas with resident populations.

PYGMY NUTHATCH *Sitta pygmaea* Vigors

Uncommon resident at upper elevations in the Guadalupe Mountains of the Trans-Pecos. This species is also present, although rare, in similar habitats in the Davis Mountains. Pygmy Nuthatches are casual winter visitors to the Chisos Mountains, El Paso County, and the western Panhandle and accidental on the South Plains. An unexpected winter record was provided by a specimen collected from Dallas County on 31 December 1966 (Pulich 1988).

BROWN-HEADED NUTHATCH *Sitta pusilla* Latham

Locally common to rare resident in the Pineywoods. This species is largely confined to mature pine and pine-hardwood forests. The Brown-headed Nuthatch's range extends from Bowie County in the extreme northeast to Chambers, Grimes, and Harris Counties in the south. Local populations of this nuthatch are adversely impacted by the removal of older, large pines that serve as potential nesting sites.

Family Certhiidae: Creepers

BROWN CREEPER *Certhia americana* Bonaparte

Uncommon to rare migrant and winter resident through the northern three-quarters of the state. Brown Creeper is rare to very rare in the southern half of the South Texas Brush Country. This species is an uncommon summer resident in the Guadalupe Mountains. There has been at least one summer sighting in the Davis Mountains (Peterson et al. 1991), but no nesting activities have been observed. Fall migrants arrive in the state in late October, and most have departed by late April.

Family Troglodytidae: Wrens

CACTUS WREN

Campylorhynchus brunneicapillus (Lafresnaye)

Uncommon to locally common resident from the Lower Rio Grande Valley, north through the Edwards Plateau to the southeastern Panhandle, as well as throughout the Trans-Pecos. The eastern edge of their range generally follows a line from Refugio County on the central coast through western Bastrop County to Wichita County on the Oklahoma border. Vagrants have been reported east to Tarrant County. Although fairly common below the Caprock Escarpment, Cactus Wrens are very rare visitors away from breeding areas in the remainder of the High Plains.

ROCK WREN *Salpinctes obsoletus* (Say)

Common resident in the western half of the state east through the Rolling Plains and locally on the Edwards Plateau. In the northern half of their range, Rock Wrens retreat during mid-winter, becoming uncommon to locally rare. They are likewise rare and very local in winter in the western South Texas Brush Country south to Falcon Dam, Starr County. This species is a vagrant across much of the remainder of the state, primarily in winter. Wandering individuals are often found near large, loose rock structures such as dams and have been reported as far east as Hopkins, Nacogdoches, and Van Zandt Counties.

CANYON WREN *Catherpes mexicanus* (Swainson)

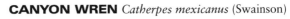

Uncommon to locally common resident in the Trans-Pecos eastward through the Edwards Plateau and southern Rolling Plains. Canyon Wrens are also common residents in the canyonlands of the southern Panhandle, although they are rare to absent in much of the northern Rolling Plains. Vagrants have been reported from Bosque, Denton, Hood, and Parker Counties in north-central Texas. This wren seldom strays far from its preferred canyon habitat.

CAROLINA WREN *Thryothorus ludovicianus* (Latham)

Common to abundant resident in the eastern two-thirds of the state. In the more arid portions of the western Rolling Plains and Edwards Plateau, this species is most often found

along riparian corridors. In the Panhandle, they occur west-ward to Oldham County in the Canadian River drainage, in the upper reaches of Palo Duro Canyon, and in Amarillo. Carolina Wrens are rare visitors, at all seasons, to the South Plains. This wren has been found with increasing regularity in the southern Trans-Pecos where a small resident population may be present in southern Brewster and Presidio Counties. Elsewhere in the region, Carolina Wrens are very rare to casual visitors.

BEWICK'S WREN *Thryomanes bewickii* (Audubon)

Uncommon to common resident in the western two-thirds of the state, east through north-central Texas and to the mouth of the Colorado River along the coast. Bewick's Wrens formerly occurred irregularly up the Coastal Prairies to San Jacinto and Jefferson Counties. This species has declined in the eastern portions of its breeding range in Texas over the last 30 to 40 years. There are two distinctive groups of Bewick's Wrens: the eastern red-backed forms and the western gray-backed forms. Red-backed individuals are rare to locally uncommon migrants and winter visitors to the eastern third of the state and have been found as far west as the eastern edge of the Edwards Plateau. Breeding populations in the remainder of the state belong to the gray-backed group.

HOUSE WREN *Troglodytes aedon* Vieillot

Common to uncommon migrant and common to rare winter resident in nearly all parts of the state. This species is most common in winter along the Coastal Prairies and in the South Texas Brush Country. As a summer resident, House Wrens are common along the Canadian River in the eastern Panhandle, becoming uncommon to rare westward to Hartley County. In the Trans-Pecos, this species is an uncommon summer resident above 7,000 feet in the Davis Mountains and rare in the Guadalupe Mountains. Migration dates fall between late March and mid-May and from mid-September to mid-November. Populations of House Wren in the highlands of Mexico are sometimes considered a separate species, the Brown-throated Wren *(T. brunneicollis)* (Brewer 2001). This form has been reported from the Lower Rio Grande Valley and Big Bend National Park, but no photographs or specimens have been obtained.

WINTER WREN *Troglodytes troglodytes* (Linnaeus)

Uncommon migrant and winter resident in the eastern two-thirds of the state, occurring most commonly in northeast and north-central Texas. Winter Wrens are found south to about the Nueces River drainage during most winters. This species is a rare to casual migrant and winter visitor through much of the remainder of the state. They are present on average between mid-October and late March. They frequent woodlots and riparian corridors and are quite vocal in the winter, especially at dawn, revealing their presence in places where they might otherwise be overlooked.

SEDGE WREN *Cistothorus platensis* (Latham)

Common to uncommon migrant through the eastern half of the state, becoming casual to rare westward across the Trans-Pecos. Sedge Wrens are uncommon to locally common winter residents along the Coastal Prairies and farther inland throughout the eastern third of the state west to the Balcones Escarpment. This wren has also been found during the winter at scattered locations across the remainder of the state and may occur as a winter resident over a larger portion of the state than is currently known. Migration is typically between late March and late May and late September to early November. There are three August records of Sedge Wren from northeast Texas (White 2002). Sedge Wren was formerly known as Short-billed Marsh Wren.

MARSH WREN *Cistothorus palustris* (Wilson)

Common winter resident in the marshes of the coast and rare to locally common winter resident elsewhere in the state. Marsh Wrens are also common to uncommon summer residents along the upper and central coasts south to Aransas County. There are isolated nesting records of this species along the Red River east of the Panhandle and along the Rio Grande in the Trans-Pecos. Fall migrants arrive in mid-September, and spring migrants are present until early May. Marsh Wren was formerly known as Long-billed Marsh Wren.

Family Cinclidae: Dippers

AMERICAN DIPPER *Cinclus mexicanus* Swainson

Casual winter visitor to the state. There are six documented records of this species for Texas; the first came from Crosby County on 2 May 1969 (TPRF 37). All records are from the western third of the state, with the exception of a 5 March 1994 record from Travis County. Dates of occurrence range between 23 October and 3 May. American Dipper has been documented from the following counties: Brewster, Crosby, Culberson (twice), El Paso, and Travis.

Family Regulidae: Kinglets

GOLDEN-CROWNED KINGLET
Regulus satrapa Lichtenstein

Uncommon to locally common migrant and winter resident in the eastern two-thirds of the state, becoming uncommon to rare westward. Golden-crowned Kinglets are casual to rare winter visitors in the southern South Texas Brush Country and Lower Rio Grande Valley. This species is somewhat irruptive: in some winters they may be scarce, and in others they may be fairly common. Golden-crowned Kinglets are generally present from mid-October to late March.

RUBY-CROWNED KINGLET
Regulus calendula (Linnaeus)

Common to abundant migrant and winter resident throughout the state. Ruby-crowned Kinglets arrive in mid-September and depart by early May. There is an extremely early fall record in early August from the Panhandle, and birds have lingered into late May on a few occasions.

Family Sylviidae:
Old World Warblers and Gnatcatchers

BLUE-GRAY GNATCATCHER
Polioptila caerulea (Linnaeus)

Rare to locally common summer resident in the eastern half of Texas, west to the Rolling Plains, and across the

Edwards Plateau to the Pecos River. Blue-gray Gnatcatchers are generally absent as a breeding species from all but the northernmost portions of the Rolling Plains and from the South Texas Brush Country, except in the oak mottes of the Coastal Sand Plain. Blue-gray Gnatcatchers are also common to uncommon summer residents in the Guadalupe and Chisos Mountains but strangely absent from the Davis Mountains. They are common to uncommon migrants throughout the state. In winter, this species is uncommon to rare on the Coastal Prairies and in the southern Trans-Pecos and common in the South Texas Brush Country. They are reported irregularly in winter from many other parts of the state, as well.

BLACK-TAILED GNATCATCHER

Polioptila melanura Lawrence

Common to uncommon resident in the western and southern Trans-Pecos and locally uncommon to rare on the southwestern Edwards Plateau, southward along the Rio Grande to the western half of the South Texas Brush Country. Black-tailed Gnatcatcher reaches the eastern limit of its range in Hidalgo County. This species is currently expanding its range eastward on the southwestern Edwards Plateau, where breeding has been noted in Edwards, Kinney, and Uvalde Counties since 1995. Vagrants have been reported from Bexar, Cameron, Duval, Goliad, Jim Wells, McMullen, and San Patricio Counties.

Family Turdidae: Thrushes

Review Species

NORTHERN WHEATEAR *Oenanthe oenanthe* (Linnaeus)

Accidental. There is one record of Northern Wheatear for the state. This species has been documented in other states along the Gulf Coast and was considered overdue for Texas at the time of its discovery.

1–6 NOV. 1994, LAGUNA ATASCOSA NWR, CAMERON CO. (TBRC 1994-165; TPRF 1310)

EASTERN BLUEBIRD *Sialia sialis* (Linnaeus)

Uncommon to locally common summer resident in the eastern half of the state to the eastern Edwards Plateau and westward along the Concho River drainage. Eastern Blue-

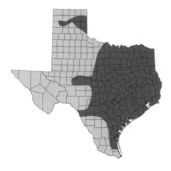

birds are also common summer residents in the eastern Panhandle westward along the Canadian River drainage to Hartley County. This species is a rare and local summer resident through the South Plains, the western Edwards Plateau, and the northern half of the South Texas Brush Country. Eastern Bluebirds have nested as far west as Brewster and Jeff Davis Counties and as far south as the Lower Rio Grande Valley. This species is a common to uncommon migrant and winter resident east of the Trans-Pecos. In the Trans-Pecos and in the Lower Rio Grande Valley, Eastern Bluebirds are rare migrants and winter residents.

WESTERN BLUEBIRD *Sialia mexicana* Swainson

Uncommon and local resident in the Davis and Guadalupe Mountains of the Trans-Pecos. Western Bluebird is an irruptive winter resident in the Trans-Pecos, although numbers can vary from locally abundant to virtually absent. This species is a rare to very rare winter visitor to the western Edwards Plateau and High Plains. Migrant Western Bluebirds arrive in late October and depart by mid-March. They are casual winter visitors farther east to the Blackland Prairies. Oberholser (1974) reports a winter sighting as far south as the Lower Rio Grande Valley but without supporting details.

MOUNTAIN BLUEBIRD *Sialia currucoides* (Bechstein)

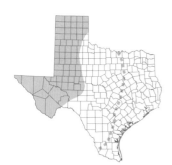

Common to uncommon migrant and winter resident in the Trans-Pecos and in the Panhandle south to the northwestern Edwards Plateau. Mountain Bluebirds are irruptive winter visitors to Texas but occur with greater predictability in the Panhandle and Trans-Pecos than farther east. This species can be virtually absent during some years and abundant during others even in the western third of the state. Mountain Bluebird is a rare winter visitor to the eastern Edwards Plateau and eastern Rolling Plains to Parker County during invasion years. There are records from virtually all areas of the state, including the Pineywoods and Lower Rio Grande Valley. This species is usually present in Texas between mid-October and late March. The single nesting record for the state, an adult with week-old fledglings, was discovered on 31 July 1995 in the Davis Mountains.

TOWNSEND'S SOLITAIRE
Myadestes townsendi (Audubon)

Common to uncommon, although irregular, migrant and winter resident in the Panhandle and Trans-Pecos. Townsend's Solitaire is an irruptive winter visitor to Texas south of the Panhandle. They are present during most years but can be virtually absent some years. During invasion years, Townsend's Solitaire is a rare winter visitor to the South Plains, Edwards Plateau, and Rolling Plains south of the Panhandle. This species has been reported east to Fannin and Hunt Counties and south to the central coast and Lower Rio Grande Valley. Townsend's Solitaires arrive in mid-October and depart in April, with a few individuals routinely lingering to mid-May.

Review Species

ORANGE-BILLED NIGHTINGALE-THRUSH
Catharus aurantiirostris (Hartlaub)

Accidental. Texas has one record of this species. An adult Orange-billed Nightingale-Thrush was mist-netted at Laguna Atascosa National Wildlife Refuge, Cameron County, in the spring of 1996 (Papish, Mays, and Brewer 1997). This record established an unexpected first for the state, as well as for the United States.

8 APR. 1996, LAGUNA ATASCOSA NWR, CAMERON CO. (TBRC 1996-59; TPRF 1493)

VEERY *Catharus fuscescens* (Stephens)

Uncommon to rare spring and very rare fall migrant in the eastern half of the state. Veery is most often encountered on the Coastal Prairies in woodland habitats. Away from the immediate coast this species is considered a rare to very rare spring migrant and a casual fall migrant. Banding data from the eastern Edwards Plateau show the species to be a rare spring migrant in central Texas (Lockwood 2001b). The few sightings from the Trans-Pecos all come from Big Bend National Park. It is possible that some of these reports actually refer to the russet-backed form of the Swainson's Thrush *(C. ustulatus).* Migrant Veeries pass through between mid-April and mid-May and from early September to late October. This species winters primarily in Brazil, and there are only two documented winter records from North America.

GRAY-CHEEKED THRUSH
Catharus minimus (Lafresnaye)

Uncommon to rare spring and very rare fall migrant in the eastern half of the state. As with the Veery, this species is most often encountered on the Coastal Prairies at stopover habitats. Away from the immediate coast this species is a rare to very rare spring migrant and a casual fall migrant. Banding data from the eastern Edwards Plateau show the species to be an occasional spring migrant in the Hill Country (Lockwood 2001b). Gray-cheeked Thrushes are present in Texas between early April and late May and from late September to early November. This species winters in northern South America, and only one documented winter record exists for the United States.

SWAINSON'S THRUSH *Catharus ustulatus* (Nuttall)

Common to uncommon spring and uncommon to rare fall migrant in the eastern half of Texas, becoming increasingly less common westward. Swainson's Thrush is probably most frequently encountered in woodland habitats along the coast but is far more likely to be observed elsewhere than Veery or Gray-cheeked Thrush. Migration periods are between early April and early June and from mid-September to early November. Swainson's Thrushes winter in South America, and there are no documented winter records from the United States. This species consists of two subspecies that were originally described as separate species, the Olive-backed Thrush *(C. swainsoni)* and the Russet-backed Thrush *(C. ustulatus)*. The regularly occurring migrants in Texas belong to the olive-backed group. Individuals of the russet-backed group may be very rare migrants through the western Trans-Pecos.

HERMIT THRUSH *Catharus guttatus* (Pallas)

Common migrant and winter resident throughout most of the state, except in winter in the Trans-Pecos, Panhandle, and South Plains where rare to uncommon. This species is an uncommon summer resident in the Davis and Guadalupe Mountains of the Trans-Pecos. There are three mid-summer records from the Panhandle, plus a reported successful nesting at Muleshoe National Wildlife Refuge, Bailey County, from 1980. Fall migrants reach Texas in mid-September, while wintering birds and spring migrants have departed by mid-May. Postbreeding dispersal from populations in the mountains accounts for the presence of Hermit Thrushes outside of breeding habitat in late summer and early fall in the Davis and Guadalupe Mountains. The Hermit Thrush is the only *Catharus* thrush expected to occur anywhere in Texas during the winter.

WOOD THRUSH *Hylocichla mustelina* (Gmelin)

Uncommon to locally common summer resident in the Pineywoods and locally uncommon to rare west to Titus and Bastrop Counties. There are also isolated breeding records from as far south as Victoria County. Wood Thrush is an uncommon to common migrant in the eastern half of the state and rare to casual in the western half. The largest concentrations of migrating birds are usually found at stopover habitats near the coast. The few isolated winter reports come from along the Coastal Prairies and the Lower Rio Grande Valley.

CLAY-COLORED ROBIN *Turdus grayi* Bonaparte

Rare resident in the Lower Rio Grande Valley. Clay-colored Robins are reported primarily from various parks in Cameron and Hidalgo Counties, but they also occur in urban areas and along the riparian corridor of the Rio Grande from Cameron County to Starr County. There are also records north to Laredo, Webb County, where nesting was documented in 2002. The population of Clay-colored Robins in the Lower Rio Grande Valley is increasing, with as many as 30 different individuals present during the spring of 2002. There are scattered winter records north of the Valley along the Coastal Prairies to Aransas County. Farther north, single records come from Huntsville, Walker County (Moldenhauer 1974), Lake Jackson, Brazoria County, and Victoria, Victoria County. A Clay-colored Robin was present in Gonzales, Gonzales County, for more than a year starting in the spring of 2001. This species was removed from the Review List in November 1998.

Review Species

WHITE-THROATED ROBIN *Turdus assimilis* Cabanis

Accidental. There are three documented records of this tropical thrush for Texas and the United States. The first was a single bird at Laguna Vista, Cameron County, discovered in 1990 (Lasley and Krzywonski 1991). The other

Review Species

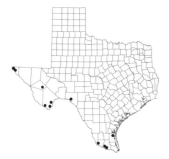

two records involved two individuals each. White-throated Robin is an uncommon resident in southern Tamaulipas and has been noted to wander during the winter in northeastern Mexico (Howell and Webb 1995).

18–25 FEB. 1990, LAGUNA VISTA, CAMERON CO. (TPRF 861)
1 FEB.–3 APR. 1998, BENTSEN–RIO GRANDE VALLEY SP, HIDALGO
  CO. (TBRC 1998-10; TPRF 1700)
1–12 MAR. 1998, SANTA ANA NWR, HIDALGO CO.
  (TBRC 1998-23; TPRF 1701)

RUFOUS-BACKED ROBIN
Turdus rufopalliatus Lafresnaye

Casual winter visitor to the Trans-Pecos and the South Texas Brush Country. Texas has 11 documented records; all occur between late October and mid-February. Rufous-backed Robin is a rare fall and winter visitor to southern Arizona, less regularly to southern New Mexico, and might be expected to occur on a more regular basis in the western Trans-Pecos. The records from the Lower Rio Grande Valley and Kenedy County are more unexpected, as Rufous-backed Robins are primarily found along the Pacific slope of Mexico.

AMERICAN ROBIN *Turdus migratorius* Linnaeus

Common to abundant migrant and winter resident throughout the state, although occurring more irregularly in the southern third. American Robins are common summer residents in the northern half of Texas and locally rare to uncommon south to the central coast. This species is increasing as a summer resident along the southern edge of the breeding range, particularly in urban areas. Although urban areas are most frequently used during the breeding season in most of the state, montane woodlands also provide nesting habitat in the Davis and Guadalupe Mountains of the Trans-Pecos.

Review Species

VARIED THRUSH *Ixoreus naevius* (Gmelin)

Casual winter visitor to the western half of the state and accidental farther east. Of the 24 documented records of Varied Thrush in Texas, 18 are from the South Plains, western Rolling Plains, and Trans-Pecos. In addition, there are three records from the Lower Rio Grande Valley, two from the upper coast, and one from Tarrant County. All docu-

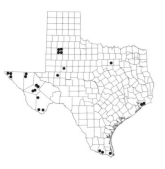

mented records occur between early October and mid-April. Three Varied Thrushes were present in a city park in Lubbock, Lubbock County, during the winter of 1999–2000. This is the only state record where more than one individual was present at a given location. There is an undocumented report of a bird present in Amarillo, Potter County, from 3 February to 31 March 1964.

Review Species

AZTEC THRUSH *Ridgwayia pinicola* (Sclater)

Accidental. Texas has four documented records of this species. Two of these records are from Big Bend National Park while the two others are from the central coast. The first for the state, and the United States, was an immature bird at Boot Spring in the Chisos Mountains (Wolf 1978). Aztec Thrush is primarily found in the mountains of western Mexico, but Howell and Webb (1995) speculate that this species may occur farther north into northeastern Mexico than currently known.

21–25 AUG. 1977, CHISOS MOUNTAINS, BREWSTER CO. (TPRF 125)
30 JAN. 1979, PORT ARANSAS, NUECES CO. (TBRC 1988-27)
31 JULY–7 AUG. 1982, BIG BEND NATIONAL PARK, BREWSTER CO.
   (TBRC 1989-22)
16–20 MAY 1996, CORPUS CHRISTI, NUECES CO.
   (TBRC 1996-71; TPRF 1496)

Family Mimidae: Mockingbirds and Thrashers

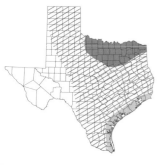

GRAY CATBIRD *Dumetella carolinensis* (Linnaeus)

Uncommon to common migrant through the eastern half of the state west to the central Edwards Plateau, becoming increasingly less common farther west. The primary migration periods are from mid-April through May and from early September through October. This species is a locally uncommon to rare winter resident along the coast and in the Lower Rio Grande Valley. Gray Catbirds have wintered at many inland locations across the state including the Panhandle and Trans-Pecos, but such occurrences are irregular. They are locally uncommon to rare summer residents across the northern portion of the state, rarely west to the Panhandle. Gray Catbirds are also very rare and local breeders in the Pineywoods.

Review Species

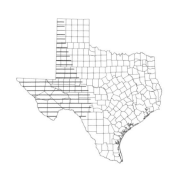

BLACK CATBIRD *Melanoptila glabrirostris* Sclater

Accidental. There is one record of Black Catbird for the state and the United States. This specimen was collected at Brownsville, Cameron County, by Frank B. Armstrong. This is the only documented record away from the species' breeding range in the Yucatan (AOU 1998).

21 JUNE 1892, BROWNSVILLE, CAMERON CO. (ANSP 42944)

NORTHERN MOCKINGBIRD
Mimus polyglottos (Linnaeus)

Abundant to common resident throughout and Texas' state bird. Mockingbirds are one of the most widespread and common birds found in Texas, and they are conspicuous by their song. Seasonal movements have been suspected in Texas, and individuals from northern migratory populations may account for apparent influxes of mockingbirds during the winter. Also, there are many reports of Northern Mockingbirds mimicking species that do not occur within their breeding territories and have also led some observers to suspect seasonal movements within the state.

SAGE THRASHER *Oreoscoptes montanus* (Townsend)

Uncommon to rare migrant and irruptive winter resident in the Trans-Pecos. Migrants generally start arriving in the state in late September, and winter residents remain until early April, although there are records from early May. The number of Sage Thrashers wintering in the state is quite variable, but they can be locally uncommon. During years when the wintering population is high in the Trans-Pecos, this species is also found with greater regularity in the Rolling Plains and Edwards Plateau and in larger numbers in the High Plains. Sage Thrasher is a casual winter visitor eastward to the Pineywoods. They are uncommon migrants through the western High Plains. There are also three July sightings from the Panhandle and another from El Paso County, probably postbreeding wanderers.

BROWN THRASHER *Toxostoma rufum* (Linnaeus)

Uncommon to locally common resident in the eastern third of the state, west across north-central Texas to the Panhandle. In addition, this species is a very rare and local

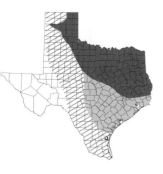

summer resident across south-central Texas to the eastern edge of the Edwards Plateau. In the Panhandle, Brown Thrasher is fairly common in the eastern half and locally common along the major rivers farther west to Hartley County. This species is a common migrant and winter resident in the eastern half of the state west to the eastern Edwards Plateau, Concho Valley, and High Plains. Brown Thrasher is a rare migrant and winter resident in the Trans-Pecos, the western Edwards Plateau, and in the South Texas Brush Country.

LONG-BILLED THRASHER

Toxostoma longirostre (Lafresnaye)

Common to uncommon resident in the South Texas Brush Country. Long-billed Thrashers range north to Matagorda County along the coast where they are very local. This species is a rare and local resident along the southern edge of the Edwards Plateau from Val Verde County east to western Bexar County. They also occur irregularly in Big Bend National Park, suggesting that its range along the Rio Grande might extend farther west than is currently known. Long-billed Thrasher has occurred as a vagrant as far north as Jeff Davis, Midland, Tom Green, Hays, and Bastrop Counties as well as along the Upper Texas Coast. A sight record also exists from Tarrant County in north-central Texas.

CURVE-BILLED THRASHER

Toxostoma curvirostre (Swainson)

Common to uncommon resident in the western half of the state. The range of Curve-billed Thrasher extends east through most of the Rolling Plains and Edwards Plateau and north along the Coastal Prairies to Calhoun and Gonzales Counties. This species has on several occasions strayed into east Texas (once to the Pineywoods), primarily between September and April. A recent study has suggested that the two subspecies groups of Curve-billed Thrasher should be considered separate species (Zink and Blackwell-Rago 2000). The two subspecies known from Texas belong to the *curvirostre* group.

CRISSAL THRASHER *Toxostoma crissale* Henry

Uncommon to locally common resident in the western and southern Trans-Pecos and rare and local in the foothills of

the Davis and Guadalupe Mountains. During the 1960s and early 1970s, Crissal Thrashers were discovered to be rare residents east to the northwestern part of the Edwards Plateau in Crockett and Irion Counties (Lockwood 2001c). Seasonal movements occur in local populations, making the species hard to find after the breeding season, which spans from February to late April.

Review Species

BLUE MOCKINGBIRD
Melanotis caerulescens (Swainson)

Accidental. There are two documented records of Blue Mockingbird for Texas. The first of these was present irregularly at Weslaco, Hidalgo County, for almost three years. This bird appears to have departed for long periods of time during its stay, primarily during the summers, although details of its occurrence are scant at best. The second bird was discovered in fall 2002 and remained into the spring. It was in juvenile plumage when initially discovered, although it molted into adult plumage soon thereafter. In the United States, there are three other documented records of this species: two in southeastern Arizona and another from south-central New Mexico.

9 MAY 1999–27 FEB. 2002, WESLACO, HIDALGO CO.
   (TBRC 1999-46; TPRF 1797)
28 SEP. 2002–26 MAY 2003, PHARR, HIDALGO CO.
   (TBRC 2002-110; TPRF 2117)

Family Sturnidae: Starlings

EUROPEAN STARLING *Sturnus vulgaris* Linnaeus

Common to abundant resident throughout most of the state, but rare to uncommon in rural areas of the western half of the state. A release of 60 individuals in New York City in 1880 is purportedly how this Old World species was introduced into the United States. The first Texas record was a bird found dead near Cove, Chambers County, in late December 1925 (Oberholser 1974). European Starlings are cavity nesters that compete with native species for available nest sites. For this reason, this species is the most problematic of the introduced birds found in Texas. Some observers have listed starlings as one of the factors responsible for the decline of Red-headed Woodpeckers.

109. Sprague's Pipit *(Anthus spragueii)* is a much-sought-after migrant and winter resident in Texas. Though not rare in some areas of the state, being familiar with the preferred winter habitat is required in order to locate this cryptic species. *Photograph by Mark W. Lockwood.*

110. The Gray Silky-flycatcher *(Ptilogonys cinereus)* is another species of the Mexican highlands that has wandered to Texas. The first record was from the Lower Rio Grande Valley, and this individual provided the second when it was found in El Paso on 12 January 1995. *Photograph by Peter Gottschling.*

111. The Olive Warbler *(Peucedramus taeniatus)* is somewhat of a taxonomic enigma. It had historically been included with the wood-warblers but is now placed in its own monotypic family. This immature male was photographed near Mount Livermore, Jeff Davis County, on 19 May 1992. *Photograph by Kelly B. Bryan.*

112. In the United States, the Colima Warbler *(Vermivora crissalis)* has long been associated only with the Chisos Mountains of Big Bend. However, the recent discovery of a territorial male in the Davis Mountains suggests a small breeding population may exist there as well. *Photograph by Vera and Bob Thornton.*

113. The Tropical Parula *(Parula pitiayumi)* is often considered a specialty of the Lower Rio Grande Valley. However, this species is in fact most common in the scattered live oak mottes of the Coastal Sand Plain in Kenedy County. This individual was photographed near Sarita, Kenedy County, on 7 May 1994. *Photograph by Mark W. Lockwood.*

114. There are three distinctive groups of Yellow Warblers *(Dendroica petechia)* that are sometimes considered separate species. Two of these occur in Texas, the typical Yellow Warbler and the "Mangrove" Warbler. The two U.S. records of Mangrove Warbler are both from Texas, and this male was at the mouth of the Rio Grande from 20 March to 6 April 1990. *Photograph by Jim Flynn.*

115. Golden-cheeked Warblers *(Dendroica chrysoparia)* are one of the earliest of the breeding warblers to return in the spring, with the first few arriving by 10 March. It is often referred to as the quintessential Texas specialty since its entire breeding range is confined within the borders of Texas. *Photograph by Mark W. Lockwood.*

116. The Swainson's Warbler *(Limnothlypis swainsonii)* is more easily heard than seen in its preferred riparian habitats. The Texas population breeds early, and they are often hard to locate after mid-July. Fall migrants seen in September and October may be from more northern populations. *Photograph by Mark W. Lockwood.*

117. Before the beginning of the twentieth century, Gray-crowned Yellowthroat
(Geothlypis poliocephala) was reported with some frequency from the Brownsville
area in the Lower Rio Grande Valley. Between 1927 and 1988 this species went
unreported from the United States, but there have been six well-documented records
since 1988. This individual was photographed at Santa Ana National Wildlife
Refuge on 25 March 2000.   *Photograph by Jim Culbertson.*

118. Slate-throated Redstarts *(Myioborus miniatus)* found in Texas belong to the northern subspecies, M. m. miniatus, found in northern and central Mexico. This individual was in the Davis Mountains from 21 to 25 June 2000. *Photograph by Kelly B. Bryan.*

119. Rufous-capped Warblers *(Basileuterus rufifrons)* have been found six times in western Val Verde County since 1993, fueling speculation that the species might be a low-density resident there. This male was mist-netted along the Devils River in 1999 and maintained a territory there for three years, attracting a female in 2001.   *Photograph by Brent Ortego.*

120. White-collared Seedeaters *(Sporophila torqueola)* have a rich and surprisingly loud, clear song that belies their small size. After being virtually extirpated from the United States in the 1950s, this species is making a slow comeback. *Photograph by Jack C. Eitniear/CSTB File Photo.*

121. Olive Sparrow *(Arremonops rufivirgatus)* has close affinities to the towhees. They are secretive and often difficult to see. Territorial males often sing from within dense tangles of brush. *Photograph by Steve Bentsen.*

122. Bachman's Sparrow *(Aimophila aestivalis)* is a habitat specialist found in open pine woodlands of the East Texas Pineywoods. Territorial males sing from an exposed perch, dropping to the grassy understory when disturbed. *Photograph by Clifford E. Shackelford.*

123. Botteri's Sparrow *(Aimophila botterii)* is restricted in Texas to grasslands from Cameron County northward through the Coastal Sand Plain. The wintering grounds of the subspecies that nests in Texas, *A. b. texana,* are unknown.
Photograph by Greg W. Lasley.

124. Sage Sparrows *(Amphispiza belli)* winter in open scrub habitats of the Trans-Pecos. This individual was photographed as it visited one of the huecos for which Hueco Tanks State Historic Site, El Paso County, is named.
Photograph by Mark W. Lockwood.

125. The secretive habits and grassland habitat of the Baird's Sparrow *(Ammodramus bairdii)* make it a difficult bird to document, clouding its actual status in Texas. The species was placed on the main Review List in 1992, although the mounting records suggest they are regular migrants through the western half of the state and possibly a winter resident. *Photograph by Greg W. Lasley.*

126. Wintering Henslow's Sparrows *(Ammodramus henslowii)* are found in damp tall-grass meadows, most often where little bluestem is a dominant grass. The secretive nature of this species made accurately determining its status in Texas difficult; it was in fact a Review Species until 1994. *Photograph by Greg W. Lasley.*

127. The winter range of Harris's Sparrow (*Zonotrichia querula*) extends from South Dakota southward through the Great Plains to the Blackland Prairies and Post Oak Savannahs of south-central Texas. They are common in vines, brush, and hedgerows within their Texas range. Recent work has suggested that the amount of black in the face of males dictates the degree of dominance an individual may have over other males. *Photograph by Mark W. Lockwood.*

128. Smith's Longspurs (*Calcarius pictus*) have a rather restricted winter range and as such are much sought after in Texas. Specific habitat requirements give this cryptic species a patchy distribution, although they can be locally uncommon. There are very few wintering areas in Texas that are publicly accessible. *Photograph by Matt White.*

129. A winter denizen of wind-swept, frosty fields of the northern United States, Snow Buntings *(Plectrophenax nivalis)* very rarely push as far south as Texas. This individual was photographed at Lake Tawakoni, Rains County, in December 1999. *Photograph by Eric Carpenter.*

130. The Crimson-collared Grosbeak *(Rhodothraupis celaeno)* is an endemic bird of northeastern Mexico that has rarely been documented in Texas. The majority of records are from the winter of 1987–88, as was this female photographed at Laguna Vista, Cameron County, on 31 January 1988. *Photograph by Mike Krzywonski.*

131. Blue Buntings *(Cyanocompsa parellina)* were first documented in Texas in the early 1980s. This species was an annual winter visitor to the Lower Rio Grande Valley between 1995 and 2002, although in most years only one or two individuals were found. This male was at Bentsen–Rio Grande Valley State Park from 30 November 1996 through 29 March 1997.
Photograph by Jim Culbertson.

132. The Varied Bunting *(Passerina versicolor)* is closely related to the Painted Bunting and has a very similar song. Another characteristic both species share is that males do not attain their bright body plumage until their second summer. First-summer males look like adult females but sing and defend territories.
Photograph by Mark W. Lockwood.

133. When Shiny Cowbirds *(Molothrus bonariensis)* invaded the Caribbean, many observers feared that they would eventually become a common resident in the southeastern United States. To date, that has not occurred, although they have been documented as far west as Texas. The first found in Texas was captured in a cowbird trap at Fort Hood, Bell County.
Photograph by Greg W. Lasley.

134. The Bronzed Cowbird *(Molothrus aeneus)* lays its eggs in other species' nests, but, unlike the Brown-headed Cowbird, the female often punctures the eggs of the host species before laying her own. In general, this cowbird is a brood parasite on similar-sized passerines, such as Northern Cardinal, Northern Mockingbird, and orioles.
Photograph by Steve Bentsen.

135. The Black-vented Oriole *(Icterus wagleri)* has only been documented in Texas on two occasions, although the first individual returned each summer for several years. This adult was photographed at Kingsville, Kleberg County.
Photograph by Mike Krzywonski.

136. Hooded Orioles *(Icterus cucullatus)* have a rather patchy distribution in Texas and are common only on the Coastal Sand Plain. The individuals of this species found in Texas have much brighter plumage than those occurring elsewhere in the United States. *Photograph by Mark W. Lockwood.*

138. Audubon's Orioles *(Icterus graduacauda)* are shy and secretive birds of dense woodlands and thickets. Their slow, whistled song is unlike that of any other oriole found in the United States. *Photograph by Steve Bentsen.*

137. The pendant nest of the Altamira Oriole *(Icterus gularis)* is often more than 2 feet long and is reminiscent of that of oropendolas. Although this species is a relatively recent addition to the Texas avifauna, Altamira Orioles appear to be declining in abundance. *Photograph by Steve Bentsen.*

139. Lesser Goldfinch *(Carduelis psaltria)* is a common resident throughout much of the western half of the state and appears to be moving eastward. Males do not obtain their black back until their second spring. This causes confusion for some observers who mistake these first-spring males for the green-backed subspecies found in California and western Arizona. *Photograph by Steve Bentsen.*

140. Lawrence's Goldfinches *(Carduelis lawrencei)* are known as regular wanderers to the southwestern United States, but these invasions have rarely included Texas. Such invasions did reach Texas in the 1950s and mid-1990s, although there are undocumented reports back to 1934. This male was at Hueco Tanks State Historic Site, El Paso County, on 27 December 1996. *Photograph by Mark W. Lockwood.*

Family Motacillidae: Wagtails and Pipits

AMERICAN PIPIT *Anthus rubescens* (Tunstall)

Common to uncommon migrant and winter resident in most of the state. American Pipits are uncommon in the southernmost reaches of the state (McKinney 1998). This pipit arrives in early October, and most depart by late April with some lingering well into May. This species was formerly called Water Pipit until that complex was divided into three species, one of which retained the common name. The American Pipit is sometimes referred to as the Buff-bellied Pipit, particularly in Old World literature.

SPRAGUE'S PIPIT *Anthus spragueii* (Audubon)

Uncommon migrant, primarily through the center of the state. This species is an uncommon to locally common winter resident along the Coastal Prairies from Galveston County south to the Lower Rio Grande Valley. They are rare to locally uncommon inland to the Post Oak Savannahs and Blackland Prairies from Williamson and Brazos Counties, south through much of the South Texas Brush Country. Wintering Sprague's Pipits are rare to locally uncommon in agricultural areas in Hudspeth County, north-central Texas, the Concho Valley, and the northwestern Edwards Plateau. These pipits are rare migrants and casual winter residents through the remainder of the state. They are typically present from early October to mid-April.

Family Bombycillidae: Waxwings

Review Species

BOHEMIAN WAXWING *Bombycilla garrulus* (Linnaeus)

Casual winter visitor to the state. Although there are only 11 documented records, this species occurred more regularly between the late 1950s and early 1970s. During that time, numerous reports were made by experienced observers in the Panhandle and across north-central Texas. Seyffert (2001) reports a flock of over 300 present in Amarillo in January 1962 and states that large flocks, sometimes numbering more than 50 individuals, were present at Palo Duro Canyon State Park, Randall County, in January 1967 and 1973. All sightings from Texas are from the winter and spring between early November and early April.

The species was first reported from the state in 1926, although the first documented record was not obtained until 26 December 1936 from Randall County.

CEDAR WAXWING *Bombycilla cedrorum* Vieillot

Common to abundant migrant and winter resident east of the Pecos River but generally considered an uncommon winter resident in the Lower Rio Grande Valley. Cedar Waxwings are common to uncommon migrants and winter residents in the Trans-Pecos. The number of waxwings present in a given area fluctuates greatly from year to year. This species is typically present from mid-October to late May with a few individuals routinely lingering into early June. In the Panhandle and Trans-Pecos, migrant Cedar Waxwings may arrive much earlier and can be present by late August. The fact that some of them have been juveniles has led to speculation that they may nest (Seyffert 1991).

Family Ptilogonatidae: Silky-flycatchers

Review Species

GRAY SILKY-FLYCATCHER
Ptilogonys cinereus Swainson

Accidental. Texas has two documented records of this species. Gray Silky-flycatchers are uncommon in northeastern Mexico as far north as western Nuevo Leon and southern Coahuila. Northern populations are at least partially migratory and are known to wander in lowland areas during winter. These factors make this species a likely candidate to occur in Texas again.

31 OCT.–11 NOV. 1985, LAGUNA ATASCOSA NWR, CAMERON CO. (TBRC 1989-37; TPRF 363)
12 JAN.–5 MAR. 1995, EL PASO, EL PASO CO. (TBRC 1995-13; TPRF 1320)

PHAINOPEPLA *Phainopepla nitens* (Swainson)

Rare to locally uncommon resident throughout most of the Trans-Pecos, where it is common only in the foothills of the Davis and Del Norte Mountains. This species has a very localized distribution in Texas, particularly during the breeding season. Phainopeplas routinely wander eastward

into other areas of the state. They are casual visitors, at all seasons, to the western Edwards Plateau and southern Rolling Plains, north to Moore County. Vagrants have been reported from virtually all other parts of the western two-thirds of the state, including from as far east as Bosque and Tarrant Counties and as far south as Hidalgo County. Populations fluctuate greatly during drought years, although some individuals are always present.

Family Peucedramidae: Olive Warblers

Review Species

OLIVE WARBLER

Peucedramus taeniatus (Du Bus de Gisignies)

Casual. There are five documented records from the Trans-Pecos and one from Briscoe County in the Panhandle. The first was found 3 May 1991 at Big Bend National Park, Brewster County (TBRC 1991-61). The first documented with a photograph was from the Davis Mountains on 19 May 1992 (TBRC 1992-72; TPRF 1094). All documented records occurred between 30 April and 19 May in the spring and 7 September to 14 November in the fall.

Family Parulidae: Wood-Warblers

BLUE-WINGED WARBLER *Vermivora pinus* (Linnaeus)

Uncommon to rare migrant in the eastern third of the state. Blue-winged Warblers are most frequently encountered along the coast, where they are uncommon, especially as a spring migrant. This species becomes increasingly rare west of the Balcones Escarpment and is considered accidental in the Trans-Pecos and the Panhandle. Blue-winged Warbler is accidental in winter with one documented record from Medina County. Others have been reported from the coast and Lower Rio Grande Valley, but supporting documentation is lacking. Average migration dates for this species are from early April to early May and from mid-August to early October. Hybrid Blue-winged and Golden-winged Warblers have been reported in Texas on numerous occasions.

Most pertain to the "Brewster's" Warbler, although the "Lawrence's" Warbler also occurs.

GOLDEN-WINGED WARBLER
Vermivora chrysoptera (Linnaeus)

Rare to uncommon migrant through the eastern third of the state. Golden-winged Warblers are significantly declining rangewide and are decidedly less common than Blue-wingeds. They are most frequently encountered at stopover habitats along the coast and are very rare to accidental in the western half of the state. Golden-winged Warblers are more frequently encountered in spring than in fall. Average migration dates are from mid-April to early May and mid-September to mid-October. A singing male was recorded in Randall County in the Panhandle on 1 June 1977.

TENNESSEE WARBLER *Vermivora peregrina* (Wilson)

Uncommon to common spring and rare to uncommon fall migrant in the eastern half of the state. As with many species of warblers, Tennessee Warblers are most commonly seen along the coast. This species is rare to casual in the western half of the state. Tennessee Warblers are a very rare winter visitor along the coast and in the Lower Rio Grande Valley. Average migration dates are from early April to mid-May and between mid-September and late October. First-winter male and adult female Tennessee Warblers can be confused with the Orange-crowned Warbler *(V. celata)*, which may account for some winter reports.

ORANGE-CROWNED WARBLER
Vermivora celata (Say)

Common to abundant migrant throughout the state. Orange-crowned Warblers are uncommon to common winter residents in much of the state, although during the winter they are generally absent above the Caprock Escarpment from Lubbock County northward through the Panhandle. Orange-crowned Warblers are especially common in winter in the southern third of the state and along the coast, where they can be locally abundant. This species is an uncommon and local summer resident in the higher elevations of the Davis and Guadalupe Mountains of the Trans-Pecos. In general, fall migrants begin arriving in early September and have departed the state by mid-May.

NASHVILLE WARBLER *Vermivora ruficapilla* (Wilson)

Uncommon to abundant migrant throughout most of the state, generally more common in fall than in spring. This warbler appears to be a circum-Gulf migrant; in spring they are less common on the upper coast as birds head north from the central coast after rounding the Gulf. This species is a rare to very uncommon migrant in the western half of the Trans-Pecos. Nashville Warbler is a locally uncommon to rare winter resident in the Lower Rio Grande Valley and very rare northward along the coast and in the South Texas Brush Country. They are casual in winter elsewhere in the state except in the Panhandle where absent. Average migration dates are from early April to mid-May and from early September to late October.

VIRGINIA'S WARBLER *Vermivora virginiae* (Baird)

Uncommon to rare migrant in the Trans-Pecos and a very rare migrant through the western High Plains. Virginia's Warblers are rare to uncommon summer residents in the upper elevations of the Davis and Guadalupe Mountains of the Trans-Pecos. Recent summer reports exist from the Chisos Mountains, but breeding activities have not been observed. A Virginia's Warbler at Santa Ana National Wildlife Refuge, Hidalgo County, from 3 January to 28 February 1991 provided the only documented winter record for Texas. The migration period for this species is from late April to mid-May and from late August to late September.

COLIMA WARBLER
Vermivora crissalis (Salvin and Godman)

Uncommon and extremely localized summer resident in the Chisos Mountains in Brewster County. This species is not known to breed anywhere else in the United States. Colima Warblers arrive in Big Bend National Park in early April, and most depart by early September, although they have been reported as early as 15 March and as late as 18 September (Wauer 1996). This species was first discovered breeding in the Chisos Mountains in 1932 (Van Tyne 1936). Single territorial males were documented in the Davis Mountains during 1999 and 2000 (Bryan and Karges 2001). There is a single sight record from the Lower Rio Grande Valley at Santa Ana National Wildlife Refuge, Hidalgo County, on 4 October 1978.

LUCY'S WARBLER *Vermivora luciae* (Cooper)

Rare to locally uncommon summer resident along the Rio Grande from southern Hudspeth County to western Brewster County in the Trans-Pecos. This species has been documented in winter from central and southern Presidio County. Lucy's Warbler has also been documented east of the Trans-Pecos on three occasions with single records from Brazoria, Kenedy, and Navarro Counties. Birds generally arrive on their breeding grounds in mid-March and depart in mid-September. Lucy's Warbler is the smallest of North American wood-warblers and one of only two cavity nesters (along with Prothonotary Warbler).

NORTHERN PARULA *Parula americana* (Linnaeus)

Uncommon to common summer resident in the eastern half of Texas. Summer residents are found west to the edge of the Rolling Plains, locally through the southern Edwards Plateau, and south to the San Antonio River on the Coastal Bend. This species is a local resident along the major rivers on the southern Edwards Plateau west to the Devils River and Independence Creek on the Pecos River. Northern Parula is rare and local south of the Edwards Plateau with single nesting records from Hidalgo and Live Oak Counties. Northern Parulas are common to uncommon migrants in the eastern half of the state, becoming increasingly less common westward. They are rare winter residents in the Lower Rio Grande Valley and casual elsewhere in the southern half of the state. This species is one of the earliest warblers to return in the spring, occasionally as early as late February, with summering birds usually on territory by mid-March. Breeding birds begin to disperse in late July, but fall migration extends at least into mid-October.

TROPICAL PARULA *Parula pitiayumi* (Vieillot)

Rare to uncommon resident along the lower coast and in the Lower Rio Grande Valley. Tropical Parulas are most common in the live oak woodlands of the Coastal Sand Plain in Kenedy and Brooks Counties. They are rare and local summer residents north along the coast to Calhoun and Victoria Counties. Wandering Tropical Parulas have been found as far north as Lubbock County but have occurred with increasing regularity in the southern Trans-Pecos, Edwards Plateau, and the upper coast during the

1990s. Territorial males have been found on the southern Edwards Plateau, and nesting is suspected along the Devils River in Val Verde County, where apparent hybrids with Northern Parula have been reported. During the summer of 2001, a pair unsuccessfully nested at Davis Mountains State Park, Jeff Davis County.

YELLOW WARBLER *Dendroica petechia* (Linnaeus)

Common to abundant migrant statewide, particularly in fall. Yellow Warblers were formerly rare summer residents in the state, nesting along the Rio Grande in the Trans-Pecos, the Edwards Plateau, the Panhandle, and at scattered locations in the eastern half of the state. Territorial males are still occasionally encountered, particularly in the Panhandle, but nesting has not been confirmed in the Panhandle since 1956 (Gray County). Strecker (1927) reported the species to be a "rather common summer resident" in McLennan County. Yellow Warbler is a rare to very rare winter visitor in the Lower Rio Grande Valley and in El Paso. The migration period is from early April to late May and from late July to mid-October. There were formerly two other species that are now considered part of the Yellow Warbler complex. One of those other subspecies groups has occurred in Texas.

"MANGROVE" WARBLER

There are two documented records of "Mangrove" Warbler for Texas. Males, presumably belonging to *D. p. oraria,* were photographed in Aransas County in 1978 and Cameron County in 1990. This distinctive subspecies group was formerly considered a separate species, *D. erithachorides.*

CHESTNUT-SIDED WARBLER
Dendroica pensylvanica (Linnaeus)

Uncommon to locally common migrant in the eastern third of the state and rare to casual westward. Chestnut-sided Warblers are most commonly encountered along the coast and are more common in spring than in fall. Migrants are generally present from mid-April to mid-May and from mid-September to late October. This species very rarely lingers into the summer, but there are a few records of birds staying into the winter. Most winter reports are from along the coast; however, there are December reports from as far north as Tarrant County in north-central Texas and Lubbock County on the South Plains.

MAGNOLIA WARBLER *Dendroica magnolia* (Wilson)

Uncommon to locally common migrant in the eastern half of the state. As with many other migrant warblers, they are encountered more frequently and in larger numbers along the coast. Magnolia Warblers are uncommon migrants west through the eastern Edwards Plateau, becoming increasingly less common westward. This species is a casual to very rare winter visitor along the coast and in the Lower Rio Grande Valley. Migration periods are typically between mid-April and late May and from early September to late October.

CAPE MAY WARBLER *Dendroica tigrina* (Gmelin)

Rare spring and very rare fall migrant in the eastern third of the state. This species is most often encountered along the upper coast. Cape May Warblers are very rare migrants elsewhere in the eastern half of the state and casual to accidental migrants in the western two-thirds of the state. Cape Mays are also casual winter visitors, with most records from the lower coast and Lower Rio Grande Valley. Spring migrants are generally found between mid-April and mid-May. In the fall, reports indicate they can occur between late August and early November.

BLACK-THROATED BLUE WARBLER
Dendroica caerulescens (Gmelin)

Rare migrant to the eastern third of the state and rare to very rare westward. Black-throated Blue Warblers are more frequently encountered in the fall than in the spring. This warbler is a very rare winter resident along the Coastal Prairies and in the Lower Rio Grande Valley, with scattered inland records north to Brazos County. Spring migration begins in mid-April and extends to mid-May with a few records from very early June. In fall, migration extends from late September to mid-November.

YELLOW-RUMPED WARBLER
Dendroica coronata (Linnaeus)

Common to abundant migrant over the entire state. Yellow-rumped Warblers are common to abundant winter resi-

dents south of the Panhandle, where they are rare to un-common. This species is a rare to locally uncommon summer resident in the higher elevations of the Davis and Guadalupe Mountains of the Trans-Pecos. Generally, fall migrants begin appearing in early September, and spring migrants are gone by mid-May. The Yellow-rumped Warbler was formerly considered two species.

"MYRTLE" WARBLER

Common to locally abundant migrant and winter resident in the eastern two-thirds of the state, becoming less common through the remainder.

"AUDUBON'S" WARBLER

Uncommon to locally common migrant and winter resident in the Trans-Pecos, Panhandle, and South Plains. They are uncommon to rare migrants and winter residents through the Rolling Plains and Edwards Plateau. "Audubon's" Warblers have been reported eastward through the Post Oak Savannahs and along the Coastal Prairies to the upper coast. This form is also an uncommon and local summer resident at the higher elevations of the Davis and Guadalupe Mountains.

BLACK-THROATED GRAY WARBLER

Dendroica nigrescens (Townsend)

Rare to uncommon migrant through the Trans-Pecos and High Plains. Black-throated Gray Warblers are very rare migrants east to Bastrop, Brazos, and Dallas Counties. This species is a rare to locally uncommon winter resident in the Lower Rio Grande Valley and a casual winter visitor along the Coastal Prairies and inland as far north as Randall County in the Panhandle. Breeding has been suspected in the Guadalupe Mountains (Newman 1974), but documentation is lacking. Migration typically occurs between late March and late April and from late August to mid-November.

GOLDEN-CHEEKED WARBLER

Dendroica chrysoparia Sclater and Salvin

Uncommon to rare summer resident in central Texas. This warbler breeds only in the Hill Country of Texas. Golden-cheeked Warblers arrive in early March and depart by early August, although they become very rare by mid-July. This species is found throughout the Balcones Canyonlands sub-region of the Edwards Plateau and northward locally to

Palo Pinto and Somervell Counties. This species was redis-covered in Dallas County in 2001 after a 35-year absence. Golden-cheekeds have occasionally been found away from breeding areas, mostly migrants seen from late July to early August. There are records from Aransas, Bastrop, Brewster, Cameron, Fayette, Galveston, Hidalgo, and Karnes Coun-ties. This Endangered songbird is a habitat specialist and nests in diverse Ashe Juniper–oak woodlands.

BLACK-THROATED GREEN WARBLER
Dendroica virens (Gmelin)

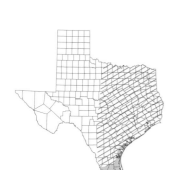

Common to uncommon migrant in the eastern half of the state, increasingly uncommon to rare farther west. Black-throated Green Warblers are uncommon to rare winter resi-dents in the Lower Rio Grande Valley and along the lower coast. They are very rare elsewhere on the coast and inland to Bexar County during this season. This species has one of the longest migration periods of any warbler: the first birds are detected in mid-March and migrants are present until mid-May, with a few lingering into early June. In the fall, they occur from mid-September to mid-November. Black-throated Greens have been found in late June and July on a number of occasions. Whether these birds sum-mered locally or were very early or very late migrants is uncertain.

TOWNSEND'S WARBLER
Dendroica townsendi (Townsend)

Uncommon to common migrant in the Trans-Pecos, pri-marily at higher elevations. Townsend's Warbler is a rare migrant east to the High Plains, where on occasion it can be locally uncommon. Migrants have been noted on rare occasions along the coast and in the Lower Rio Grande Valley as well. This species is a casual to very rare migrant in most of the remainder of the state west of the Pineywoods. In winter, Townsend's Warblers are very rare in riparian woodlands along the Rio Grande and its tributaries from El Paso County to Brewster County and in the Lower Rio Grande Valley. This species has been found in winter in other areas of the state, although most records are from the coast. Townsend's Warblers migrate through Texas from mid-April to mid-May and between late August and early October.

HERMIT WARBLER *Dendroica occidentalis* (Townsend)

Rare to very rare migrant primarily through the mountains of the Trans-Pecos. This species has most frequently been encountered in the Chisos Mountains, although they may be equally common in the Davis Mountains. East of the Pecos River, Hermit Warbler is casual to accidental, with records from as far east as the upper coast and as far north as Bailey and Castro Counties on the High Plains. The only documented winter record consists of two males present at Anzalduas County Park, Hidalgo County, from December 1998 through March 1999. The typical migration period is from mid-April to mid-May and mid-August to mid-September. This species hybridizes with Townsend's Warblers in Oregon and Washington (Dunn and Garrett 1997), but to date no hybrids have been reported in Texas.

BLACKBURNIAN WARBLER *Dendroica fusca* (Müller)

Uncommon to locally common spring migrant in the eastern half of the state, west to the Balcones Escarpment. On the eastern Edwards Plateau and Rolling Plains, Blackburnian Warblers are rare spring migrants, becoming very rare farther west. In fall, they are casual to rare migrants throughout the state. As with many other species of warblers, Blackburnians are most commonly encountered as migrants along the immediate coast. One was reported from Rancho Viejo, Cameron County, in February 1998. Blackburnian Warblers winter in northern South America, and this individual may have been an extraordinarily early migrant. The migration periods are between mid-April and mid-May and from early September to early November.

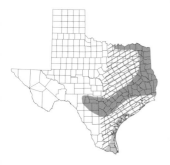

YELLOW-THROATED WARBLER
Dendroica dominica (Linnaeus)

Uncommon to locally common summer resident in the eastern third of Texas. On the Edwards Plateau, they are uncommon to rare and confined to riparian corridors. This species is a common to uncommon migrant in the eastern half of the state, especially along the coast. Farther west, they are rare migrants, becoming casual in the Trans-Pecos and High Plains. Yellow-throated Warblers are rare to locally uncommon winter residents along the coast and in the Lower Rio Grande Valley. There are isolated winter records inland to Travis County and the southern half of the Pineywoods. This species arrives early in the spring and is often on territory by mid-March, although migration continues through late April. Fall migration extends from late July to early November. A specimen of the yellow-lored subspecies, *D. d. dominica,* has been reported from Aransas County, although the status of this subspecies as a migrant in Texas is unknown. Texas birds are predominantly, if not completely, the white-lored subspecies, *D. d. albilora.*

GRACE'S WARBLER *Dendroica graciae* Baird

Uncommon to very locally common summer resident in the higher elevations of the Davis and Guadalupe Mountains of the Trans-Pecos. This species is rarely seen during migration, even in the Trans-Pecos. There are very few reports east of the Pecos River, fewer still that are documented. Despite a small number of reports, there are no documented winter records for Texas. Spring migrants are first seen in the Trans-Pecos in early April, and summer residents often linger to mid-September.

PINE WARBLER *Dendroica pinus* (Wilson)

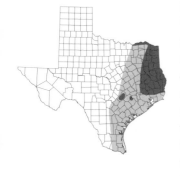

Common resident in the pine forests of East Texas and the "Lost Pines" area of Bastrop and northeast Caldwell Counties of central Texas. They are very local in Austin, Colorado, Fayette, and Washington Counties, as well. This species is a rare migrant west to the High Plains and a casual migrant in the Trans-Pecos. Pine Warblers are uncommon to common winter residents in the eastern third of the state west to Parker and Travis Counties, becoming uncommon to rare southward to the Lower Rio Grande Valley. Wintering birds have been noted as far west as Big Bend National Park, Brewster County. They are frequently encountered along the coast during that season and can be locally common. It is unclear if these wintering birds represent migrants from northern populations or are dispersing from breeding areas in east and central Texas. The timing of migration is not well defined, although birds seen away from the Pineywoods are typically noted from early October through late March and occasionally early April.

PRAIRIE WARBLER *Dendroica discolor* (Vieillot)

Rare to uncommon summer resident in the eastern quarter of the state, south to Hardin and Montgomery Counties.

This species is a rare to uncommon migrant in the eastern third and along the coast, becoming very rare to casual elsewhere. Prairie Warblers have been encountered far more frequently in the western half of the state in the fall than in the spring. This species has been reported during the winter, though rarely, at scattered locations across the state including the Trans-Pecos and northeast and central Texas. Winter sightings are most frequent along the Coastal Prairies and in the Lower Rio Grande Valley. Prairie Warblers arrive in Texas in mid-April and have usually departed by late September, occasionally lingering into early October. This species uses regenerating clearcuts and other disturbed areas of small, often dense, stands of young trees for nesting. As a result, habitat is available at a particular location for only a few years before the trees mature to a point where they are no longer suitable for nesting.

PALM WARBLER *Dendroica palmarum* (Gmelin)

Rare to locally uncommon migrant in the eastern two-thirds of the state west to the Pecos River. Palm Warblers are locally uncommon winter residents along the upper and central coasts, becoming rare along the lower coast and in the Lower Rio Grande Valley. Away from the Coastal Prairies, they are rare to casual winter visitors inland to the Balcones Escarpment, with scattered winter records even farther inland. Palm Warblers typically arrive from late August to early September and depart between mid-April and early May. Two subspecies are found in the state, *D. p. palmarum* from the western United States and *D. p. hypochrysea* from the east. Of these, *D. p. palmarum* is more common than the yellower *D. p. hypochrysea*, which is rare, although the exact status of the latter is unclear.

BAY-BREASTED WARBLER
Dendroica castanea (Wilson)

Uncommon to common spring migrant and rare to locally uncommon fall migrant in the eastern half of the state. During the fall, this species is most frequently encountered on the upper and central coasts. In the western half of the state, they are casual migrants and accidental in the Trans-Pecos. The typical migration periods extend from late April to mid-May and late September to late October, with a few individuals occasionally lingering into early November. The migration windows of Bay-breasted Warbler are among the shortest of the warblers passing through Texas.

BLACKPOLL WARBLER *Dendroica striata* (Forster)

Uncommon to rare spring migrant and very rare fall migrant along the coast. Blackpoll Warblers are rare to very rare migrants inland with records from all regions of the state. Winter records are extremely rare, assuming the birds were correctly identified, although there is one documented record from El Paso. Female and first-winter individuals pose difficult identification problems when separating them from other *Dendroica* species, particularly dull-plumaged Pine and Bay-breasted Warblers. Migration is from mid-April to late May and from late August to early October.

CERULEAN WARBLER *Dendroica cerulea* (Wilson)

Uncommon to rare spring and very rare to casual fall migrant through the eastern half of the state. Cerulean Warblers are rarely encountered away from the immediate coast. There are no documented records from the Panhandle and only one from the Trans-Pecos involving a bird at Big Bend National Park, Brewster County, on 5 October 1992. Like the Blackpoll Warbler, first-winter birds pose identification problems. Migration falls between early April and early May and from early August to mid-September. This species was formerly a summer resident in northeast Texas from Cooke and Dallas Counties eastward (Oberholser 1974).

BLACK-AND-WHITE WARBLER
Mniotilta varia (Linneaus)

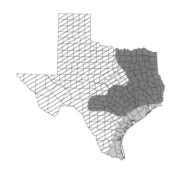

Uncommon to common summer resident in the eastern half of the state west into the Edwards Plateau, where more localized, and rare to uncommon south of Nueces County. There are a number of midsummer records from the Panhandle and South Plains without evidence of nesting. Black-and-white Warblers are uncommon to common spring and fall migrants throughout most of the state, becoming rare in the western Trans-Pecos. They can be locally abundant along the coast during migration. The migration periods for this species are from early March to mid-May and from late July to early November, with territorial birds often in place by 10 March in the southern portions of the breeding range. This species is a rare to uncommon winter resident in the southern third of the state and very rare north to north-central Texas and along the upper coast.

AMERICAN REDSTART *Setophaga ruticilla* (Linnaeus)

Rare to uncommon and very local summer resident in the forested areas of east Texas southwest to Fort Bend County. American Redstart is an uncommon to locally common migrant in the eastern half of the state and rare to uncommon in the western half. The breeding range has decreased significantly in recent decades as it formerly included the Colorado River watershed to Lavaca County (Oberholser 1974). Away from the known breeding range, this species is a rare summer visitor to virtually all regions, including Dallam and Hemphill Counties in the Panhandle. American Redstart is a rare winter resident in the Lower Rio Grande Valley and along the lower coast, becoming very rare elsewhere along the coast inland to Grimes and Washington Counties. There are documented winter records from El Paso and Tarrant Counties. Typical migration periods are from mid-April to early June and from mid-August to mid-October.

PROTHONOTARY WARBLER

Protonotaria citrea (Boddaert)

Rare to locally common summer resident in the eastern half of the state, west to the edge of the Rolling Plains southward to the central coast. Prothonotary Warblers are uncommon to common migrants through the eastern half of the state and along the coast, becoming rare to very rare farther west. During the winter, this species is very rare along the coast and in the Lower Rio Grande Valley. Migrants generally are present between mid-March and late May and from early August to early October. Prothonotary Warblers are one of only two cavity-nesting warblers in North America. This species breeds primarily in swampy habitats and in creek and river bottom forests.

WORM-EATING WARBLER

Helmitheros vermivorus (Gmelin)

Uncommon to locally common migrant in the eastern third of the state, although primarily encountered along the coast. Worm-eating Warbler is a rare to uncommon migrant westward to the Balcones Escarpment and very rare to casual

farther west. They are rare and local summer residents in the central and southern portions of the Pineywoods. Dense woodland thickets in association with bay-gallberry holly bogs constitute their preferred nesting habitat. Because of habitat loss, this species has a more restricted breeding range today. Worm-eating Warblers are casual to accidental winter visitors along the coast. The migration period occurs between late March and early May and from late August to early October.

SWAINSON'S WARBLER

Limnothlypis swainsonii (Audubon)

Uncommon to locally common summer resident in the eastern third of the state. Swainson's Warblers are very local summer residents at a few locations west to Aransas, Bastrop, and Victoria Counties. As a migrant, they are very rare to uncommon in the eastern third of the state west to about the edge of the Rolling Plains, although most commonly encountered along the upper coast south to the Coastal Bend. Swainson's Warblers are casual to accidental migrants in the western half of the state. This species migrates through Texas between late March and early May and from late July to early October.

OVENBIRD *Seiurus aurocapilla* (Linnaeus)

Uncommon to common migrant through the eastern half of the state, becoming increasingly less common farther west. Ovenbirds are encountered in greatest numbers along the coast. This species is a rare to uncommon winter resident in the Lower Rio Grande Valley, becoming rare northward along the coast. They are very rare during the winter inland in the southern half of the state east of the Edwards Plateau, with one record from Lubbock County on the South Plains. The primary migration period for Ovenbirds is from early April, occasionally late March, to early May and from late August to late October. Although they are a summer resident in Arkansas and southeast Oklahoma very close to the Texas border, no breeding records exist from Texas.

NORTHERN WATERTHRUSH

Seiurus noveboracensis (Gmelin)

Common to uncommon migrant in the eastern half of the state, becoming uncommon to rare west to the Trans-Pecos.

As with many warblers, migrant Northern Waterthrushes are most frequently encountered along the coast, becoming rare to uncommon inland. This species is a very rare winter visitor along the coast, becoming rare and more regular in the Lower Rio Grande Valley. In general, Northern Waterthrush migrates later, in both spring and fall, than the Louisiana Waterthrush. The migration period is between mid-April and mid-May and from late August to mid-October.

LOUISIANA WATERTHRUSH
Seiurus motacilla (Vieillot)

Uncommon summer resident in the eastern third of the state and rare to locally uncommon west across the southern Edwards Plateau. This species is an uncommon migrant through the eastern two-thirds of the state, becoming rare to casual farther west. Louisiana Waterthrushes have been reported in the eastern half of the state during winter, but documentation is lacking. The primary migration period lasts from mid-March to late April and from mid-July to mid-September.

KENTUCKY WARBLER *Oporornis formosus* (Wilson)

Rare to locally uncommon summer resident in the eastern quarter of the state, locally west to Bastrop, Grayson, and McLennan Counties. Kentucky Warblers formerly were rare summer residents on the southeastern Edwards Plateau. They are uncommon to common migrants in the eastern third of the state, becoming increasingly less common west to the eastern Edwards Plateau and Rolling Plains. In the western half of the state, Kentucky Warblers are casual migrants only in the spring. This species is very rare in winter on the coast and in the Lower Rio Grande Valley. The migration period is from early April to early May and from late July to mid-September.

Review Species

CONNECTICUT WARBLER *Oporornis agilis* (Wilson)

Casual migrant through the eastern half of the state. Texas has eight documented records of this species, most from the fall. The dates of occurrence range from 30 April to 14 May and from 5 September to 10 October. Five of the records are from the upper coast, two from north-central Texas, and one from the Edwards Plateau. The first docu-

mented record was a bird photographed at High Island on 16 September 1978 (TPRF 140). There are undocumented sightings from other areas. This species may be confused with other species of *Oporornis* as well as Nashville Warbler *(Vermivora ruficapilla)*.

MOURNING WARBLER

Oporornis philadelphia (Wilson)

Uncommon to rare migrant in the eastern half of the state and very rare to casual in the western half. Mourning Warblers are circum-Gulf migrants and therefore rare on the upper coast in spring. In general, they are much more commonly encountered during the fall. This species migrates between very late April and early June and from early September to late October. There are a few reports of birds lingering into early winter. Mourning Warblers are among the latest of the warblers to arrive in the spring.

MACGILLIVRAY'S WARBLER

Oporornis tolmiei (Townsend)

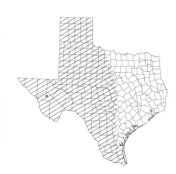

Uncommon to rare migrant through the western half of the state and rare to very rare eastward through the Blackland Prairies and central and lower coasts. During the winter, this species is a very rare visitor to the coast, with reports from as far north as Jefferson County. Migration occurs between early April and early June and from late August to early October. The migratory pathways of Mourning and MacGillivray's overlap through the eastern Rolling Plains, Edwards Plateau, and South Texas Brush Country. MacGillivray's Warbler is a rare and very local summer resident at the highest elevations of the Davis Mountains. Nesting was suspected in the vicinity of Mount Livermore in 2001 and confirmed in 2002.

COMMON YELLOWTHROAT

Geothlypis trichas (Linnaeus)

Rare to locally common summer resident in the northeastern part of the state and the Panhandle. Common Yellowthroats are uncommon to locally common summer residents south through the eastern third of the state and along the Coastal Prairies to the central coast. This species is also a locally uncommon summer resident along the entire length of the

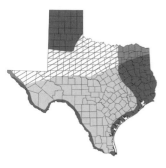

Rio Grande. There have been isolated nesting records from virtually all of the remaining areas of the state. They are common to uncommon migrants throughout the state. In winter, Common Yellowthroat is uncommon to locally common across much of the southern half of Texas but are generally rare to locally uncommon in the Trans-Pecos and Edwards Plateau. In the northern half of the state, they winter locally but are absent from most of the Panhandle. The "Brownsville" Yellowthroat, *G. t. insperata,* a subspecies with a very restricted range, is found only around resacas in southern Cameron County, where it is very rare and local. Summering birds found farther west in the Lower Rio Grande Valley belong to *G. t. chryseola.* The migration of this species in Texas is complicated and hard to discern; however, it generally falls from mid-March to mid-May and from early September to late October.

Review Species

GRAY-CROWNED YELLOWTHROAT
Geothlypis poliocephala Baird

Casual visitor during all seasons to the Lower Rio Grande Valley. Prior to the twentieth century this species was a rare to uncommon spring and summer resident in the Lower Rio Grande Valley, primarily in Cameron County. The reasons for the decline of Gray-crowned Yellowthroats in Texas are unclear. Records from prior to the twentieth century suggest that this species was present between early February to early July and fairly common. Between May 1890 and May 1894, a minimum of 34 specimens were collected from the Brownsville area, possibly along with many others that are now apparently lost. Since 1927 there are only six documented records of the species, all occurring since 1988. This species is also known as Ground Chat and is sometimes placed in a separate genus, *Chamaethlypis* (AOU 1998).

HOODED WARBLER *Wilsonia citrina* (Boddaert)

Uncommon to common summer resident in the eastern quarter of the state. Very localized breeding populations of Hooded Warblers also exist in Bastrop, Colorado, and Matagorda Counties, the westernmost to be found in North America. They are also reported to breed in Aransas County (Jones 1992). This species is an uncommon to common migrant in the eastern third of the state west to the Balcones

Escarpment and can be locally common to abundant along the coast. Hooded Warblers are very rare to casual migrants in the western two-thirds of the state. There is a midsummer record from Randall County in the Panhandle. Hooded Warblers are rare winter visitors in extreme southern Texas north to the central coast with only scattered records farther north and west. Migration periods are typically between mid-March and early May and from late August to mid-October.

WILSON'S WARBLER *Wilsonia pusilla* (Wilson)

Uncommon to common migrant throughout the state. Wilson's Warblers are most common in migration in the Trans-Pecos, Panhandle, and South Plains where they can be abundant. This species is generally less common in the spring than in the fall. Wilson's Warblers are uncommon winter residents in the southern third of the state ranging north to near the Balcones Escarpment and Matagorda Bay. Elsewhere they are rare to very rare. Two summer records of singing Wilson's Warblers from the Panhandle probably represent late migrants, as there are no nesting records for Texas. Migration runs from early April to mid-May and from late August to mid-October. In many parts of the western third of the state this species is second only to the Yellow-rumped Warbler *(Dendroica coronata)* in terms of relative abundance.

CANADA WARBLER *Wilsonia canadensis* (Linnaeus)

Uncommon to rare spring migrant in the eastern half of the state. Canada Warblers are more commonly encountered along the coast where they can be locally common. This species is a common to uncommon fall migrant in the eastern half of the state west to the central Edwards Plateau and very rare to casual in the western half. There is one documented winter record from Cameron County. Canada Warblers are generally found from mid-April to mid-May and from late August to mid-October.

Review Species

RED-FACED WARBLER *Cardellina rubrifrons* (Giraud)

Very rare late summer and fall migrant to the Chisos Mountains in the Trans-Pecos. Red-faced Warbler is an accidental visitor elsewhere in the state. There are 28 documented records; the first was a bird collected in El Paso County on

17 August 1890. Seventeen come from the Chisos Mountains, mostly from August, although there are several spring records. With greater observer awareness of the timing of occurrence of this species, Red-faced Warblers have been found annually during August since 1999. Curiously, there are only single records from the Guadalupe and Davis Mountains. The four documented records from east of the Pecos River refer to single individuals found in Bastrop, Calhoun, Cameron, and Comal Counties. There are 17 reports of Red-faced Warblers from prior to the development of the Review List in 1987 for which there is no documentation on file at Texas A&M University.

PAINTED REDSTART *Myioborus pictus* (Swainson)

Rare and irregular spring and summer visitor to the Chisos Mountains. The population of Painted Redstarts in Texas has fluctuated greatly over the past 100 years (Wauer 1996). Between 1976 and 1989, they were uncommon summer residents in the Chisos Mountains and nested in the Davis Mountains in 1992. The summer population in Texas is probably directly affected by the species' abundance in the nearby Sierra del Carmen of northern Coahuila, Mexico. Since the late 1970s, this species has been a very rare to casual visitor to other areas of the Trans-Pecos, High Plains, Edwards Plateau, upper coast, and Lower Rio Grande Valley. Painted Redstarts should be looked for in the Chisos Mountains from late March to mid-October.

Review Species

SLATE-THROATED REDSTART
Myioborus miniatus (Swainson)

Accidental. Texas has seven documented records of this species, five of them from the Trans-Pecos. There are three records from Big Bend National Park, all from the Boot Springs area of the Chisos Mountains. The other two Trans-Pecos records are from the Davis Mountains, and both were discovered in a very steep mesic canyon that includes a small patch of aspens near the summit of Mount Livermore. Two of the Trans-Pecos records involved males that sang vigorously, but neither remained on territory. The final two records are from much more unexpected locations. Two adults were at Corpus Christi, Nueces County, on 10 April 2002 (TBRC 2002-49; TPRF 2032), and one adult was at Pharr, Hidalgo County, on 12–13 March 2003 (TBRC 2003-17; TPRF 2118).

Review Species

GOLDEN-CROWNED WARBLER
Basileuterus culicivorus (Deppe)

Casual winter visitor to the Lower Rio Grande Valley with one record from the central coast. There are 16 documented records of this widespread tropical warbler for the state. Golden-crowned Warblers have not been documented elsewhere in the United States. The first record involved a bird collected at Brownsville, Cameron County, on 6 January 1892. Other than a single record from Nueces County, all others are from Cameron and Hidalgo Counties. The majority of records fall between 23 October and 6 April. There are two documented spring records: one from 30 April 1995 (Hidalgo County) and another from 24–29 April 2001 (Nueces County). An adult mist-netted at Laguna Atascosa National Wildlife Refuge on 12 August 2001 provided the only summer record.

Review Species

RUFOUS-CAPPED WARBLER
Basileuterus rufifrons (Swainson)

Very rare visitor. This species was first documented in Texas on 10 February 1973 at Falcon Dam, Starr County. Since then there have been 19 others. Rufous-capped Warblers have occurred in every month of the year with the greatest number of records from January to May. The majority of records have come from Brewster and Val Verde Counties. This species has been found almost annually between 1997 and 2001 along the Devils River drainage of central Val Verde County where it may be a low-density resident. The species may have also nested in Webb County (Arnold 1980), but there are no definite nesting records for the state.

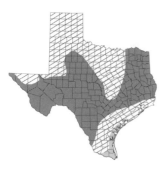

YELLOW-BREASTED CHAT *Icteria virens* (Linnaeus)

Common to uncommon summer resident through most of the Trans-Pecos, Edwards Plateau, and Pineywoods. Yellow-breasted Chats are uncommon and local summer residents in the western half of the South Texas Brush Country and locally in the Panhandle, southward through the Rolling Plains. Although this species is considered a summer resident throughout much of the state, populations are small in many areas and breeding is highly localized. Chats are uncommon to common migrants through the eastern two-thirds of the state, becoming less common farther west. Typical migration dates are from early April to early May and late August to mid-October. Yellow-breasted Chat is a rare to very rare winter resident in the Lower Rio Grande Valley northward to the central coast.

Family Thraupidae: Tanagers

HEPATIC TANAGER *Piranga flava* (Vieillot)

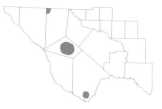

Uncommon to locally common summer resident in the Chisos, Davis, and Guadalupe Mountains of the Trans-Pecos. Hepatic Tanagers are very rarely seen during migration in the Trans-Pecos away from their breeding habitat. This species is accidental during migration east of the Trans-Pecos, with records north to Bailey and Castro Counties and east to Bexar and Gonzales Counties. There are several winter records from just east of the Balcones Escarpment in Bastrop and Gonzales Counties as well as others from Brazoria, Cameron, and Nueces Counties. The breeding population arrives in mid-April and is present until mid-October.

SUMMER TANAGER *Piranga rubra* (Linnaeus)

Rare to locally common summer resident in most of the state, although generally absent from the High Plains, Rolling Plains, the southern South Texas Brush Country, and the highest elevations of the Trans-Pecos. Summer Tanagers are uncommon to common migrants in all regions. They are rare winter residents along the coast and the Lower Rio Grande Valley, with isolated records inland to Bastrop, Bexar, Dallas, Llano, Nacogdoches, Tarrant, and Travis Counties. Migration lasts from early April to mid-May and from mid-August to late October.

SCARLET TANAGER *Piranga olivacea* (Gmelin)

Uncommon to locally common spring and rare fall migrant in the eastern third of Texas. Scarlet Tanagers are most frequently encountered along the coast. This species is a very rare to casual migrant in the western two-thirds of the state. In the fall, Scarlet Tanagers are very rarely found away from the coast. Migration falls between early April and mid-May and from early September to mid-October. There are a few summer sightings from the eastern third of the state and one mid-June sighting of a first-year male from Potter County in the Panhandle that might have been an exceptionally late migrant.

WESTERN TANAGER *Piranga ludoviciana* (Wilson)

Uncommon to locally common summer resident in the Guadalupe and Davis Mountains of the Trans-Pecos. Western Tanagers are uncommon to common migrants in the Trans-Pecos and High Plains, becoming increasingly less common eastward. Most records from the eastern half of the state are from the spring, possibly due to the fact that breeding-plumaged males are more readily recognizable. This species is rare in the winter along the coast and in the Lower Rio Grande Valley. There are isolated winter records from virtually all other areas of the state including as far north as Randall County in the Panhandle. Spring migrants arrive in late April and are present through May. Postbreeding wanderers can be found almost anywhere in the Trans-Pecos beginning in early July. Fall migrants are generally present from late August until early October.

Review Species

FLAME-COLORED TANAGER
Piranga bidentata Swainson

Accidental. There are five documented records of this species in Texas. The first four records were from the mountains of the southern Trans-Pecos. Surprisingly, the remaining record was from South Padre Island, Cameron County. This species has been found with increasing frequency in southeastern Arizona since the early 1990s. In many cases, males discovered in the spring have remained through the summer and paired with Western Tanagers, sometimes producing offspring.

14–19 APR. 1996, PINE CANYON, BIG BEND NP, BREWSTER CO.
  (TBRC 1996-64; TPRF 1488)
20–22 APR. 1996, CHISOS BASIN, BIG BEND NP, BREWSTER CO.
  (TBRC 1996-65; TPRF 1489)
1–5 OCT. 2001, DAVIS MOUNTAINS, JEFF DAVIS CO.
  (TBRC 2001-122; TPRF 2014)
11–14 APR. 2002, SOUTH PADRE ISLAND, CAMERON CO.
  (TBRC 2002-50; TPRF 2028)
27–28 APR. 2002, BOOT SPRING, BIG BEND NP, BREWSTER CO.
  (TBRC 2002-55; TPRF 2029)

Family Emberizidae: New World Sparrows

WHITE-COLLARED SEEDEATER
Sporophila torqueola (Bonaparte)

Uncommon to rare resident along the Rio Grande from Starr County north through Webb County. White-collared

Seedeaters have been reported irregularly east to Hidalgo County. There is also a recent report from Kenedy County where five were found on 30 August 1997 and another near Quemado, Maverick County, on 4 May 2002. This species was more widespread in the Lower Rio Grande Valley but was virtually extirpated from the United States in the late 1950s and early 1960s, as much of its habitat was converted to croplands. It has been suggested that the decline was closely tied to the heavy use of herbicides and pesticides, including DDT (Oberholser 1974).

Review Species

YELLOW-FACED GRASSQUIT
Tiaris olivacea (Linnaeus)

Accidental. There are two records for the state. The Texas records refer to *T. o. pusilla,* the subspecies found from central Tamaulipas and Nuevo Leon, Mexico, south through northern Central America. The 1990 record is the first for the United States, although there are now several additional records from Florida, of the Caribbean subspecies *T. o. olivacea.*

22–24 JAN. 1990, SANTA ANA NWR, HIDALGO CO.
  (TBRC 1990-23; TPRF 859)
11–29 JUNE 2002, BENTSEN–RIO GRANDE VALLEY SP, HIDALGO CO.
  (TBRC 2002-75; TPRF 2031)

OLIVE SPARROW *Arremonops rufivirgatus* (Lawrence)

Common resident throughout the South Texas Brush Country. Olive Sparrows reach the northern limits of their range on the southern edge of the Edwards Plateau where they have a discontinuous distribution, but they are primarily found from central Val Verde County east to Uvalde County. Along the Coastal Prairies, they are found north to Refugio County. Olive Sparrows are casual to very rare visitors north to Wilson and Bexar Counties.

GREEN-TAILED TOWHEE *Pipilo chlorurus* (Audubon)

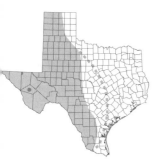

Rare to locally uncommon summer resident at higher elevations of the Davis and Guadalupe Mountains in the Trans-Pecos. This species is also a common to uncommon migrant and winter resident in the western half of the state, east through the High Plains south of the Panhandle, western Edwards Plateau, and the western South Texas Brush Country. Green-tailed Towhee becomes increasingly rare and irregular farther east but has occurred in all regions of the state. Fall migrants arrive in early September, and spring migrants have generally departed by mid-May.

SPOTTED TOWHEE *Pipilo maculatus* Swainson

Uncommon to locally common summer resident in the mountains of the Trans-Pecos. This species is a common migrant and winter resident throughout the western two-thirds of the state, east to the Blackland Prairies region. Spotted Towhee becomes increasingly rare farther east, primarily as a winter visitor. Migrants and wintering individuals are generally present between early October and early May. The elevation of Spotted and Eastern Towhees to the species level in 1995 has focused more attention on "rufous-sided" towhees. The range limits of these two species will undoubtedly continue to be better defined in coming years.

EASTERN TOWHEE *Pipilo erythrophthalmus* (Linnaeus)

Uncommon to rare migrant and winter resident in the eastern third of the state. Eastern Towhees are found regularly westward through the Blackland Prairies region where they are significantly outnumbered by Spotted Towhees. Eastern Towhee is a casual visitor farther west, with scattered records from the High Plains, Rolling Plains, Edwards Plateau, and Trans-Pecos. There are also records from as far south as the Lower Rio Grande Valley. Fall migrants arrive as early as mid-October, and the wintering population has generally departed by early April. Territorial male Eastern Towhees have been found with increasing regularity during the late spring and early summer in the Pineywoods since the late 1990s, although nesting has not been confirmed. The only documented breeding record for Texas involved a nest found in Harrison County on 31 July 1914.

CANYON TOWHEE *Pipilo fuscus* Swainson

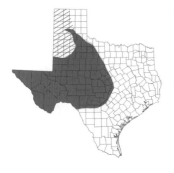

Common to uncommon resident in the Trans-Pecos east to the canyonlands of the southern Panhandle, the South Plains, western Rolling Plains, and western Edwards Plateau. This species becomes uncommon to rare and local on the eastern Rolling Plains and eastern Edwards Plateau. Canyon Towhee is an uncommon migrant and rare winter visitor to the remainder of the western Panhandle. There have also been isolated reports, primarily during the winter, from north-central Texas and the central coast.

CASSIN'S SPARROW *Aimophila cassinii* (Woodhouse)

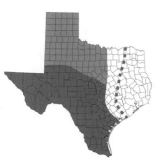

Common to abundant summer resident in the Panhandle and western South Plains, becoming locally common to rare in the remainder of the western two-thirds of the state. Breeding populations of Cassin's Sparrow are also found farther east to a line from western Tarrant County south to Matagorda Bay, where they are uncommon to rare. This species has wandered as far east as Delta, San Augustine, and Rains Counties. Cassin's Sparrows arrive on the breeding grounds in late March and early April and remain through October. This species is an uncommon to rare winter resident within the breeding range in the Trans-Pecos, western Edwards Plateau, and south through the South Texas Brush Country and occurs irregularly as far north as the South Plains (Lubbock County).

BACHMAN'S SPARROW

Aimophila aestivalis (Lichtenstein)

Uncommon and local resident in the Pineywoods. Bachman's Sparrows are found west to about Leon and Henderson Counties and south to Harris County. This species occurred as far west as Cooke, Lee, and Navarro Counties until the late 1880s (Oberholser 1974). Bachman's Sparrow is a habitat specialist found primarily in pine forests where the understory is composed of tall grasses, sometimes with scattered patches of shrubs and pine regeneration. Management with prescribed fire maintains this habitat type.

BOTTERI'S SPARROW *Aimophila botterii* (Sclater)

Uncommon to local summer resident on the lower coastal plain from southern Kleberg County southward. There have been isolated breeding records up the coast to San Patricio County and inland to Duval County. Botteri's Sparrows are present from late March through early October. There have been periodic winter reports, but this species is not believed to regularly winter in the state. An unexpected find was a pair of Botteri's Sparrows in Presidio County in June 1997 (Adams and Bryan 1999). The Texas coastal population belongs to *A. b. texana,* but the individuals found in the Trans-Pecos represent another subspecies, possibly *A. b. arizonae* or *A. b. botterii.*

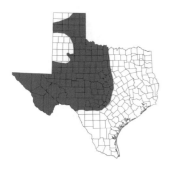

RUFOUS-CROWNED SPARROW
Aimophila ruficeps (Cassin)

Common to uncommon and local resident in the western two-thirds of the state. Rufous-crowned Sparrow ranges eastward through the Rolling Plains to Somervell and Bosque Counties in north-central Texas, and to the eastern and southern edges of the Edwards Plateau. On the South Plains and portions of the Panhandle, this species is rare and local. Rufous-crowneds are very rare winter visitors away from the breeding grounds. They are rare, but regular, in the western half of the South Texas Brush Country as far south as Starr County during this season. One was discovered well east of the normal range at Monument Hill, Fayette County, on 1 January 1998.

AMERICAN TREE SPARROW
Spizella arborea (Wilson)

Locally common winter resident in the Panhandle. American Tree Sparrow is a rare to very rare and irregular winter visitor to the South Plains eastward to northeast Texas and a casual winter visitor to the Trans-Pecos. This species arrives on the wintering grounds in mid-November, occasionally mid-October, and is present until early April. A single bird was recorded in Randall County on 3 May 1973. Historic reports indicate that American Tree Sparrows occurred outside of the Panhandle in greater numbers until the 1950s. For example, they were reported on Christmas Bird Counts as far south as the Edwards Plateau with some regularity in the late 1930s and 1940s. Currently, this species is best considered a vagrant in the eastern two-thirds of the state south of the stated range, where there are very few well-documented records. One of those records was a bird photographed on a petroleum platform in Louisiana waters at Garden Banks, 50 miles south of the mouth of the Sabine River, in April 1998.

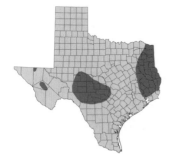

CHIPPING SPARROW *Spizella passerina* (Bechstein)

Chipping Sparrow has a rather disjunct breeding distribution in the state. They are common residents on the Edwards Plateau and locally abundant in the Guadalupe and Davis Mountains. In the Pineywoods, Chipping Sparrows are uncommon summer residents. They are common to abundant migrants and winter residents in nearly all parts of the state. This species is less common as a winter resident on the South Plains and irregular in the Panhandle. Migrants are generally present between mid-March and late April and from late September to mid-November

CLAY-COLORED SPARROW *Spizella pallida* (Swainson)

Common to uncommon migrant through much of the state. Clay-colored Sparrows are an uncommon to rare and irregular migrant in the western half of the Trans-Pecos, primarily in the fall, and very rare in the eastern third of the state. Migrants pass through between early April and late May and from mid-September to late October. This species is an uncommon to rare winter resident in the western South Texas Brush Country. They are also very irregular, although sometimes uncommon, winter visitors north to the southern Rolling Plains and western Edwards Plateau and west to the Davis Mountains. Clay-colored Sparrows are rare to very rare winter visitors along the coast, in the western half of the Trans-Pecos, and north to the Panhandle.

BREWER'S SPARROW *Spizella breweri* Cassin

Common to uncommon migrant in the western third of the state. This species is a rare to locally abundant winter resident in the Trans-Pecos and a rare and irregular winter visitor from the southern Panhandle south to the Lower Rio Grande Valley. Brewer's Sparrows have been found farther east, both as winter visitors and as migrants, with records from the upper coast and Brazos and San Augustine Counties. The migration periods are from mid-March to early May and from mid-September through October. Brewer's Sparrows were found breeding in the Panhandle in the 1870s, but there are no recent nesting records (Seyffert 1985a, 2001). Recent studies suggest that the two subspecies of Brewer's Sparrow, *S. b. breweri* and *S. b. taverneri,* should be considered separate species (Klicka et al. 1999). The status and distribution of *S. b. breweri* is provided in this account. The status of "Timberline" Sparrow, *S. b. taverneri,* is not well known, but it appears to be a rare migrant through the Trans-Pecos and possibly the western Edwards Plateau. The easternmost record of this subspecies in the state is a specimen from Irion County. The winter range of *S. b. taverneri* is unknown but may include parts of the Trans-Pecos.

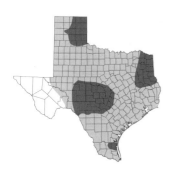

FIELD SPARROW *Spizella pusilla* (Wilson)

The breeding distribution of this species is interesting because of the scattered populations across the state. Field Sparrows are an uncommon resident in the northern half of the Pineywoods, the eastern Panhandle westward along the Canadian River Valley to Oldham County, the Edwards Plateau, and in Brooks and Kenedy Counties. Field Sparrows may also breed on the Stockton Plateau in the eastern Trans-Pecos, although Thornton (1951) did not report them. They are also suspected of breeding in Victoria County and north-central Texas, but no confirmed records exist. This species is a common to uncommon migrant and winter resident throughout most of the state. In the central and western Trans-Pecos, Field Sparrow is a rare to very rare migrant and irregular winter visitor. Migrant periods are from mid-March to early May and late September to early November.

BLACK-CHINNED SPARROW

Spizella atrogularis (Cabanis)

Uncommon summer resident in the mountains of the central Trans-Pecos. Black-chinned Sparrow is generally less numerous in the winter within its breeding range because most individuals move to lower elevations. In the Franklin Mountains, El Paso County, this species is an uncommon winter resident but is rare during the breeding season. There are scattered reports east of the Pecos River including Garza, Howard (TPRF 197), Lubbock, Midland, Randall, and San Patricio Counties.

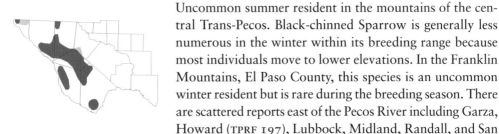

VESPER SPARROW *Pooecetes gramineus* (Gmelin)

Uncommon to common migrant and winter resident throughout most of the state. This species is a rare winter resident in the southern Panhandle and generally absent farther north. Fall migrants begin to arrive in the state in early September, and spring migrants can be found as late as early May. Vesper Sparrow is also a casual summer visitor to the High Plains, with most records from July.

LARK SPARROW *Chondestes grammacus* (Say)

Common to uncommon migrant and summer resident throughout most of the state. Lark Sparrows are uncommon and local breeders in southern Hudspeth County but

generally absent from the most arid habitats in the southern and western Trans-Pecos. They are rare and very local in summer in the Pineywoods. This species is a locally uncommon winter resident on the Blackland Prairies and Post Oak Savannahs, Coastal Prairies, and in the South Texas Brush Country. Lark Sparrows are rare to casual winter residents in the remainder of the eastern half of the state as well as on the Edwards Plateau, north to the southern Panhandle and west to the southeastern Trans-Pecos.

BLACK-THROATED SPARROW

Amphispiza bilineata (Cassin)

Common to abundant resident in the western half of the state away from the High Plains. Black-throated Sparrows are common in the Trans-Pecos, western Edwards Plateau, and through the South Texas Brush Country. This species is uncommon and more local on the eastern Edwards Plateau north through the Rolling Plains to Palo Pinto County. Black-throated Sparrows nest, possibly irregularly, in the Panhandle in the Palo Duro Canyon but are casual visitors elsewhere on the High Plains. There are scattered records from east of the breeding range, although they are unrecorded in the Pineywoods.

SAGE SPARROW *Amphispiza belli* (Cassin)

Uncommon migrant and local winter resident in the western and central Trans-Pecos. Sage Sparrow is a very rare to casual migrant and winter visitor to the High Plains. These sparrows arrive in mid-October and are present until mid-March. They have also been reported from the western edge of the Edwards Plateau but without supporting documentation (Lockwood 2001b). Recent studies suggest that the Sage Sparrow may be more than one species (Johnson and Martin 1992). The individuals found in Texas belong to the eastern subspecies, *A. b. nevadaensis*.

LARK BUNTING *Calamospiza melanocorys* Stejneger

Uncommon and irregular summer resident in the Panhandle, primarily in the northern half of the region. Lark Bunting is a rare and irregular nesting species south through the South Plains to the northwestern portion of the Edwards Plateau (Wiedenfeld 1983; Kostecke, Floyd, and Stogner 2001). Midsummer records from the grasslands in the central Trans-Pecos suggest that nesting may occur there as well. This species is an abundant to uncommon migrant and winter resident in the western half of the state, east through the Rolling Plains and western Edwards Plateau, and south to the central coast and the Lower Rio Grande Valley. Lark Buntings are occasional migrants and rare and irregular winter visitors east to the Pineywoods. Migrant Lark Buntings begin moving south as early as late July, and northbound birds can be found through mid-May.

SAVANNAH SPARROW

Passerculus sandwichensis (Gmelin)

Abundant to uncommon migrant and winter resident throughout the state. Fall migrants arrive in mid-September, with the bulk of the winter population present by early November. Wintering birds begin to depart in early April, and migrants are present as late as mid-May. Savannah Sparrow is a casual summer visitor to the western Panhandle and a vagrant farther south (Travis and Kleberg Counties).

GRASSHOPPER SPARROW

Ammodramus savannarum (Gmelin)

Rare to locally common summer resident in most of the state. On the Edwards Plateau, this species typically nests during the spring and has departed by mid-summer. In mid-elevation grasslands in the Trans-Pecos, Grasshopper Sparrows are present only in summer and typically arrive in July. They are very rare and local in the Pineywoods at all seasons and an uncommon to common migrant west of the Pineywoods. This species is also a rare to locally common winter resident throughout most of the state, although it appears that most birds winter south of the Nueces River. Grasshopper Sparrows are absent from the Panhandle in winter and generally absent from other areas of the High Plains and Rolling Plains.

BAIRD'S SPARROW *Ammodramus bairdii* (Audubon)

Review Species

Very rare to rare migrant in the western half of the state. There are 42 documented state records, with the majority from the High Plains, Concho Valley, and Trans-Pecos. Migrants have been documented between early April and late May and mid-September and early November. Baird's Sparrow is also a very rare and local winter resident in the

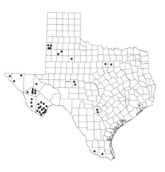

Trans-Pecos and possibly on the South Plains. The only documented winter records from the High Plains are three specimens collected out of 14 individuals observed between November 1976 and January 1977 at Muleshoe National Wildlife Refuge, Bailey County (Grzybowski 1982). The species is very elusive and probably occurs more commonly and regularly than is currently known. Its grassland habitat and skulking behavior make it difficult to document, as indicated by the more than one hundred undocumented reports.

HENSLOW'S SPARROW

Ammodramus henslowii (Audubon)

Rare to very rare migrant and winter resident in the eastern third of the state. Henslow's Sparrows are regular winter residents east of the Brazos River drainage but only casual visitors to north-central Texas, with reports from Cooke, Dallas, Delta, and Rains Counties. Henslow's Sparrows are very rare during the winter along the Coastal Prairies south to San Patricio County. In general, this species is present in Texas from mid-October to early April. There are scattered reports from farther west to Travis and Bexar Counties and one record from the Panhandle involving a single bird found in Oldham County on 6 May 2000. Formerly, a resident endemic population was found in Harris County, *A. h. houstonensis,* which is now considered extinct (Arnold 1983; Arnold and Garza 1998).

LE CONTE'S SPARROW

Ammodramus leconteii (Audubon)

Uncommon to locally common migrant in the eastern third of the state, becoming uncommon to rare west to the High Plains and western Edwards Plateau. Le Conte's Sparrows are also an uncommon to common winter resident in the eastern third of the state, including the upper and central coasts. They become uncommon to rare westward to the eastern Edwards Plateau and the Concho Valley and southward along the Coastal Prairies to Cameron County. Le Conte's Sparrows are irregular to rare and local winter residents west to the central Trans-Pecos and southern Panhandle. This species is generally present from early October to early May. A singing male found in Ochiltree County on 25 June 1994 provided the only summer record for the state.

NELSON'S SHARP-TAILED SPARROW

Ammodramus nelsoni Allen

Uncommon to locally common winter resident along the coast south to Nueces County, rare and local south to the Rio Grande. Despite being a common winter resident on the coast, this species is rarely detected inland during migration (White 1999). Migrant Nelson's Sharp-tailed Sparrows have been found primarily in the eastern third of the state, although there is one documented record from as far west as Reeves County (TPRF 221). Fall migrants generally arrive on the coast in early to mid-October and depart for the breeding grounds by early May. Specimens of the Saltmarsh Sharp-tailed Sparrow *(A. caudacutus)* had been previously reported from Texas (TOS 1995); however, upon examination they were identified as *A. nelsoni*.

SEASIDE SPARROW *Ammodramus maritimus* (Wilson)

Uncommon to locally common resident along the coast south to Aransas County, rare and local south to the Rio Grande. The only documented inland record of Seaside Sparrow for Texas was a single bird mist-netted and photographed on 14 December 1974 near Waco, McLennan County. The bird was present until at least mid-March 1975.

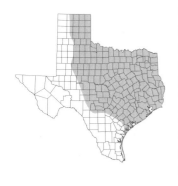

FOX SPARROW *Passerella iliaca* (Merrem)

Common to uncommon migrant and winter resident from the eastern Panhandle and Edwards Plateau eastward. This species is a rare to locally uncommon winter resident on the High Plains, western Edwards Plateau, and the Trans-Pecos. Fox Sparrows are generally absent from the South Texas Brush Country, with only a few scattered records. Fall migrants begin to arrive in mid-October but are very rare before mid-November. Wintering individuals and migrants depart by early March, with a few lingering as late as early May. Recent work has suggested that the subspecies groups of Fox Sparrow may represent three or four species (Zink 1994). The Fox Sparrows occurring in Texas are part of the eastern or "Red" group and belong to two subspecies, *P. i. iliaca* and *P. i. zaboria*. There are reports of the "Slate-colored" Fox Sparrow, *P. i. schistacea,* from the western Panhandle and western Trans-Pecos, but there are no well-documented records of this subspecies for Texas.

SONG SPARROW *Melospiza melodia* (Wilson)

Common to uncommon migrant and winter resident throughout most of the state. Song Sparrow is rare to very rare in the South Texas Brush County, especially in the Lower Rio Grande Valley. A few individuals arrive in late September, but this species is not common until mid-November. Winter residents begin to depart in early March and are rare by early April, although a few birds have lingered into early May in the Panhandle (Seyffert 2001).

LINCOLN'S SPARROW *Melospiza lincolnii* (Audubon)

Common to uncommon migrant throughout the state. Lincoln's Sparrow is an uncommon to locally rare winter resident in much of the Panhandle and eastward across north-central Texas to the Pineywoods. This species is common to locally abundant as a winter resident throughout the remainder of the state. The migration periods are from late March to mid-May and from mid-September through November. On occasion, they have been found as early as mid-August and have lingered in spring as late as early June.

SWAMP SPARROW *Melospiza georgiana* (Lathum)

Common migrant through the eastern half of the state, becoming uncommon and increasingly local westward through the Trans-Pecos. Swamp Sparrows are uncommon winter residents in most areas of the state. They occur most commonly in the Pineywoods and along the upper and central coasts and less commonly in the Panhandle. They normally arrive in mid-October and depart in mid-April.

WHITE-THROATED SPARROW
Zonotrichia albicollis (Gmelin)

Abundant to common migrant and winter resident in the eastern half of the state. White-throated Sparrows become uncommon to rare west to the eastern Trans-Pecos and south through the South Texas Brush Country to the Rio Grande. This species is a rare and local winter visitor to the western Trans-Pecos. They generally arrive in mid-October and remain through April, with a few stragglers lingering into early May. There are three summer records of White-throated Sparrow from the northeastern corner of the state. Two of these records are from Van Zandt County in late

June. A third is from Delta County on 7 August 1998; this specimen was probably an extraordinarily early migrant.

HARRIS'S SPARROW *Zonotrichia querula* (Nuttall)

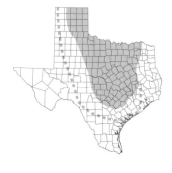

Uncommon to locally common winter resident in the central portion of the state. Harris's Sparrows are found from the central Panhandle and eastern Edwards Plateau east through the Blackland Prairie and Oak Savannahs regions. They are rare on the Coastal Prairies to San Patricio County and are casual to Cameron County. This species is a rare visitor to the Pineywoods in the east and the Trans-Pecos in the west. Harris's Sparrows can generally be found between early November and late March; however, a few individuals routinely linger as late as early May in north-central Texas and in the Panhandle. This species formerly occurred more commonly on the South Plains.

WHITE-CROWNED SPARROW
Zonotrichia leucophrys (Foster)

Abundant to uncommon migrant and winter resident throughout the northern two-thirds of the state, becoming uncommon southward to the Rio Grande. White-crowned Sparrow is somewhat local in distribution within the Pineywoods during winter. Migrants arrive as early as mid-September and remain as late as late May. Two identifiable subspecies groups of White-crowned Sparrow winter in the state. White-lored individuals belong to *Z. l. gambelii,* which breed in the northern Rocky Mountains. Most of the black-lored individuals belong to *Z. l. leucophrys,* which breed in the boreal forest of Canada. The other black-lored subspecies, *Z. l. oriantha,* breeds in the southern Rocky Mountains and is a fall and late spring migrant in the Trans-Pecos and possibly farther east (Dunn, Garrett, and Alderfer 1995).

Review Species

GOLDEN-CROWNED SPARROW
Zonotrichia atricapilla (Gmelin)

Very rare winter visitor to the western half of the state. There are 28 documented records from the state; almost half of them are from the Trans-Pecos. Eight records are scattered from the Panhandle south to the Edwards Plateau. Those remaining include two from the South Texas Brush Country (Live Oak County), one from Brazos County,

and three, including two specimens, from Orange County. All occurred between 23 October and 24 May. There are 16 reports of Golden-crowned Sparrows from prior to the development of the Review List in 1987 for which there is no documentation on file at Texas A&M University.

DARK-EYED JUNCO *Junco hyemalis* (Linnaeus)

Uncommon to abundant migrant and winter resident throughout the northern two-thirds of the state. Dark-eyed Juncos are less common and more irregular on the Texas coast and are rare in the South Texas Brush Country. Generally, this species can be found in Texas between mid-October and mid-April, although individuals have been found as early as mid-September and lingered into late May. They are common summer residents in the upper elevations of the Guadalupe Mountains. The four subspecies groups in this taxon were formerly considered separate species and all occur in Texas.

"SLATE-COLORED" JUNCO

Common to abundant in the eastern two-thirds of the state, becoming increasingly less common westward. Slate-colored Junco is rare to locally uncommon in the Trans-Pecos and South Texas Brush Country.

"WHITE-WINGED" JUNCO

Casual visitor to the Panhandle. There are nine reports, including three documented records, from the Panhandle and a single report from the South Plains. The first confirmed occurrence in the state was a specimen collected in Briscoe County on 19 December 1968 (Weske 1974). "White-winged" Junco has also been documented once in the Trans-Pecos (El Paso County). The Texas Bird Records Committee is interested in receiving details on any "White-winged" Juncos found in Texas.

"OREGON" JUNCO

Common to uncommon migrant and winter resident in the western half of the state. "Oregon" Juncos occur uncommonly east to Van Zandt County and the Central Brazos Valley. They are casual to rare farther east and south. Interesting midsummer records come from Crosby and Jeff Davis Counties. This group also includes the "Pink-sided" Junco.

"GRAY-HEADED" JUNCO

Common to rare migrant and winter resident in the Trans-

Pecos and Panhandle south to the Concho Valley. There are a few scattered records from other parts of the state, including individuals in Brooks and Dallas Counties. This group includes the "Red-backed" Junco, which is a common breeding bird at upper elevations in the Guadalupe Mountains and an uncommon and local winter resident elsewhere in the Trans-Pecos.

Review Species

YELLOW-EYED JUNCO *Junco phaeonotus* Wagler

Casual visitor to the Trans-Pecos. There are seven documented records of this species for the state: four from Guadalupe Mountains National Park, two from Big Bend National Park, and one from El Paso County. There are records from all seasons, and no pattern to the occurrence of Yellow-eyed Junco in the state is discernable.

McCOWN'S LONGSPUR

Calcarius mccownii (Lawrence)

Abundant to uncommon winter resident on the High Plains and Rolling Plains, south to the northwestern Edwards Plateau. McCown's Longspur is a rare to locally uncommon winter resident east through north-central Texas and south through the Blackland Prairies. In the Trans-Pecos, they are irregular winter visitors. This species is a vagrant along the coast and to the South Texas Brush Country. Oberholser (1974) reported that McCown's Longspurs were regular winter visitors to the South Texas Brush Country prior to 1900. This species generally arrives in late October and is present until mid-March with a few lingering into early April.

LAPLAND LONGSPUR *Calcarius lapponicus* (Linnaeus)

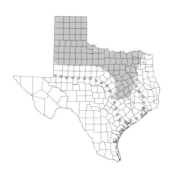

Uncommon to abundant winter resident in the Panhandle east to north-central Texas. Lapland Longspur is rare through the remainder of the eastern half of Texas. During invasion years, they can be locally common as far south as Bexar County and east to Harris County. This longspur is a rare winter visitor to the South Plains and very rare south to the Concho Valley. Lapland Longspur is considered accidental in the Trans-Pecos, with most records coming from the northern portion of that region. They generally arrive in mid- to late November and are gone by early March.

SMITH'S LONGSPUR *Calcarius pictus* (Swainson)

Locally uncommon to rare migrant and winter resident to eastern north-central and northeast Texas. Smith's Longspurs are a casual winter visitor as far south as Brazos and Guadalupe Counties. This species usually arrives in late November, and most have departed by early March. Despite the restricted winter range, this species has been detected in many other areas of the state, including the central coast (Calhoun County), Edwards Plateau (Schleicher County), Pineywoods (Gregg, Nacogdoches, Smith, and Walker Counties), South Plains (Crosby County), and Trans-Pecos (Brewster, El Paso, and Jeff Davis Counties). Many of these reports, as well as those from the Panhandle, are undocumented.

CHESTNUT-COLLARED LONGSPUR

Calcarius ornatus (Townsend)

Common to uncommon winter resident to the High Plains, Rolling Plains, and Trans-Pecos. Chestnut-collared Longspur is also an uncommon to rare winter visitor east through north-central Texas and south through the Blackland Prairies and Edwards Plateau. This species is a very rare visitor along the coast and south through the South Texas Brush Country. Chestnut-collared Longspurs are present in Texas between mid-October and early April.

Review Species

SNOW BUNTING *Plectrophenax nivalis* (Linnaeus)

Accidental. Texas has five documented records of this species. The first record was a bird found at Lake Livingston, Polk County, in 1977 (Bryan, Gallucci, and Moldenhauer 1978). Snow Bunting are found south to the central Great Plains during a normal winter. When food crops are poor and sometimes after particularly strong storms, these birds may be pushed much farther south. During these invasions, Snow Buntings are sometimes found in numbers across the southeastern United States and into the southern Great Plains.

21–23 DEC. 1977, LAKE LIVINGSTON, POLK CO. (SHSU 1001)
29 DEC. 1983, 16 MI. N OF DALHART, DALLAM CO.
  (TBRC 1984-12)
9 MAY 1988, CHISOS BASIN, BIG BEND NATIONAL PARK,
  BREWSTER CO. (TBRC 1988-214)
27 NOV. 1993, LAKE BALMORHEA, REEVES CO. (TBRC 1994-7)
26 DEC. 1999–15 JAN. 2000, LAKE TAWAKONI, RAINS CO.
  (TBRC 1999-116; TPRF 1858)

Family Cardinalidae: Cardinals and Allies

Review Species

CRIMSON-COLLARED GROSBEAK
Rhodothraupis celaeno (Deppe)

Casual winter visitor to the Lower Rio Grande Valley. There are eight documented records of this species from Texas and the United States, two of them outside the Lower Rio Grande Valley. Single individuals, both in female-type plumage, were found at Laredo, Webb County, and Aransas National Wildlife Refuge, Aransas County. Interestingly, five of the records from the Lower Rio Grande Valley come from the winter of 1987–88 and two others from the winter of 1985–86. The remaining record is from midsummer, involving a bird at Bentsen–Rio Grande Valley State Park, Hidalgo County, from 28 June to 1 July 1974 (TPRF 244). Crimson-collared Grosbeaks are endemic to northeastern Mexico.

NORTHERN CARDINAL *Cardinalis cardinalis* (Linnaeus)

Common to abundant resident throughout most of the state. In the Trans-Pecos, Northern Cardinals are uncommon to locally common residents in the southern counties and rare visitors at all seasons to the northern counties. Despite the irregular occurrence of this species in the northern Trans-Pecos, there are scattered nesting records. In the Panhandle, they are rare and local residents in the far western counties. Northern Cardinals use many habitats, including urban areas, making them one of the more conspicuous members of our state's avifauna.

PYRRHULOXIA *Cardinalis sinuatus* Bonaparte

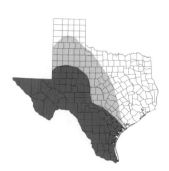

Common to uncommon resident in the southwestern portion of the state. Resident populations occur as far north as the southern South Plains, east to the western Edwards Plateau, and south to the Lower Rio Grande Valley. Pyrrhuloxias are notorious for wandering north after the breeding season and are uncommon winter visitors to the entire South Plains. They are irregular, but increasing, north to the southern Panhandle. During migration and winter, this species is an irruptive wanderer eastward into north-central Texas and to the upper coast. Pyrrhuloxias have significantly expanded their range in Texas over the past century. Oberholser (1974) postulated that this was the result of the northward invasion of honey mesquite *(Prosopis glandulosa)*.

ROSE-BREASTED GROSBEAK
Pheucticus ludovicianus (Linnaeus)

Common to uncommon migrant in the eastern half of the state, becoming increasingly rare farther west. As with many migrants, Rose-breasted Grosbeak is encountered much more frequently along the coast than inland. This species is primarily found between early April and late May and between mid-September and early November. Rose-breasted Grosbeaks are rare winter visitors along the coast and in the Lower Rio Grande Valley. A few isolated reports of wintering individuals have come from inland locations, including as far north as Amarillo, Randall County. This species is also a casual summer visitor to the High Plains and northern Rolling Plains and accidental in other areas of the state.

BLACK-HEADED GROSBEAK
Pheucticus melanocephalus (Swainson)

Common migrant and summer resident in the mountains of the Trans-Pecos and a casual summer visitor to the Panhandle and South Plains. They are uncommon to rare migrants throughout the Trans-Pecos east to the High Plains, northern Rolling Plains, and western Edwards Plateau, and south through the Lower Rio Grande Valley, becoming increasingly less common farther east. Black-headed Grosbeaks are found annually during migration as far east as north-central Texas and the central coast. This species migrates through the state between early April and late May and from early August to late October. Fall migrants are occasionally noted as early as late July. They are very rare and irregular winter visitors along the coast and inland as far north as Randall County.

Review Species

BLUE BUNTING *Cyanocompsa parellina* (Bonaparte)

Very rare and irregular winter visitor to the Lower Rio Grande Valley. The majority of records occur from mid-November to mid-March, although individuals have lingered as late as early April. Of the 27 accepted records for the state, 19 are from Hidalgo County, four from Starr County, two from Cameron County, and the remaining two from Brazoria County on the upper coast. Despite the rarity of this species in the state, and the United States, undocumented reports are received almost every winter.

BLUE GROSBEAK *Passerina caerulea* (Linnaeus)

Locally common to uncommon summer resident through most of the state. Blue Grosbeaks are uncommon to rare in the Blackland Prairie and Post Oak Savannah regions, as well as the Coastal Prairies north of Aransas County. This species is a common to uncommon migrant throughout the state. Blue Grosbeaks arrive in Texas in early April (early May in much of the Trans-Pecos) and are present on the breeding grounds through August. Fall migrants are common until mid-October, with some lingering well into November. Blue Grosbeaks occasionally linger into early winter, particularly along the coast and in extreme southern Texas, and are very rare winter residents near the Rio Grande in southern Brewster and Presidio Counties.

LAZULI BUNTING *Passerina amoena* (Say)

Uncommon migrant through the Trans-Pecos, Panhandle, and South Plains, becoming increasingly less common eastward. Migrants pass through the state from early April to late May and between early August and early October. Lazuli Bunting is a much more common migrant in fall than spring. Inexplicably, this species has not been reported in the fall from the Edwards Plateau (Lockwood 2001b), and it is virtually unknown during the fall in north-central Texas, where it occurs annually in small numbers in the spring. Lazuli Bunting is a rare summer resident in the Panhandle, although nesting records are few (Seyffert 2001). The only other nestings are from Kerr County, where Lacey (1911) reportedly collected egg sets from two nests in 1903. They are rare to very rare winter residents in the Lower Rio Grande Valley and along the coast north to Aransas County. This species is casual elsewhere along the coast and inland south of the Balcones Escarpment. There is a winter sighting from Randall County in the Panhandle on 3 December 1984.

INDIGO BUNTING *Passerina cyanea* (Linnaeus)

Common to locally abundant summer resident in the eastern half of the state. Breeding populations of Indigo Buntings are found west to the western Edwards Plateau, eastern Rolling Plains, and the eastern Panhandle. They are also present in the western Panhandle along the Canadian River drainage to Oldham County. This species occasion-

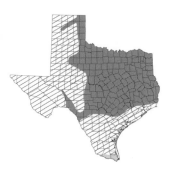

ally breeds in riparian habitats in the Trans-Pecos, with nesting records from El Paso, Hudspeth, and Jeff Davis Counties. Indigo Buntings are abundant migrants through the eastern half of Texas, becoming increasingly less common westward. Migrants pass through the state between late March and late May and from mid-August to early November. This species is rare to locally uncommon in winter in the Lower Rio Grande Valley and, to a lesser extent, along the coast. There are also isolated records of overwintering birds inland to the southern Edwards Plateau.

VARIED BUNTING *Passerina versicolor* (Bonaparte)

Locally uncommon to rare summer resident in the southern Trans-Pecos and eastward to the southwestern Edwards Plateau. This species is a rare and local summer resident in the western half of the South Texas Brush Country and the Lower Rio Grande Valley (Lockwood 1995). There are isolated summer records from the eastern Edwards Plateau and one from Tom Green County. Varied Bunting is a very rare winter resident in southern Brewster and Presidio Counties, primarily during wet cycles. They are very rare spring migrants along the lower and central coasts as far north as Corpus Christi. Isolated reports of spring migrants have been received far from the normal breeding areas, including Calhoun, Chambers, El Paso, Galveston, Lubbock, Midland, and Potter Counties.

PAINTED BUNTING *Passerina ciris* (Linnaeus)

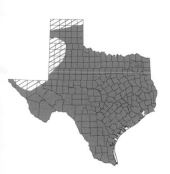

Uncommon to common summer resident throughout most of the state. Painting Buntings are uncommon to common migrants throughout Texas. Migrants begin passing through Texas in early April. Summer residents arrive on the breeding grounds in late April and remain until early September. Fall migrants may linger, particularly along the coast, into early November. Painted Buntings are very rare winter residents in the Lower Rio Grande Valley and along the coast and are casual inland to Lubbock and Presidio Counties.

DICKCISSEL *Spiza americana* (Gmelin)

Uncommon to locally abundant summer resident and migrant east of the Pecos River. Breeding populations of Dickcissels fluctuate greatly depending on environmental

conditions. If conditions are favorable when migrants arrive, breeding activities commence almost immediately. During drought years when conditions are less favorable, they continue their migration, and evidence of breeding can be difficult to find. For similar reasons, Dickcissel is an uncommon to rare fall migrant in the Trans-Pecos but a very rare and local summer resident in the eastern half of the region. This species winters in northern South America, but a few well-documented winter records have come from along the coast and inland to Dallas, Grayson, and Lubbock Counties. One of the more interesting occurrences in the state was an unprecedented influx of birds along the upper and central coasts during late January and February 1999.

Family Icteridae:
Blackbirds, Meadowlarks, and Orioles

BOBOLINK *Dolichonyx oryzivorus* (Linnaeus)

Uncommon to rare spring and very rare fall migrant in the eastern third of the state. Bobolink is a casual to accidental spring migrant in the remainder of the state. There are documented records in the Trans-Pecos from El Paso, Jeff Davis, and Reeves Counties and in the Panhandle from Carson and Moore Counties. Spring migrants are present between early April and late May with a peak from late April to mid-May. The fall migration period is not as well defined, but there are records from mid-August to late October. One documented winter record exists for the state involving a bird at Brazos Bend State Park, Fort Bend County, on 27 December 1995.

RED-WINGED BLACKBIRD
Agelaius phoeniceus (Linnaeus)

Abundant to locally uncommon resident throughout the state. Red-winged Blackbirds are more localized during the breeding season because of the spotty availability of nesting habitat, particularly in the western half of the state. They are more widespread and often found in large flocks during the remainder of the year, as migrants join the resident population. Some wintering roosts reportedly contain a million or more birds.

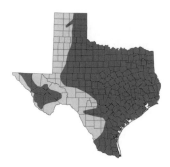

EASTERN MEADOWLARK *Sturnella magna* (Linnaeus)

Common to locally uncommon resident through the eastern half of the state west to the eastern Panhandle and south along the Coastal Prairies to the Rio Grande. Eastern Meadowlark is a rare to very rare and local summer resident in the western half of the High Plains, south to the interior of the South Texas Brush Country. During winter, they are uncommon to rare and more widespread through the western half of the state, including the South Texas Brush Country. Taxonomic studies have suggested that the southwestern subspecies of Eastern Meadowlark, *S. m. lilianae*, may be a separate species (Lanyon 1962; Sibley and Monroe 1990). This subspecies is an uncommon resident in the mid- and upper elevation grasslands of the central Trans-Pecos west to northeastern El Paso County and has been documented in Kinney and Val Verde Counties in the winter. There is a summer record of this subspecies from Lamb County on the South Plains.

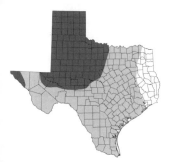

WESTERN MEADOWLARK *Sturnella neglecta* Audubon

Common to uncommon resident in portions of the western half of the state, east through the Rolling Plains and western Edwards Plateau. There is an isolated nesting record from Brooks County. The summer distribution of this species in the Trans-Pecos is not well understood but appears to be limited primarily to agricultural areas of Hudspeth and El Paso Counties and perhaps similar niches elsewhere. There is only minimal overlap in nesting habitat with Eastern Meadowlarks in mid-elevation grasslands. Western Meadowlark is common to abundant during the winter through the western half of the state, east to the Blackland Prairies and south through the South Texas Brush Country, and it is locally uncommon east to the Pineywoods, where it is very rare but regular. There is evidence that Western Meadowlarks use agricultural fields more extensively during winter than do the Eastern. Winter residents are generally present from October through early April.

YELLOW-HEADED BLACKBIRD
Xanthocephalus xanthocephalus (Bonaparte)

Common to uncommon migrant in the western half of the state, becoming increasingly less common eastward to the Pineywoods and Upper Texas Coast, where it is rare.

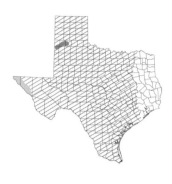

The migration periods are between early April and late May and mid-July and early November. Yellow-headed Blackbirds are also very local summer residents in the Panhandle, with established breeding colonies primarily located in the southwestern sector (Seyffert 2001). The largest colonies occur in Castro County, with additional nesting sites in nearby Parmer, Swisher, and Bailey Counties and north to Hansford County when conditions are favorable. Yellow-headed Blackbirds are rare and irregular in winter in most areas of the state, except in the western Trans-Pecos, where they are locally abundant in El Paso and Hudspeth Counties with flocks that can sometimes exceed 20,000 individuals.

RUSTY BLACKBIRD *Euphagus carolinus* (Müller)

Rare to locally uncommon migrant and winter resident in the eastern third of the state. The majority of wintering birds are found from north-central Texas eastward and southward through the Pineywoods. This species has become less common and more irregular in the state in recent decades. Pulich (1961b) reported winter roosts of up to 5,000 individuals in the mid-1950s in Tarrant County. Concentrations of 500 to 600 birds are now noteworthy. Rusty Blackbird is a very rare to casual visitor to the western half of the state, with records as far west as El Paso County. They are accidental in extreme southern Texas, with only one report from the Lower Rio Grande Valley. Rusty Blackbirds are generally present in Texas from mid-November to late March.

BREWER'S BLACKBIRD

Euphagus cyanocephalus (Wagler)

Common to locally abundant migrant and winter resident throughout most of Texas. Brewer's Blackbirds are most common in the western half of the state, becoming less common farther east. They are locally uncommon to rare in the Lower Rio Grande Valley and southern South Texas Brush Country. Migrants arrive in mid-September, and most have departed by early May. The only two documented nesting records for the state are a nest with eggs collected in Wilbarger County in 1928 and a nest discovered in Jeff Davis County in 2000 (Bryan and Karges 2001). Additional reported nestings have come from Crosby, Jeff Davis, and Lubbock Counties.

COMMON GRACKLE *Quiscalus quiscula* (Linnaeus)

Common to uncommon summer resident in the eastern two-thirds of the state, west through the High Plains and central Edwards Plateau, and south to the Guadalupe River drainage in the Coastal Prairies. The breeding range has expanded westward since the 1950s, and Common Grackles are now present very locally in urban areas on the western Edwards Plateau and locally as far west as Pecos, Reeves County. This species is an abundant migrant and winter resident in the eastern third of the state, becoming increasingly less common westward through the eastern Rolling Plains and Edwards Plateau. Common Grackles are rare and local in winter throughout the South Texas Brush Country and the eastern half of the Trans-Pecos; however, they are largely absent from the Panhandle. Beginning in the mid-1990s, small numbers of Common Grackles have wintered irregularly in El Paso County.

BOAT-TAILED GRACKLE *Quiscalus major* Vieillot

Uncommon to locally abundant resident along the upper and central coasts. Boat-tailed Grackles are most common on the upper coast, becoming increasingly less so south to Nueces County. This species is accidental south to Willacy and Cameron Counties. Boat-tailed Grackles are almost exclusively found within 30 miles of the Gulf of Mexico. This species was formerly considered conspecific with Great-tailed Grackle under the name Boat-tailed Grackle.

GREAT-TAILED GRACKLE

Quiscalus mexicanus (Gmelin)

Abundant resident throughout most of the southern half of the state. They are also common, though largely limited to urban areas, northward through the state to the Oklahoma border, including the Panhandle. In the Pineywoods, this species is a very rare resident, particularly away from urban areas. Similarly, in the Trans-Pecos, Great-tailed Grackles are common to abundant in urban areas and rare to absent otherwise. Great-tailed Grackles have greatly expanded their range over the past century. Found primarily in the South Texas Brush Country prior to 1910, by 1960 they had colonized the remaining Coastal Prairie and much of the central portion of the state, with breeding documented as far north as north-central Texas and the southern

Panhandle. The remainder of the state, west of the Pineywoods, had been colonized by the mid-1980s.

Review Species

SHINY COWBIRD *Molothrus bonariensis* (Gmelin)

Casual. Texas has nine documented records of this species. The first two were males captured in cowbird traps on Fort Hood in Bell and Coryell Counties. All but one of the subsequent records have come from the coast. Shiny Cowbirds have undergone a range expansion over the past two decades. This expansion included a march northward through the islands of the Caribbean to southern Florida. Many observers speculated that this species would soon colonize the southeastern United States; however, that has not happened, and Shiny Cowbirds are still rare even in southern Florida. All Texas records are of the distinctive males.

BRONZED COWBIRD *Molothrus aeneus* (Wagler)

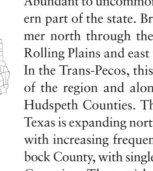

Abundant to uncommon summer resident in the southwestern part of the state. Bronzed Cowbirds are found in summer north through the Edwards Plateau to the southern Rolling Plains and east up the coast to Matagorda County. In the Trans-Pecos, this species occurs in the southern half of the region and along the Rio Grande to El Paso and Hudspeth Counties. The Bronzed Cowbird population in Texas is expanding northward, and birds are being reported with increasing frequency in summer as far north as Lubbock County, with single sightings from Randall and Tarrant Counties. They withdraw from the Trans-Pecos and Edwards Plateau during the winter and are locally uncommon winter residents in the South Texas Brush Country. Bronzed Cowbirds are rare up the Coastal Prairies to Harris County in winter.

BROWN-HEADED COWBIRD
Molothrus ater (Boddaert)

Common to locally abundant summer resident throughout the state, except in the southern South Texas Brush Country where uncommon. During the winter, the majority of Brown-headed Cowbirds withdraw from the Trans-Pecos and from upland habitats of the Edwards Plateau. Small numbers remain in these regions throughout the season and may even be locally abundant at roost sites such as feed lots. In the eastern half of the state, the number of wintering birds increases greatly as migrants bolster the resident population. In the Panhandle, these migrants congregate in large flocks during the fall and remain into early winter before dispersing (Seyffert 2001). Brown-headed Cowbirds form large winter roosts, with numbers at some sites estimated as high as 2,000,000 individuals.

Review Species

BLACK-VENTED ORIOLE *Icterus wagleri* Sclater

Accidental. Texas has four documented records of this oriole, three of which involve a single individual. An adult Black-vented Oriole was discovered on 27 September 1968 at Rio Grande Village, Big Bend National Park, Brewster County. What is believed to be the same individual returned for the summer of 1969, during which time it was captured and banded. This bird once again returned to the same location during the summer of 1970 (Wauer 1970). The other Texas record involved an adult at Kingsville, Kleberg County, in 1989.

27 SEPT. 1968, RIO GRANDE VILLAGE, BBNP, BREWSTER CO.
 (TPRF 31)
26 APR.–27 SEPT. 1969, RIO GRANDE VILLAGE, BBNP, BREWSTER CO.
17 APR.–10 OCT. 1970, RIO GRANDE VILLAGE, BBNP, BREWSTER CO.
17 JUNE–4 OCT. 1989, KINGSVILLE, KLEBERG CO.
 (TBRC 1989-176; TPRF 781)

ORCHARD ORIOLE *Icterus spurius* (Linnaeus)

Uncommon to locally common summer resident in the eastern two-thirds of the state and locally uncommon to rare farther west. This species is particularly scarce from the western High Plains south through the South Texas Brush Country. In the Trans-Pecos, Orchard Orioles are locally uncommon in riparian habitats in the southern half of the region and along the Rio Grande floodplain in extreme southeastern El Paso and Hudspeth Counties. They are common to uncommon migrants in the state west to the central Trans-Pecos, becoming rare in the remainder of that region. Migration periods last from mid-March to mid-May and late July to mid-November. There are isolated winter reports, primarily along the Coastal Prairies. Most are probably late migrants, but there are valid records of birds overwintering. Orchard Orioles have declined greatly in recent decades. A distinctive subspecies, *I. s. fuertesi,* which is endemic to northeastern Mexico, has been documented in Cameron County on three occasions. This subspecies is known as the Fuertes's or Ochre Oriole and was previously considered a separate species.

HOODED ORIOLE *Icterus cucullatus* Swainson

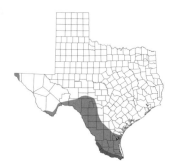

Uncommon and local summer resident on the southwestern Edwards Plateau and south through the South Texas Brush Country to the Lower Rio Grande Valley. Hooded Orioles are rare and local summer residents in El Paso County and along the Rio Grande from southern Presidio County eastward to Terrell County. The breeding population is generally present between mid-March and mid-September. The highest density of Hooded Orioles occurs in the oak woodlands of Kenedy and Brooks Counties. This species is an occasional visitor to the Davis and Guadalupe Mountains, and vagrants have been reported as far north as Bailey, Crosby, and Randall Counties and as far east as northeast Texas and the upper coast. Hooded Oriole is a rare and local winter resident in the Lower Rio Grande Valley.

BULLOCK'S ORIOLE *Icterus bullockii* (Swainson)

Common summer resident in the western half of the state. Summering Bullock's Orioles can be found east to the central Rolling Plains, central Edwards Plateau, and South Texas Brush Country. They are irregular breeders east to the Balcones Escarpment and the central coast. Bullock's Orioles are common to uncommon migrants through the western half of the state, becoming very rare east to Bastrop and Tarrant Counties. Migration is generally from late March to mid-May and late July to late September. This species is a very rare winter visitor to virtually all areas of the state, including the Pineywoods. This oriole was formerly known as Northern Oriole when it was considered conspecific with the Baltimore Oriole *(I. galbula)*.

ALTAMIRA ORIOLE *Icterus gularis* (Wagler)

Uncommon resident in the Lower Rio Grande Valley. Altamira Orioles occur upriver to at least northern Zapata County. They have been reported as far north as Kleberg and La Salle Counties, but records north of the Lower Rio Grande Valley are very few and need documentation. Altamira Oriole was first documented in Texas in 1938 (Burleigh 1939) and seen infrequently through the 1940s. The first documented nesting record did not come until

1951. This species underwent an impressive population growth beginning in the early 1960s. Some observers suspect, however, that Altamira Oriole numbers in Texas are now declining.

AUDUBON'S ORIOLE *Icterus graduacauda* Lesson

Locally uncommon to rare resident in the South Texas Brush Country north to Goliad and Dimmit Counties although generally absent from Cameron and eastern Hidalgo Counties. There is a report of two nesting pairs from Val Verde County in 1941; however, the possibility exists that these were misidentified Scott's Orioles. This species is a casual visitor northward to Bexar, Medina, and Val Verde Counties, and vagrants have been documented in Bastrop, Edwards, and Midland (TPRF 66) Counties. The highest concentrations of Audubon's Orioles in Texas are found in the open oak woodlands of Kenedy and Brooks Counties.

BALTIMORE ORIOLE *Icterus galbula* (Linnaeus)

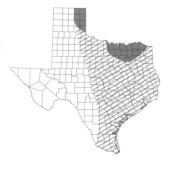

Locally uncommon summer resident in the eastern third of the Panhandle where hybrids with Bullock's Orioles may be encountered. They are rare to uncommon and local summer residents in north-central Texas, becoming very rare and local south through the Pineywoods. Baltimore Orioles are common to uncommon migrants in the eastern half of the state, becoming increasingly less common west to the Pecos River and casual farther west. Migrants pass through the state between mid-March and mid-May and from late August to mid-November. This species is a rare winter visitor along the coast, and there are several winter records from inland locations. Baltimore Oriole was formerly considered conspecific with Bullock's Oriole under the name Northern Oriole.

SCOTT'S ORIOLE *Icterus parisorum* Bonaparte

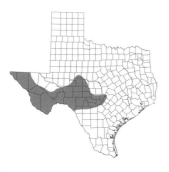

Uncommon to common summer resident in the Trans-Pecos eastward across the southern half of the Edwards Plateau. Scott's Orioles arrive on the breeding grounds in late March and are usually present through late September. There are several records of individuals lingering into early winter, especially in the Trans-Pecos. Unexpected winter records include single birds in Collingsworth County in the Panhandle on 1 December 2001 and in Walker County from 18 January to 1 March 1970. Scott's Orioles have wandered north to the southern Panhandle and east along the Coastal Prairies during other seasons. There are a few records from the South Texas Brush County, including an individual at Brownsville, Cameron County, on 1 March 1994.

Family Fringillidae: Finches and Allies

Review Species

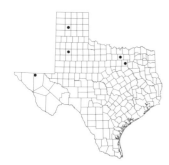

PINE GROSBEAK *Pinicola enucleator* (Linnaeus)

Accidental. Texas has five documented records of this species. Eight additional sightings of Pine Grosbeak from the Panhandle were made prior to the development of the Review List in 1987. Among these is a female found alive in Pampa, Gray County, during December 1933 that subsequently died. Including those reports, the majority of Pine Grosbeak sightings from Texas occurred between 10 October and 15 March.

24 NOV. 1969, DALLAS, DALLAS CO. (WFVZ 49829)
21–24 NOV. 1984, AMARILLO, POTTER CO. (TPRF 336)
1 MAY 1988, LUBBOCK, LUBBOCK CO. (TBRC 1988-232)
28 DEC. 1990, LEWISVILLE, DENTON CO. (TBRC 1991-10)
24 NOV. 2000, GUADALUPE MOUNTAINS NP, CULBERSON CO.
   (TBRC 2000-104; TPRF 1942)

PURPLE FINCH *Carpodacus purpureus* (Gmelin)

Uncommon to rare and irregular winter visitor to the northeastern portion of the state. Purple Finches were a more regular and widespread winter resident in Texas prior to the 1980s. Formerly, they regularly occurred west to the eastern Rolling Plains and Edwards Plateau. In general, this species is now absent from the upper coast. Purple Finches are very rare to casual winter visitors to the western half of the state, including the Trans-Pecos. They are typically found between early December and early April.

CASSIN'S FINCH *Carpodacus cassinii* Baird

Rare and irregular winter visitor in the Trans-Pecos. This species exhibits an irruptive pattern of occurrence throughout most of that region and may occur annually only in the Guadalupe Mountains. Nine major winter incursions into the Trans-Pecos have been reported since 1960, with a few individuals remaining through the summer. Cassin's Finch is a very rare to casual winter visitor to the High Plains and

Edwards Plateau and is accidental farther east. There is one record of a single bird on South Padre Island, Cameron County, from 8 to 10 November 2000. Winter residents are generally present from mid-November to late March.

HOUSE FINCH *Carpodacus mexicanus* (Müller)

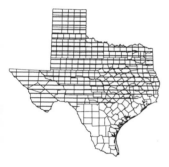

Uncommon to locally common resident throughout most of the state. During the 1990s, the population of House Finches introduced to the eastern United States expanded westward and the native western population continued to expand eastward meeting in central Texas. This species has now been reported from nearly every county in the state. House Finches are still rare to very rare along the contact zone, which include the area just east of the Balcones Escarpment and south to the central coast. They are also very rare in the South Texas Brush Country south and east of Laredo, Webb County.

RED CROSSBILL *Loxia curvirostra* Linnaeus

Rare and irregular resident of the higher elevations of the Guadalupe Mountains and possibly the Davis Mountains. Red Crossbills are rare and irregular winter visitors elsewhere in the state, occurring most regularly in El Paso County. This species is irruptive, and several small invasions have pushed into the northern two-thirds of the state. Despite these events, Red Crossbills have not been reported from all areas of the state. The first known occurrence in the Pineywoods was in November 1996 (Schaefer 1998). On rare occasions, Red Crossbills have lingered into the summer, and there are potential breeding records from the Pineywoods and Taylor County. Recent research has suggested that more than one species may be included under Red Crossbill (Growth 1993). Specimens of four subspecies have been collected in Texas, although the status and movements of any particular subspecies are unknown. Separating these subspecies in the field is very difficult at best.

Review Species

WHITE-WINGED CROSSBILL
Loxia leucoptera Gmelin

Accidental. There are seven documented records of this northern finch for the state. White-winged Crossbills are rare residents in the southern Rocky Mountains to northern New Mexico, although the birds occurring in Texas

probably originate from more northern populations. A sub-stantial southward movement of White-winged Crossbills occurred during the winter of 2001–2002. Many individu-als reached the southern Great Plains, including the Texas Panhandle, where four individuals were documented from separate locations. The first record for the state was a male in Lubbock, Lubbock County, from 28 December 1975 to 8 March 1976 (TPRF 94). The dates of occurrence of Texas records range from mid-December to mid-March.

Review Species

COMMON REDPOLL *Carduelis flammea* (Linnaeus)

Accidental. Texas has seven documented records of this species. The first five records are from the winter, with dates of occurrence between 25 November and 1 March. The first state record involved six birds at Buffalo Lake Na-tional Wildlife Refuge, Randall County, from 25 Novem-ber 1965 to 16 January 1966 (TBRC 1978-2). The other winter records come from Dallas, Jeff Davis, Ochiltree, and Somervell Counties. The most recent records are also the most unexpected: an adult Common Redpoll was well docu-mented at Laguna Vista, Cameron County, from 28 to 30 May 2002 (TBRC 2002-66; TPRF 2023), and another was photographed at Galveston, Galveston County, on 18–19 June 2002 (TBRC 2002-90; TPRF 2044).

PINE SISKIN *Carduelis pinus* (Wilson)

Common to abundant migrant and winter visitor through-out the northern two-thirds of the state and rare farther south. The occurrence of Pine Siskins in any given area can be very irregular, from common one winter to virtually absent the next, although they are more regular in the north-ern third of the state. Pine Siskins generally arrive in Texas in late September, with most departing by late April, al-though a few may linger into late May or, occasionally, early June. There are breeding records from the Trans-Pecos, Panhandle, and northeast Texas. In most cases these nest-ing records are from May and early June. Lingering siskins should be carefully monitored to determine if they are nesting.

LESSER GOLDFINCH *Carduelis psaltria* (Say)

Uncommon to locally abundant summer resident through-out the western half of the state south to the Lower Rio

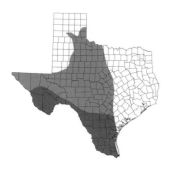

Grande Valley. They are generally rare and very local on the High Plains. This species has wandered eastward to the edge of the Pineywoods and to the upper coast. Most individuals retreat from the northern half of the breeding range during winter, but a few individuals may remain. Lesser Goldfinches are uncommon to rare winter residents in the southern Trans-Pecos and eastward through the South Texas Brush Country. The Lesser Goldfinches that occur in Texas are of the black-backed subspecies, *C. p. psaltria*. Green-backed immature males of this subspecies are often confused with the western subspecies, *C. p. hesperophilus*, which has never been documented in Texas. Closer study to determine the subspecific identity of birds found in the Franklin Mountains, El Paso County, is needed, however.

Review Species

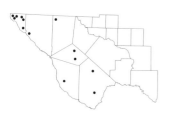

LAWRENCE'S GOLDFINCH *Carduelis lawrencei* Cassin

Accidental. Texas has 13 documented records of this western finch. The occurrence of Lawrence's Goldfinch in Texas has been primarily linked to irruptive events. One of these incursions took place in the 1950s; unfortunately, there is no supporting documentation. The first documented record for the state was a male photographed at Hueco Tanks State Historical Park, El Paso County, on 7 December 1984 (TBRC 1988-101; TPRF 533). All but two of the remaining records were part of an invasion during the winter of 1996–97. All records but one have occurred between 12 October and 10 March, and several of these represent multiple birds. A flock of up to 23 individuals was present in El Paso during January 1997. There is one very unexpected summer record for the state involving an adult male at Guadalupe Mountains National Park, Culberson County, from 5 to 7 June 2002 (TBRC 2002-73; TPRF 2023).

AMERICAN GOLDFINCH *Carduelis tristis* (Linnaeus)

Uncommon to abundant winter resident throughout the state. The occurrence of American Goldfinch is somewhat irregular; consequently there can be considerable fluctuation in the number of birds present in a given area from one year to the next. The wintering population is less influenced by these irruptions than that of Pine Siskins and the rare northern finches. American Goldfinches generally arrive in Texas in late September and depart by mid-May, but it is not uncommon for them to linger into late May or even early June, thus acquiring alternate plumage. This species is a very rare and local summer resident in portions of northeast Texas and in Hemphill County in the northeastern Panhandle.

EVENING GROSBEAK

Coccothraustes vespertinus (Cooper)

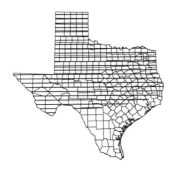

Rare and very irregular winter visitor to the northern half of the state and the Trans-Pecos. Evening Grosbeaks are absent from the state during most years. Minor invasions have occurred more frequently in the Trans-Pecos and Panhandle than in other areas of the state. Larger invasions of this species into the Pineywoods happened four times between 1968 and 1975. Evening Grosbeaks have appeared in Texas as early as late August and lingered as late as mid-June. There is one midsummer report of two pairs of Evening Grosbeaks in the Guadalupe Mountains on 10 July 1988.

Family Passeridae: Old World Sparrows

HOUSE SPARROW *Passer domesticus* (Linnaeus)

Locally abundant resident in urban areas across the state. House Sparrows are common to locally rare in rural areas and are generally found near human habitations. They are native to Europe and were introduced to the United States in several releases during the early 1850s in Brooklyn, New York. The population rapidly expanded, and they are naturalized throughout most of North America.

APPENDIX A:
PRESUMPTIVE SPECIES LIST

For a species to be accepted on the Texas list, at least one record must be supported by specimen, photograph, or tape-recording. However, the Committee may accept sight records for species not currently on the state list that are supported by written details only. Such species are added to this "Presumptive Species List," so named because it can be safely presumed that they have, in all probability, occurred in Texas. If subsequent records are documented by specimen, photograph, or tape-recording, the species is then moved to the state list.

murre species (*Uria* sp.)
There is a single sight record of a murre for Texas. An apparent adult murre was observed at Lake O' the Pines, Marion County, from 19 to 20 March 1994 (TBRC 1994-70). The bird was initially identified as a Common Murre *(Uria aalge)*. The Committee accepted the sight record only as murre species because Thick-billed Murre *(U. lomvia)* could not be ruled out. Detailed descriptions of the bird did eliminate Long-billed Murrelet *(Brachyramphus perdix)* as an alternative identification, however.

White-crowned Pigeon *Patagioenas leucocephala* Linnaeus
There is one accepted sight record of White-crowned Pigeon for Texas. A single adult was observed on Green Island, Cameron County, on 24 June and again on 2 July 1989 (TBRC 1989-186). The closest populations of this species to Texas are found in southern Florida and along the eastern coast of the Yucatan Peninsula.

Black Swift *Cypseloides niger* (Gmelin)
There is one accepted sight record of Black Swift in Texas. A small group of Black Swifts was observed in the Franklin Mountains, El Paso County, on 22 August 1985 (TBRC 1994-172). Black Swift is probably a very rare, but regular, fall migrant through the Trans-Pecos. They have been reported on several other occasions. The inherent difficulty in photographing swifts makes obtaining documentation needed to add this species to the main list even more difficult.

Social Flycatcher *Myiozetetes similes* (Spix)
There is a single accepted sight record for this species in the state. A Social Flycatcher was present at Anzulduas County Park, Hidalgo County, from 17 March to 5 April 1990 (TBRC 1990-83). Many people observed this individual, but no photographs were obtained. Social Flycatcher occurs in northeastern Mexico north to southern Tamaulipas.

Crescent-chested Warbler *Parula superciliosa* (Hartlaub)
There is a single accepted sight record for this species for Texas. A singing male was discovered in the Chisos Mountains of Big Bend National Park, Brewster County, on 2 June 1993 (TBRC 1993-90). Crescent-chested Warbler is found as far north as central Nuevo Leon and western Chihuahua in Mexico.

APPENDIX B:
NON-ACCEPTED SPECIES

There are published reports of a number of species for Texas that have not, for a variety of reasons, been accepted by the Texas Bird Records Committee. The following list includes species that have been frequently attributed to Texas, accompanied by the original citation or the most widely circulated reference. This list excludes those species for which a captive origin is overwhelmingly likely. It also excludes those species whose geographic range and habits likewise argue overwhelmingly against natural occurrence in Texas (e.g., Red-breasted Goose, San Blas Jay, Orange-breasted Bunting). The citations listed as Audubon Field Notes, American Birds, and Field Notes all refer to the Texas column that appears quarterly in the periodical currently known as *North American Birds,* published first by the National Audubon Society and later (since 1999) by the American Birding Association.

White-tailed Tropicbird *Phaethon lepturus* Daudin
Oberholser 1974. Prior to the first documented record of Red-billed Tropicbird, this species was thought to be the tropicbird most likely to occur in the state.

Little Egret *Egretta garzetta* (Linnaeus)
Field Notes 52:87

Scarlet Ibis *Eudocimus ruber* (Linnaeus)
Oberholser (1974) mentions two specimens collected from the state, although neither was apparently saved. A Scarlet Ibis was photographed at Green Island, Cameron County, in June 1972. Further investigation determined that a Scarlet Ibis had escaped earlier that spring from the Gladys Porter Zoo in Brownsville.

Barnacle Goose *Branta leucopsis* (Bechstein)
Oberholser (1974), Bolen (1987)

Sharp-tailed Grouse *Tympanuchus phasianellus* (Linnaeus)
Oberholser (1974) listed the Sharp-tailed Grouse as hypothetical based on reports of the species from the northwestern Panhandle from the nineteenth century. This species had apparently disappeared from Texas by 1906. Sharp-tailed

Grouse was formerly a resident in the extreme western Panhandle of Oklahoma (Sutton 1967), and Ligon (1961) reported them from northeastern New Mexico in the vicinity of Raton, Colfax County. Today, none of these populations are extant. Apparently, no specimens collected in Texas of Sharp-tailed Grouse were ever preserved.

Limpkin *Aramus guarauna* (Linnaeus)
There are three reports of Limpkin from Texas (Oberholser 1974). One of these refers to a specimen reportedly collected at Brownsville, Cameron County, now housed at the American Museum of Natural History (AMNH 79775). Colonel Field and E. C. Greenwood supposedly collected this specimen on 23 May 1889. Recent investigations have determined that Greenwood was on a collecting trip to the marshes near Tampico, Mexico, during the spring of 1889. While on this expedition, Greenwood contracted a fever and returned to Brownsville where he died later that summer (S. Casto, pers. comm.). It seems clear that Field and Greenwood were not together during the spring of 1889. They were business partners selling bird and mammal specimens, which may account for the label data listing them both as the collectors of the Limpkin specimen. There is a distinct possibility that the bird was collected in Tampico. For this reason, the TBRC has not included Limpkin on the official state list.

Common Crane *Grus grus* (Linnaeus)
Tacha, Martin, and Patterson (1981)

Pacific Golden-plover *Pluvialis fulva* (Gmelin)
North American Birds 53:300

Wood Sandpiper *Tringa glareola* Linnaeus
American Birds 32:227

Bristle-thighed Curlew *Numenius tahitiensis* (Gmelin)
American Birds 29:712

Bar-tailed Godwit *Limosa lapponica* (Linnaeus)
Audubon Field Notes 21:522, Oberholser (1974)

Blue Ground-Dove *Claravis pretiosa* (Ferrari-Perez)
American Birds 28:662

Smooth-billed Ani *Crotophaga ani* Linnaeus
Oberholser (1974)

Vaux's Swift *Chaetura vauxi* (Townsend)
Oberholser (1974), American Birds 34:795. Quite likely to occur as a very rare fall or winter vagrant (e.g., specimens from Louisiana), but identification difficulties continue to cloud all reports. There are more than 15 sight reports to date, many with written notes. The difficulty in obtaining documentation hampers acceptance.

Antillean Crested Hummingbird
Orthorhynchus cristatus (Linnaeus)
The origin of the single specimen from Galveston County, housed at the American Museum of Natural History, is dubious (Pulich 1968; Oberholser 1974).

Black-crested Coquette *Paphosia helenae* (DeLattre)
American Birds 30:96. There have been numerous reports of "coquette" hummingbirds in Texas. To date, all such reports that included photographs have been identified as clear-winged sphinx moths of the genus *Aellopos*.

Rufous-tailed Hummingbird *Amazilia tzacatl* (De la Llave)
Oberholser (1974) reported that J. C. Merrill and Robert Ridgway identified two separate Rufous-tailed Humming-birds during June and July 1876 at Fort Brown, Cameron County. Neither bird was preserved, nor is there compelling evidence that would eliminate Buff-bellied Hummingbird.

Plain-capped Starthroat *Heliomaster constantii* (DeLattre)
Wauer (1996)

Amazon Kingfisher *Chloroceryle amazona* (Latham)
Field Notes 51:85

Lineated Woodpecker *Dryocopus lineatus* (Linnaeus)
Field Notes 51:771

Bridled Titmouse *Baeolophus wollweberi* (Bonaparte)
American Birds 35:839

Black-capped Gnatcatcher *Polioptila nigriceps* Baird
American Birds 39:321

Bendire's Thrasher *Toxostoma bendirei* (Coues)
Peterson (1960). None of the many sight reports to date of Bendire's Thrasher have satisfactorily ruled out immature (or simply misidentified) Curve-billed Thrasher.

Bachman's Warbler *Vermivora bachmanii* (Audubon)
Oberholser (1974)

Fan-tailed Warbler *Euthlypis lachrymosa* (Bonaparte)
North American Birds 54:303

Abert's Towhee *Pipilo aberti* Baird
H. S. Peters (1931) reported collecting two Abert's Towhees in El Paso County on 19 and 20 April 1930. Apparently neither specimen was preserved.

Worthen's Sparrow *Spizella wortheni* Ridgway
American Birds 44:294

Saltmarsh Sharp-tailed Sparrow
Ammodramus caudacutus (Gmelin)
Oberholser (1974) reported two specimens of this species from Texas, but subsequent examination of both specimens showed them to be Nelson's Sharp-tailed Sparrows.

Yellow Grosbeak *Pheucticus chrysopeplus* (Vigors)
Wauer (1996)

Hooded Grosbeak *Coccothraustes abeillei* (Lesson)
Lasley et al. (1982)

APPENDIX C: EXOTICS AND BIRDS OF UNCERTAIN ORIGIN

This short list includes species that are not native to Texas and for which no established populations exist. This group can be divided into two categories. The first category includes species that originate from individuals intentionally released into the wild and includes Mute Swan, Chukar, and Ringed Turtle-Dove. The second group includes several psittacids that have been encountered in the Lower Rio Grande Valley. None of these parrots are known to be reproducing, and only a small number of individuals are present. There is a remote possibility that some of these species could occur as vagrants from northeastern Mexico.

Mute Swan *Cygnus olor* (Gmelin)
Feral Mute Swans can be found in urban and other areas throughout the state. Some of these individuals are breeding and free-flying. This Old World species is not considered to be an established exotic in Texas, and therefore is not included on the official state list. Any swan discovered in Texas, however, should be carefully examined to eliminate the possibility of Mute Swan.

Chukar *Alectoris chukar* (Gray)
Chukars are occasionally found throughout the state. During the 1940s and 1950s, the Texas Parks and Wildlife Department attempted to introduce this species to the Panhandle and the Trans-Pecos. Neither attempt was successful, but private individuals continue to hold and release these Asian game birds.

Ringed Turtle-Dove *Streptopelia risoria* (Linnaeus)
Ringed Turtle-Dove apparently still persists locally on the Upper Texas Coast and possibly elsewhere. Local escapees have been found throughout the state, and hybrids with Eurasian Collard-Doves *(S. decaocto)* have been noted in scattered locations along the upper and central coasts. The validity of this taxon has been debated in recent years.

Orange-fronted Parakeet *Aratinga canicularis* (Linnaeus)
Although this species is frequently encountered in Texas,

Orange-fronted Parakeet is an obvious escapee. This species is found along the Pacific slope of Mexico and south to Costa Rica.

White-fronted Parrot *Amazona albifrons* (Sparrman)
Ten White-fronted Parrots were found in a mixed parrot flock in Brownsville, Cameron County, in 1999. Single individuals of this species are often encountered in Red-crowned Parrot flocks.

Lilac-crowned Parrot *Amazona finschi* (Sclater)
This species is frequently reported from the Lower Rio Grande Valley. Some of these reports undoubtedly refer to female Red-crowned Parrots, which show extensive blue in the crown. Lilac-crowned Parrots are endemic to the Pacific slope of Mexico.

Red-lored Parrot *Amazona autumnalis* (Linnaeus)
Red-lored Parrots are usually found in flocks with other parrots. As with some of the other exotic psittacids found in the Lower Rio Grande Valley, Red-loreds are generally found singly, although as many as 15 have been reported from a single winter flock. This species occurs in northeastern Mexico but is more narrowly confined to heavy tropical forests than is the Red-crowned Parrot.

Yellow-headed Parrot *Amazona oratrix* Ridgway
Yellow-headed Parrots occur in northeastern Mexico within 150 miles of the Rio Grande. This species is regularly encountered and occasionally seen in small flocks in the Lower Rio Grande Valley.

APPENDIX D:
LIST OF REVIEW SPECIES

REVIEW LIST A

The list below includes species that have occurred four or fewer times per year in Texas over a ten-year average. The TBRC requests documentation for review for these species, as well as any bird not yet accepted on the Texas State List.

Yellow-billed Loon
Red-necked Grebe
Yellow-nosed Albatross
White-chinned Petrel
Stejneger's Petrel
Black-capped Petrel
Greater Shearwater
Sooty Shearwater
Manx Shearwater
Wilson's Storm-Petrel
Leach's Storm-Petrel
Red-billed Tropicbird
Blue-footed Booby
Brown Booby
Red-footed Booby
Jabiru
Greater Flamingo
Brant
Trumpeter Swan
Eurasian Wigeon
American Black Duck
White-cheeked Pintail
Garganey
King Eider
Harlequin Duck
Barrow's Goldeneye
Masked Duck
Snail Kite
Northern Goshawk
Crane Hawk
Roadside Hawk
Short-tailed Hawk
Collared Forest-Falcon
Paint-billed Crake
Spotted Rail

Double-striped Thick-knee
Collared Plover
Northern Jacana
Spotted Redshank
Wandering Tattler
Eskimo Curlew
Surfbird
Red-necked Stint
Sharp-tailed Sandpiper
Purple Sandpiper
Curlew Sandpiper
Ruff
Red Phalarope
Long-tailed Jaeger
Little Gull
Black-headed Gull
Heermann's Gull
Black-tailed Gull
Mew Gull
Thayer's Gull
Iceland Gull
Slaty-backed Gull
Yellow-footed Gull
Western Gull
Great Black-backed Gull
Kelp Gull
Elegant Tern
Roseate Tern
Arctic Tern
Brown Noddy
Black Noddy
Ruddy Ground-Dove
Ruddy Quail-Dove
Mangrove Cuckoo
Dark-billed Cuckoo

Snowy Owl
Northern Pygmy-Owl
Mottled Owl
Stygian Owl
Northern Saw-whet Owl
White-collared Swift
Green Violet-ear
Green-breasted Mango
White-eared Hummingbird
Berylline Hummingbird
Violet-crowned Hummingbird
Costa's Hummingbird
Allen's Hummingbird
Elegant Trogon
Red-breasted Sapsucker
Ivory-billed Woodpecker
   (presumed extirpated in Texas)
Greenish Elaenia
Tufted Flycatcher
Buff-breasted Flycatcher
Greater Pewee
Dusky-capped Flycatcher
Sulphur-bellied Flycatcher
Piratic Flycatcher
Tropical Kingbird
Thick-billed Kingbird
Gray Kingbird
Fork-tailed Flycatcher
Rose-throated Becard
Masked Tityra
Yellow-green Vireo
Black-whiskered Vireo
Yucatan Vireo
Clark's Nutcracker
Black-billed Magpie
Tamaulipas Crow

Gray-breasted Martin
Black-capped Chickadee
American Dipper
Northern Wheatear
Orange-billed Nightingale-
   Thrush
Clay-colored Robin
White-throated Robin
Rufous-backed Robin
Varied Thrush
Aztec Thrush
Black Catbird
Blue Mockingbird
Bohemian Waxwing
Gray Silky-flycatcher
Olive Warbler
Connecticut Warbler
Gray-crowned Yellowthroat
Red-faced Warbler
Slate-throated Redstart
Golden-crowned Warbler
Rufous-capped Warbler
Flame-colored Tanager
Yellow-faced Grassquit
Baird's Sparrow
Golden-crowned Sparrow
Yellow-eyed Junco
Snow Bunting
Crimson-collared Grosbeak
Blue Bunting
Shiny Cowbird
Black-vented Oriole
Pine Grosbeak
White-winged Crossbill
Common Redpoll
Lawrence's Goldfinch

REVIEW LIST B

Subspecies under special study by the TBRC. Records of these species will be formally reviewed by the TBRC.

(Great White) Heron
Green-winged (Eurasian) Teal
Yellow (Mangrove) Warbler
Dark-eyed (White-winged) Junco
Orchard (Fuertes's) Oriole

SELECTED REFERENCES

Adams, M. T., and K. B. Bryan. 1999. Botteri's Sparrow in Trans-Pecos, Texas. *Texas Birds* 1:6–13.

Albers, R. P., and F. R. Gehlbach. 1990. Choices of feeding habitat by relict Montezuma Quail in central Texas. *Wilson Bull.* 102:300–308.

Aldrich, J. W. 1944. Geographic variation of Bewick's Wrens in the eastern United States. *Occas. Papers Mus. Zool., La. State Univ.* No. 18:305–309.

———. 1946. Speciation in the white-cheeked geese. *Wilson Bull.* 58:94–103.

———. 1968. Population characteristics and nomenclature of the Hermit Thrush. *Proc. U.S. Natl. Mus.* 124 (36–37):1–33.

Allen, A. A., and P. P. Kellogg. 1937. Recent observations of the Ivory-billed Woodpecker. *Auk* 54:164–84.

Allen, J. A. 1891. Capture of *Geothlypis poliocephola* in Cameron County, Texas. *Auk* 8:316.

American Birding Association Checklist Committee. 1986. Report of the ABA Checklist Committee for 1986. *Birding* 18:333–40.

American Ornithologists' Union. 1957. *A.O.U. check-list of North American birds.* 5th ed. Baltimore: American Ornithologists' Union.

———. 1983. *A.O.U. check-list of North American birds.* 6th ed. Lawrence, Kans.: Allen Press, Inc.

———. 1998. *A.O.U. check-list of North American birds.* 7th ed. Washington, D.C.: American Ornithologists' Union.

Arnold, K. A. 1968. Olivaceous Flycatcher in the Davis Mountains of Texas. *Bull. Texas Ornith. Soc.* 2:28.

———. 1972. Crested titmice in Cottle and Foard Counties. *Bull. Texas Ornith. Soc.* 5:23.

———. 1975. First record of the Greater Shearwater from the Gulf of Mexico. *Auk* 92:394–95.

———. 1978a. A Jabiru *(Jabiru mycteria)* specimen from Texas. *Auk* 95:611–12.

———. 1978b. First United States record of Paint-billed Crake *(Neocrex erythrops). Auk* 95:745–46.

———. 1980. Rufous-capped Warbler and White-collared Seedeater from Webb County, Texas. *Bull. Texas Ornith.* Soc. 13:27.

———. 1983. New subspecies of Henslow's Sparrow *(Ammodramus henslowii). Auk* 100:504–505.

———. 1984a. *Check-list of the birds of Texas.* Waco: Texas Ornithological Society.

———. 1984b. Decisions of the TOS Bird Records Committee for 1984. *Bull. Texas Ornith. Soc.* 17:18–19.

———. 1985. Decisions of the TOS Bird Records Committee for 1985. *Bull. Texas Ornith. Soc.* 18:31–32.

———. 1994. First specimen of Clark's Grebe for Texas: An environmental casualty. *Bull. Texas Ornith. Soc.* 27:26–28.

Arnold, K. A., and N. C. Garza, Jr. 1998. Populations and habitat requirements of breeding Henslow's Sparrow in Harris County, Texas. *Bull. Texas Ornith. Soc.* 31:42–49.

Arnold, K. A., and J. C. Henderson. 1973. First specimen of Arctic Loon from Texas. *Auk* 90:420–21.

Arnold, K. A., and E. A. Kutac, eds. 1974. *Check-list of the birds of Texas.* Waco: Texas Ornithological Society.

Arvin, J. C. 1980. The Golden-crowned Warbler: An 88-year-old "new" species for the avifauna of the United States. *Birding* 12:10–11.

Attwater, H. P. 1887. Nesting habits of Texas birds. *Ornithologist and Oologist* 12:103–105, 123–25.

———. 1892. List of birds observed in the vicinity of San Antonio, Bexar County, Texas. *Auk* 9:229–38, 337–45.

Bailey, V. 1905. *Biological survey of Texas.* Washington D.C.: United States Department of Agriculture.

Banks, R. C., C. Cicero, J. L. Dunn, A. W. Kratter, P. C. Rasmussen, J. V. Remsen, Jr., J. D. Rising, and D. F. Stotz. 2003. Forty-third supplement to the American Ornithologists' Union check-list of North American birds. *Auk* 119:897–906.

Beavers, R. A. 1977. First specimen of Allen's Hummingbird, *Selasphorus sasin* (Trochilidae) from Texas. *Southwest. Nat.* 21:285.

Bent, A. C. 1940. Life histories of North American birds, cuckoos, goatsuckers, hummingbirds and their allies. *U.S. Natl. Mus. Bull.* 176.

Biaggi, V., Jr. 1960. The birds of Culberson County, Texas, with notes on ecological aspects. Part II. Annotated list of the birds (continued). Newsletter, Texas *Ornith. Soc.* 8(10):1–20.

Blacklock, G. W., and J. Peabody. 1983. Two specimen records of Leach's Storm-Petrel for Texas. *Bull. Texas Ornith. Soc.* 16:34.

Blankenship, T. L., and J. T. Anderson. 1993. A large concentration of Masked Duck *(Oxyura dominica)* on the Welder Wildlife Refuge, San Patricio County, Texas. *Bull. Texas Ornith. Soc.* 26:19–21.

Bolen, E. G. 1987. A specimen record of the Barnacle Goose in Texas. *Southwest. Nat.* 32:506–507.

Brewer, D. 2001. *Wrens, dippers and thrashers.* New Haven, Conn.: Yale University Press.

Brown, N. C. 1882a. Description of a new race of *Peucaea ruficeps* from Texas. *Bull. Nutt. Ornith. Club* 7:26.

———. 1882b. A reconnaissance in southwestern Texas. *Bull. Nutt. Ornith. Club* 7:33–42.

———. 1884. A second season in Texas. *Auk* 1:120–24.

Brush, T. 1998. Recent nesting and current status of Red-billed Pigeon along the Lower Rio Grande in southern Texas. *Bull. Tex. Ornith. Soc.* 31:22–26.

———. 1999a. Current status of Northern Beardless-Tyrannulet and Tropical Parula in Bentsen–Rio Grande Valley State Park and Santa Ana National Wildlife Refuge, Southern Texas. *Bull. Texas Ornith. Soc.* 32:2–12.

———. 1999b. The Hook-billed Kite: A reclusive, snail eating raptor of the Lower Rio Grande Valley. *Texas Birds* 1(2): 26–32.

———. 2000. First nesting record of Blue Jay *(Cyanocitta cristatata)* in Hidalgo County. *Bull. Texas Ornith. Soc.* 33:35–36.

Brush, T., and J. C. Eitniear. 2002. Status and recent nesting of Muscovy Duck *(Cairina moschata)* in the Rio Grande Valley, Texas. *Bull. Texas Ornith. Soc.* 35:12–14.

Bryan, K., T. Gallucci, G. Lasley, M. Lockwood, and D. H. Riskind. 2003. *A checklist of Texas birds.* Austin: Natural Resources Program, Texas Parks and Wildlife Dept.

Bryan, K., T. Gallucci, and R. Moldenhauer. 1978. First record of the Snow Bunting for Texas. *Amer. Birds* 32:1070.

Bryan, K. B. 1999. *Birds of Big Bend Ranch and vicinity: A field checklist.* Austin: Natural Resources Program, Texas Parks and Wildlife Dept.

Bryan, K. B., and J. Karges. 2001. Recent changes to the Davis Mountains avifauna. *Texas Birds* 3(1):41–53.

Bryan, K. B., and M. W. Lockwood. 2000. Gray Vireo in Texas. *Texas Birds* 2(2):18–24.

Buechner, H. K. 1946–47. Birds of Kerr County, Texas. *Trans. Kans. Acad. Sci.* 49:357–62.

Burleigh, T. D. 1939. Alta Mira Oriole in Texas: An addition to the A. O. U. "check-list." *Auk* 56:87–88.

Burleigh, T. D., and G. H. Lowery, Jr. 1940. Birds of the Guadalupe Mountain region of western Texas. *Occas. Papers Mus. Zool.,* La. State Univ., No. 8.

Burt, D. B., D. Burt, T. C. Maxwell, and D. G. Tarter. 1987. Clapper Rail *(Rallus longirostris)* in west-central Texas. *Texas J. Sci.* 39:378.

Cahn, A. R. 1922. Notes on the summer avifauna of Bird Island, Texas. Condor 24:169–80.

Casto, S., and H. W. Garner. 1969. Photographic evidence for the occurrence of the Dipper in west Texas. *Bull. Texas Ornith. Soc.* 3:29.

Casto, S. D. 2001. Additional records of the Passenger Pigeon in Texas. *Bull. Tex. Ornith. Soc.* 34:5–16.

———. 2002. The early history of ornithology in Texas. *Occ. Publ. Texas Ornith. Soc.,* No. 4.

Central Texas Audubon Society. 1997. *Checklist of the birds of McLennan County, Texas.* Waco, Tex.: Cord Communications.

Chapman, B. P., P. A. Buckley, and F. G. Buckley. 1979. First photographic record of Greater Flamingo in Texas. *Bull. Texas Ornith. Soc.* 12:20–21.

Clark, C. 1982. Jabiru in the United States. *Birding* 14:8–9.

Clum, N. J., and T. J. Cade. 1994. Gyrfalcon. In *Birds of North America,* No. 114, edited by A. Poole and F. Gill. Washington, D.C.: Acad. Nat. Sci., Philadelphia, and Amer. Ornith. Union.

Cooksey, M. 1998. A pre-1996 North American record of Stygian Owl. *Field Notes* 52:265–66.

Cottam, C., E. Bolen, and R. Zink. 1975. Sabine's Gull on south Texas coast. *Southwest. Nat.* 20:134–35.

Dalquest, W. W., and L. D. Lewis. 1955. Whistling Swan and Snowy Owl in Texas. *Condor* 57:243.

D'Anna, W., D. DiTommaso, B. Potter, J. Skelly, and S. Skelly. 1999. First Texas record of Black-tailed Gull. *Texas Birds* 1(2):20–24.

Davis, L. I. 1945a. Brasher's Warbler in Texas. *Auk* 62:146.

———. 1945b. Rose-throated Becard nesting in Cameron County, Texas. *Auk* 62:316–17.

———. 1945c. Yellow-green Vireo nesting in Cameron County, Texas. *Auk* 62:146.

Davis, W. B. 1940. Birds of Brazos County, Texas. *Condor* 42:81–85.

Delacour, J. 1954. *The waterfowl of the world.* Vol. 1. London: Country Life, Ltd.

Delnicki, D. 1978. Second occurrence and first successful nesting record of the Hook-billed Kite in the United States. *Auk* 95:427.

Devine, A. B., D. Gendron, and D. G. Smith. 1978. Occurrence of the Coppery-tailed Trogon in Hidalgo County, Texas. *Bull. Texas Ornith. Soc.* 11:52.

Dickerman, R. W. 1964. A specimen of Fuertes' Oriole, *Icterus fuertesi,* from Texas. *Auk* 81:433.

Dittman, D. L., and G. W. Lasley. 1992. How to document rare birds. *Birding* 24:145–59.

Dresser, H. E. 1865. Notes on birds of southern Texas. *Ibis* 1:312–30.

Dunn, J. L., and K. L. Garrett. 1997. *A field guide to warblers of North America.* Boston: Houghton Mifflin Co.

Dunn, J. L., K. L. Garrett, and J. K. Alderfer. 1995. White-crowned Sparrow subspecies: Identification and distribution. *Birding* 27:182–200.

Duvall, A. J. 1943. Breeding Savannah Sparrows of the southwestern United States. *Condor* 45:237–38.

Eitniear, J, C., and T. Rueckle. 1996. Noteworthy avian breeding records from Zapata County, Texas. *Bull. Texas Ornith. Soc.* 29:43–44

Eubanks, T. L., Jr. 1994. Status and distribution of the Piping Plover in Texas. *Bull. Texas Ornith. Soc.* 27:19–25.

Eubanks, T. L., Jr., and J. Morgan. 1989. First photographic documentation of a live White-collared Swift from the United States. *Amer. Birds* 43:258–59.

Farmer, M. 1990. A Herring Gull nest in Texas. *Bull. Texas Ornith. Soc.* 23:27–28.

Fischer, D. L. 1979. Black-billed Cuckoo *(Coccyzus erythrophthalmus)* breeding in south Texas. *Bull. Texas Ornith. Soc.* 12(1):25.

Fleetwood, R. J., and J. L. Hamilton. 1967. Occurrence and nesting of the Hook-billed Kite *(Chondrohierax uncinatus)* in Texas. *Auk* 84:598–601.

Flippo, M., and J. M. Selleck. 1999. *Bird checklist: Big Bend National Park, Texas.* Big Bend Natural History Association.

Freeman, B. 1996. *Birds of Bastrop, Buescher, and Lake Bastrop State Parks: A field checklist.* Austin: Natural Resources Program, Texas Parks and Wildlife Dept.

———. 2003. *Birds of the oaks and prairies of Texas: A field checklist.* Austin: Texas Parks and Wildlife Dept.

Gallucci, T. 1979. Successful breeding of Lucy's Warbler in Texas. *Bull. Texas Ornith. Soc.* 12:37–41.

Gallucci, T., and J. G. Morgan. 1987. First documented record of the Mangrove Cuckoo for Texas. *Bull. Texas Ornith. Soc.* 20:2–6.

Gee, J. P., and C. E. Edwards. 2000. Interesting gull records from north-east Tamaulipas, Mexico. *Cotinga* 13:65, 67.

Gould, F. W. 1969. *Texas plants: A checklist and ecological summary.* Texas Agric. Experiment Stat. Misc. Publ. No. 585 (revised).

Grieb, J. R. 1970. The shortgrass Canada Goose population. *The Wildlife Soc. Monogr.* 22. Washington, D.C.

Griscom, L. L., and M. S. Crosby. 1925. Birds of the Brownsville region, southern Texas. *Auk* 42:432–40, 519–37.

———. 1926. Birds of the Brownsville region, southern Texas. *Auk* 43:18–36.

Growth, J. G. 1993. Call matching and positive assortative mating in Red Crossbill. *Auk* 110:398–401.

Grzybowski, J. A. 1982. Population structure in grassland bird communities during winter. *Condor* 84:137–51.

Grzybowski, J. A., J. W. Arterburn, W. A. Carter, J. S. Turner, and D. W. Verser. 1992. *Date guide to the birds of Oklahoma.* 2d ed. Oklahoma Ornithological Society.

Guthery, F. S., and J. C. Lewis. 1979. Sandhill Cranes in coastal counties of southern Texas: Taxonomy, distribution, and populations. In *Proc. 1978 Crane Workshop,* edited by J. C. Lewis, 121–28. Fort Collins: Colorado State University Printing Service.

Hagar, C. N., and F. M. Packard. 1952. *Check-list of the birds of the central coast of Texas.* Rockport, Tex.: C. N. Hager and F. M. Packard.

Haucke, H. H., and W. H. Kiel, Jr. 1973. Jabiru in south Texas. *Auk* 90:675–76.

Hawkins, A. S. 1945. Bird life of the Texas Panhandle. *Panhandle-Plains Historical Review* 18:110–50.

Haynie, C. B. 1989. First photographic record of Common Redpoll in Texas. *Bull. Texas Ornith. Soc.* 22:18–20.

———. 1992a. Texas Bird Records Committee report for 1991. *Bull. Texas Ornith. Soc.* 25:2–12.

———. 1992b. Texas Bird Records Committee report for 1992. *Bull. Texas Ornith. Soc.* 25:30–41.

———. 1993. Texas Bird Records Committee report for 1993. *Bull. Texas Ornith. Soc.* 26:2–14.

———. 1994. Texas Bird Records Committee report for 1994. *Bull. Texas Ornith. Soc.* 28:30–41.

———. 1996. Texas Bird Records Committee report for 1995. *Bull. Texas Ornith. Soc.* 29:2–10.

———. 1998. Texas Bird Records Committee report for 1996. *Bull. Texas Ornith. Soc.* 31:7–21.

Heidrich, P., C. Koenig, and M. Wink. 1995. Bioacoustics, taxonomy, and molecular systematics in American Pygmy Owls. *Stuttgarter Beitraege zur Naturkunde Serie a (Biologie)* 534:1–47.

Heindel, M. 1996. Solitary Vireos. *Birding* 28:458–71.

Hoffman, J. C. 1999. Timing of migration of Short-billed Dowitchers and Long-billed Dowitchers in Northeastern Oklahoma. *Bull. Okla. Ornith. Soc.* 32:21–29.

Horvath, E., and J. Karges. 2000. First Texas record of Buff-breasted Flycatcher. *Texas Birds* 2(1):4–7.

Howell, S. N. G., J. Correa S., and J. Garcia B. 1993. First record of Kelp Gull in Mexico. *Euphonia* 2:71–80.

Howell, S. N. G., and S. Webb. 1995. *A guide to the birds of Mexico and northern central America.* Oxford: Oxford University Press.

Hubbard, J. P., and D. M. Niles. 1975. Two specimen records of the Brown Jay from southern Texas. *Auk* 92:797–98.

Husak, M. S., and T. C. Maxwell. 2000. A review of 20th century range expansion and population trends of the Golden-fronted Woodpecker *(Melanerpes aurifrons):* Historical and ecological perspectives. *Texas J. Sci.* 52(4):275–84.

James, P. 1963. Freeze loss in the Least Grebe *(Podiceps dominicus)* in Lower Rio Grande Delta of Texas. *Southwest. Nat.* 8:45–46.

James, P., and A. Hayes. 1963. Elf Owl rediscovered in lower Rio Grande Delta of Texas. *Wilson Bull.* 75:179–82.

Johnson, N. K., and J. A. Martin. 1992. Macrogeographic patterns of morphometric and genetic variation in the Sage Sparrow complex. *Condor* 94:1–19.

Jones, B. 1992. *A birder's guide to Aransas National Wildlife Refuge.* Albuquerque, N.Mex.: Southwest Natural and Cultural Heritage Association.

Jury, G. W. 1976. First record of White-winged Crossbill *(Loxia leucoptera)* for Texas. *Bull. Texas Ornith. Soc.* 9:7.

Kincaid, E. B. 1956. Ringed Kingfisher at Austin, Texas. *Wilson Bulletin* 68:324–25.

Kirn, A. J., and R. W. Quillin. 1927. *Birds of Bexar County, Texas.* San Antonio, Tex: Witte Memorial Museum.

Klicka, J., R. M. Zink, J. C. Barlow, W. B. McGillivray, and T. J. Doyle. 1999. Evidence supporting the recent origin and species status of the Timberline Sparrow. *Condor* 101(3):577–88.

Kostecke, R., A. Floyd, and C. Stogner. 2001. *Birds of the Texas South Plains.* Llano Estacado Audubon Society.

Kutac, E. A., and S. C. Caran. 1993. *Birds and other wildlife of south central Texas.* Austin: University of Texas Press.

Lacey, H. 1903. Notes on the Texas Jay. *Condor* 5:151–53.

———. 1911. The birds of Kerrville, Texas, and vicinity. *Auk* 28:200–19.

———. 1912. Additions to birds of Kerrville, Texas. *Auk* 29:254.

Langham, J. M. 1980. Golden-crowned Warbler in Texas: A documented record for the ABA checklist area. *Birding* 12:8–9.

Lanyon, W. E. 1962. Specific limits and distribution of meadowlarks of the desert grassland. *Auk* 79:183–207.

Lasley, G. W. 1984. First Texas specimen of the White-collared Swift. *Amer. Birds* 38:370–71.

———. 1988. Texas Bird Records Committee report for 1987. *Bull. Texas Ornith. Soc.* 21:25–32.

———. 1989. Texas Bird Records Committee report for 1988. *Bull. Texas Ornith. Soc.* 22:2–14.

———. 1990. Texas Bird Records Committee report for 1989. *Bull. Texas Ornith. Soc.* 23:6–9.

———. 1991. Texas Bird Records Committee report for 1990. *Bull. Texas Ornith. Soc.* 24:2–15.

Lasley, G. W., D. A. Easterla, C. W. Sexton, and D. A. Bartol. 1982. Documentation of the Red-faced Warbler in Texas and a review of its status in Texas and adjacent areas. *Bull. Texas Ornith. Soc.* 15:8–14.

Lasley, G. W., and J. P. Gee. 1991. The first nesting record of the Hutton's Vireo *(Vireo huttoni)* east of the Pecos River, Texas. *Bull. Texas Ornith. Soc.* 24:23–24.

Lasley, G. W., and M. Krzywonski. 1991. First United States record of the White-throated Robin. *Amer. Birds* 45:230–31.

Lasley, G. W., and T. Pincelli. 1986. Gray Silky-flycatcher in Texas. *Birding* 18:34–36.

Lasley, G. W., C. W. Sexton, and D. Hillsman. 1988. First record of the Mottled Owl in the United States. *Amer. Birds* 42:23–24.

Lee, D. S., and S. W. Cardiff. 1993. Status of the Arctic Tern in the coastal and offshore waters of the southeastern United States. *J. Field Ornith.* 64:158–68.

Lethaby, N., and J. Bangma. 1998. Identifying Black-tailed Gull in North America. *Birding* 30:470–83.

Ligon, J. S. 1961. *New Mexico birds and where to find them.* Albuquerque: University of New Mexico Press.

Lloyd, W. L. 1887. The birds of Tom Green and Concho Counties, Texas. *Auk* 4:181–93, 289–99.

Lockwood, M. W. 1992. First breeding record of *Aechmophorus* grebes in Texas. *Bull. Texas Ornith. Soc.* 25:64–66.

———. 1995. A closer look: Varied Bunting. *Birding* 27(2):110–13.

———. 1997. A closer look: Masked Duck. *Birding* 29(5):386–90.

———. 1998. Texas Bird Records Committee report for 1997. *Bull. Texas Ornith. Soc.* 31:50–62.

———. 1999a. Possible anywhere: Fork-tailed Flycatcher. *Birding* 31:126–39.

———. 1999b. Texas Bird Records Committee report for 1998. *Bull. Texas Ornith. Soc.* 32:26–37.

———. 2000. Texas Bird Records Committee report for 1999. *Bull. Texas Ornith. Soc.* 33:13–22.

———. 2001a. *Birds of the Edwards Plateau: A field checklist.* Austin: Texas Parks and Wildlife.

————. 2001b. *Birds of the Texas Hill Country*. Austin: University of Texas Press.

————. 2001c. Texas Bird Records Committee report for 2000. *Bull. Texas Ornith. Soc.* 34:1–4.

————. 2002. Texas Bird Records Committee report for 2001. *Bull. Texas Ornith. Soc.* 35:1–10.

Lockwood, M. W., and T. W. Cooper. 1999. A Texas hybrid: Cinnamon x Green-winged Teal. *Texas Birds* 1(2):38–40.

Lockwood, M. W., and C. E. Shackelford. 1998. The occurrence of Red-breasted Sapsucker and suspected hybrids with Red-naped Sapsucker in Texas. *Bull. Texas Ornith. Soc.* 31:2–6.

Loetscher, F. W., Jr. 1956. Masked Duck and Jacana at Brownsville, Texas. *Auk* 73:291.

Lyndon B. Johnson School of Public Affairs. 1978. *Preserving Texas' natural heritage*. Austin: The University of Texas at Austin. Policy Research Project Report 31:1–34.

McAlister, W. H. 2002. *Birds of Matagorda Island: A field checklist*. Austin: Natural Resources Program, Texas Parks and Wildlife.

MacInnes, C.D., and E. B. Chamberlain. 1963. The first record of Double-striped Thick-knee in the United States. *Auk* 80:79.

McKinney, B. 1998. *A checklist of Lower Rio Grande birds*. Rancho Viejo, Tex.: B. McKinney.

McKenzie, P. M., and M. B. Robbins. 1999. Identification of adult male Rufous and Allen's hummingbirds, with specific comments on dorsal coloration. *Western Birds* 30:86–93.

Marshall, J. T. 1967. *Parallel variation in North and Middle American Screech-Owls*. Monographs of the Western Found. Vert. Zool., No. 1.

Maxwell, T. C. 1977. First record of Heermann's Gull for Texas. *Southwest. Nat.* 22:282–83.

————. 1979. Vireos (Aves: Vireonidae) in west-central Texas. *Southwest. Nat.* 24:223–29.

————. 1980. Significant nesting records of birds from western Texas. *Bull. Texas Ornith. Soc.* 13:2–6.

Maxwell, T. C., and M. S. Husak. 1999. Common Black-Hawk nesting in west-central Texas. *J. Raptor Res.* 33:270–71

Meitzen, T. G. 1963. Additions to the known breeding range of several species in south Texas. *Auk* 80:368–69.

Miller, F. W. 1959. The Barrow's Goldeneye in Texas. *Condor* 61:434.

Moldenhauer, R. R. 1974. First Clay-colored Robin collected in the United States. *Auk* 91:839–40.

More, R. L., and J. K. Strecker. 1929. The summer birds of Wilbarger County, Texas. *Contr. Baylor Univ. Mus.*, No. 20.

Morgan, J. G., and T. L. Eubanks, Jr. 1979. First documentation of Connecticut Warbler in Texas. *Bull. Texas Ornith. Soc.* 12:21–22.

Morgan, J. G., and L. M. Feltner. 1985. A neotropical bird flies north: the Greenish Elaenia. *Amer. Birds* 39:242–44.

Morgan, J. G., T. L. Eubanks, V. Eubanks, and L. N. White. 1985. Yucatan Vireo appears in Texas. *Amer. Birds* 39:244–46.

Neck, R. W. 1986. Expansion of Red-crowned Parrot, *Amazona viridigenalis,* into southern Texas and changes in agricultural practices in northern Mexico. *Bull. Texas Ornith. Soc.* 19:6–12.

———. 1989. Winter Whooping Cranes in the Texas Hill Country in 1854. *Bull. Texas Ornith. Soc.* 22:15–16.

Nehrling, H. 1882. List of birds observed at Houston, Harris County, Texas, and in the counties Montgomery, Galveston and Fort Bend. *Bull. Nuttall Ornith. Club* 7:6–13, 166–75, 222–25.

Neill, R. L. 1975. *The birds of the Buescher Division.* University of Texas Environmental Science Park at Smithville. Pub. No. 3.

Newfield, N. L. 1983. Records of Allen's Hummingbird in Louisiana and possible Rufous x Allen's Hummingbird hybrids. *Condor* 85:253–54.

Newman, G. A. 1974. Recent bird records from the Guadalupe Mountains, Texas. *Southwest. Nat.* 19:1–7.

Oberholser, H. C. 1974. *The bird life of Texas.* Austin: University of Texas Press.

Oring, L. W. 1964. Notes on the birds of Webb County, Texas. *Auk* 81:440.

Papish, R., J. L. Mays, and D. Brewer. 1997. Orange-billed Nightingale-Thrush: First record for Texas and the U.S. *Birding* 29:128–30.

Parkes, K. C. 1950. Further notes on the birds of Camp Barkeley, Texas. *Condor* 52:91–93.

Parkes, K. C., D. P. Kibbe, and E. L. Roth. 1978. First records of the Spotted Rail *(Pardirallus maculatus)* for the United States, Chile, Bolivia, and western Mexico. *Amer. Birds* 32:295–99.

Patten, M. A. 2000. Changing seasons. *North American Birds* 54:146–48.

Patten, M. A., and G. W. Lasley. 2000. Range expansion of the Glossy Ibis in North America. *North American Birds* 54:241–47.

Pemberton, J. R. 1922. A large tern colony in Texas. *Condor* 24:37–42.

Peters, H. S. 1931. Abert's Towhee, a new bird for Texas. *Auk* 48:274–75.

Peterson, J. J., G. W. Lasley, K. B. Bryan, and M. Lockwood. 1991. Additions to the breeding avifauna of the Davis Mountains. *Bull. Texas Ornith. Soc.* 24:39–48.

Peterson, J. J., and B. R. Zimmer. 1998. *Birds of the Trans Pecos.* Austin: University of Texas Press.

Peterson, R. T. 1960. *A field guide to the birds of Texas.* Boston: Houghton Mifflin Co.

———. 1973. *A field guide to Mexican birds.* Boston: Houghton Mifflin Co.

Pettingell, N. 1967. Eskimo Curlew: Valid records since 1945. *Bull. Texas Ornith. Soc.* 1(3 and 4):14, 21.

Phillips, A. R. 1950. The Great-tailed Grackles of the southwest. *Condor* 52:78–81.

———. 1986. *The known birds of North and Middle America.* Part 1. Privately published.

Phillips, H. W., and W. A. Thornton. 1949. The summer resident birds of the Sierra Vieja range in southwestern Texas. *Texas J. Sci.* 1:101–31.

Phillips, J. N. 1998. A survey of wintering Rufous Hummingbirds in Texas. *Bull. Texas Ornith. Soc.* 31:65–67.

Pulich, W. M. 1955. A record of the Mexican Crossbill *(Loxia curvirostra stricklandi)* from Fort Worth, Texas. *Auk* 72:299.

———. 1961a. A record of the Yellow Rail from Dallas County, Texas. *Auk* 78:639–40.

———. 1961b. *Birds of Tarrant County.* Fort Worth, Tex.: Allen Press.

———. 1968. The occurrence of the Crested Hummingbird in the United States. *Auk* 85:322.

———. 1971. Some fringillid records for Texas. Condor 73:111.

———. 1976. *The Golden-cheeked Warbler, a bioecological study.* Austin: Texas Parks and Wildlife Dept.

———. 1979. *The birds of Tarrant County.* 2d ed. Fort Worth, Tex: Branch Smith, Inc.

———. 1988. *The birds of north central Texas.* College Station: Texas A&M University Press.

Pulich, W. M., and J. E. Parrot. 1977. The occurrence of the Gray Vireo east of the Pecos River. *Southwest. Nat.* 21:551–52.

Pulich, W. M., Jr. 1982. Documentation and status of Cory's Shearwater in the western Gulf of Mexico. *Wilson Bull.* 94:381–85.

Quillin, R. W. 1935. New bird records from Texas. *Auk* 52:324–25.

Quinn, T. W., G. F. Shields, and A. C. Wilson. 1991. Affinities of the Hawaiian Goose based on two types of mitochondrial DNA data. *Auk* 108:585–93.

Rappole, J. H., and G. W. Blacklock. 1985. *Birds of the Texas Coastal Bend: Abundance and distribution.* College Station: Texas A&M University Press.

Robinson, J. A., and G. Aumaun. 1997. An American Woodcock nest in Galveston County, Texas. *Bull. Texas Ornith. Soc.* 30:20–23.

Runnels, S. R. 1975. Rose-throated Becard in Jeff Davis County, Texas. *Condor* 77:221.

———. 1980. Louisiana Heron *(Hydranassa tricolor)* breeding in north central Texas. *Bull. Texas Ornith. Soc.* 13:23.

Rupert, J. R., and T. Brush. 1996. Red-breasted Mergansers, *Mergus serrator,* nesting in southern Texas. *Southwest. Nat.* 41:199–200.

Rylander, K. 2002. *The behavior of Texas birds.* Austin: University of Texas Press.

Schaefer, R. R. 1998. First county records of Red Crossbill in the Pineywoods region of eastern Texas. *Bull. Texas Ornith. Soc.* 31:63–64.

Schmidt, J. R. 1976. First nesting record of Anna's Hummingbird in Texas. *Bull. Texas Ornith. Soc.* 9:6–7.

Seyffert, K. D. 1984. Wintering White-throated Swifts in the Texas Panhandle. *Bull. Oklahoma Ornith. Soc.* 17:31.

———. 1985a. The breeding birds of the Texas Panhandle. *Bull. Texas Ornith. Soc.* 18:7–20.

———. 1985b. A first nesting of the Wilson's Phalarope in Texas. *Bull. Texas Ornith. Soc.* 18:27–29.

———. 1988. Breeding status of the Eared Grebe in the Texas Panhandle. *Bull. Oklahoma Ornith. Soc.* 21:5–6.

———. 1991. Does the Cedar Waxwing nest in the Texas Panhandle? *Bull. Texas Ornith. Soc.* 24:54–56.

———. 1993. Nesting of the Yellow-headed Blackbird in the Panhandle of Texas. *Bull. Oklahoma Ornith. Soc.* 26:1–4.

———. 2001. *Birds of the Texas Panhandle.* College Station: Texas A&M University Press.

Sexton, C. W. 1999. The Vermilion Flycatcher in Texas. *Texas Birds* 1(2):41–45.

Shackelford, C. E. 1998. Compilation of published records of the Ivory-billed Woodpecker in Texas: Voucher specimens verses sight records. *Bull. Texas Ornith. Soc.* 31:35–41.

Shackelford, C. E., D. Saenz, and R. R. Schaefer. 1996. Sharp-shinned Hawks nesting in the Pineywoods of eastern Texas and western Louisiana. *Bull. Texas Ornith. Soc.* 29:23–25.

Shackelford, C. E., and G. G. Simons. 1999. *An annual report of the Swallow-tailed Kite in Texas: A survey and monitoring project for 1998.* Austin: Texas Parks and Wildlife Dept.

Sibley, C. G., and B. L. Monroe, Jr. 1990. *Distribution and taxonomy of birds of the world*. New Haven, Conn.: Yale University Press.

Simmons, G. F. 1925. *Birds of the Austin region*. Austin: The University of Texas.

Singley, J. A. 1887. Observations on eggs collected in Lee County, Texas, etc. *Ornithologist and Oologist* 12: 163–65.

Slack, D. R., and K. A. Arnold. 1985. Nesting of the Magnificent Hummingbird in Jeff Davis County, Texas. *Bull. Texas Ornith. Soc.* 18:27.

Smith, A. P. 1916. Additions to the avifauna of Kerr Co., Texas. *Auk* 33:187–93.

Stevenson, J. C. 1937. The Alaska Longspur and Oregon Horned Lark in Texas. *Condor* 39:44.

Stevenson, J. O. 1942. Whooping Cranes in Texas in summer. *Condor* 44:40–41.

Stewart, R. E., and J. W. Aldrich. 1956. Distinction of maritime and prairie populations of Blue-winged Teal. *Proc. Biol. Soc. Washington* 69:29–36.

Stiles, F. G. 1972. Age and sex determination in Rufous and Allen's hummingbirds. *Condor* 74:25–32.

Strecker, J. K., Jr. 1912. The birds of Texas: An annotated check list. *Baylor Univ. Bull.* 25:1–69.

———. 1927. *Notes on the Ornithology of McLennan County Texas*. Baylor University Press. Bull. No. 1.

Stringham, E. 1948. *Kerrville, Texas, and its birds*. Kerrville, Tex.: Pacot Publications.

Stutzenbaker, C. D. 1988. *The Mottled Duck, its life history, ecology and management*. Austin: Texas Parks and Wildlife Department.

Sutton, G. M. 1967. *Oklahoma birds*. Norman: University of Oklahoma Press.

Tacha, R. C., D. C. Martin, and C. T. Patterson. 1981. Common Crane *(Grus grus)* sighted in west Texas. *Southwest. Nat.* 25:569.

Tarrant County Bird Records Committee. 2000. *A bar graph of the birds of Tarrant County*. 2nd ed. Fort Worth, Tex.: Fort Worth Audubon Society.

Telfair, R. C., II. 1980. Additional inland nesting records in Texas of four species of colonial waterbirds. *Bull. Texas Ornith. Soc.* 13:11–13.

———. 1995. Neotropic Cormorant *(Phalacrocorax brasiliannus)* population trends and dynamics in Texas. *Bull. Texas Ornith. Soc.* 28:1, 7–16.

Texas Ornithological Society. 1995. *Checklist of the birds of Texas*. 3d ed. Austin, Tex: Capital Printing.

Thompson, W. L. 1952. Summer birds of the Canadian "breaks" in Hutchinson County, Texas. *Texas J. Sci.* 4:220–29.

———. 1953. The ecological distribution of the birds of the Black Gap area, Brewster County, Texas. *Texas J. Sci.* 5:158–77.

Thornton, W. A. 1951. Ecological distribution of the birds of the Stockton Plateau in northern Terrell County, Texas. *Texas J. Sci.* 3:413–30.

Tomlinson, R. E., D. D. Dolton, R. R. George, and R. E. Mirarchi. 1994. Mourning Dove. In: *Migratory shore and upland game bird management in North America,* edited by T. C. Tacha and C. E. Braun. Washington, D.C.: International Association of Fish and Wildlife Agencies.

Trautman, M. B. 1964. A specimen of the Roadside Hawk, *Buteo magnirostris griseocauda,* from Texas. *Auk* 81:435.

Travis Audubon Society. 1994. *Birds of the Austin, Texas Region.* Austin, Tex: Travis Audubon Society.

Traweek, M. S. 1978. *Texas waterfowl production survey.* Fed. Aid Proj. No. W–106-R–5. Final report. Austin: Texas Parks and Wildlife Dept.

Van Tyne, J. 1936. *The discovery of the nest of the Colima Warbler* (Vermivora crissalis). Univ. Michigan Mus. Zool., Misc. Publ. No. 33.

Van Tyne, J., and G. M. Sutton. 1937. *The birds of Brewster County, Texas.* Univ. Ann Arbor: Michigan Mus. Zool., Misc. Publ. No. 37.

Wauer, R. H. 1967. First Thick-billed Kingbird record for Texas. *Southwest Nat.* 12:485–86.

———. 1970. The occurrence of the Black-vented Oriole, *Icterus wagler,* in the United States. *Auk* 87:811–12.

———. 1996. *A field guide to birds of the Big Bend.* Houston: Gulf Publishing.

———. 2001. Breeding Avifaunal Baseline for Big Bend National Park. *Occ. Publ. Texas Ornith. Soc.* No. 3.

Wauer, R. H., P. C. Palmer, and A. Windham. 1994. The Ferruginous Pygmy-Owl in south Texas. *Amer. Birds* 47:1071–76.

Weeks, R., and M. A. Patten. 2000. First Texas record of Yellow-footed Gull. *Texas Birds* 2(1):25–33.

Weske, J. S. 1974. White-winged Junco in Texas. *Condor* 76:119.

Wetmore, A., and H. Friedmann. 1933. The California Condor in Texas. *Auk* 35:37–38.

Wheeler, B. K., and W. S. Clark. 1995. *A photographic guide to North American raptors.* San Diego, Calif.: Academic Press.

White, M. 1999. Inland occurrences of Nelson's Sharp-tailed Sparrow. *Texas Birds* 1(1):34–39.

———. 2000. Range expansion of Fish Crow in northeast Texas. *Bull. Texas Ornith. Soc.* 33:6–9.

———. 2002. *Birds of Northeast Texas.* College Station: Texas A&M University Press.

Wiedenfeld, C. C. 1983. Lark Buntings *(Calamospiza melanocorys)* breeding in the Edwards Plateau of Texas. *Bull. Texas Ornith. Soc.* 16:32–33.

Williams, S. O. 1987. A Northern Jacana in Trans-Pecos Texas. *Western Birds* 18:123–24.

Wolf, D. E. 1978. First record of an Aztec Thrush in the United States. *Amer. Birds* 32:156–57.

Wolf, D. E, C. E. Shackelford, G. G. Luneau, and C. D. Fisher. 2001. *Birds of the Pineywoods of eastern Texas: A field checklist.* Austin: Texas Parks and Wildlife Dept.

Wolfe, L. R. 1956. *Check-list of the birds of Texas.* Lancaster, Penn.: Intelligencer Printing Co.

———. 1965. *Check list of the birds of Kerr County, Texas.* Kerrville, Tex.: L. R. Wolfe.

Wright, J. S., and P. C. Wright. 1997. Stygian Owl in Texas. *Field Notes* 51:950–52.

Yovanovich, G. D. L. 1995. Collared Plover in Uvalde, Texas. *Birding* 27:102–104.

Zimmer, B., and K. Bryan. 1993. First United States record of the Tufted Flycatcher. *Amer. Birds* 47:48–50.

Zink, R. M. 1994. The geography of mitochondrial DNA variation, population structure, hybridization, and species limits in the Fox Sparrow *(Passerella iliaca).* *Evolution* 48:96–111.

Zink, R. M., and R. C. Blackwell-Rago. 2000. Species limits and recent population history in the Curve-billed Thrasher. *Condor* 102:881–86.

Zinn, K. S. 1977. Olivaceous Cormorants nesting in north central Texas. *Southwest. Nat.* 21:556–57.

INDEX

ISBN 1-58544-284-4